CHOOSE YOUR INFOSEC PATH

AN INTERACTIVE CYBERSECURITY ADVENTURE FOR BEGINNERS

Alexander J. Roxon

Apress®

Choose Your InfoSec Path: An Interactive Cybersecurity Adventure for Beginners

Alexander J. Roxon
London, UK

ISBN-13 (pbk): 978-1-4842-7035-6   ISBN-13 (electronic): 978-1-4842-7036-3
https://doi.org/10.1007/978-1-4842-7036-3

Managing Director, Apress Media LLC: Welmoed Spahr
Acquisitions Editor: Susan McDermott
Development Editor: Rita Fernando
Coordinating Editor: Rita Fernando

Cover designed by eStudioCalamar

Distributed to the book trade worldwide by Springer Science+Business Media New York, 1 New York Plaza, New York, NY 100043. Phone 1-800-SPRINGER, fax (201) 348-4505, e-mail orders-ny@springer-sbm.com, or visit www.springeronline.com. Apress Media, LLC is a California LLC and the sole member (owner) is Springer Science + Business Media Finance Inc (SSBM Finance Inc). SSBM Finance Inc is a Delaware corporation.

For information on translations, please e-mail booktranslations@springernature.com; for reprint, paperback, or audio rights, please e-mail bookpermissions@springernature.com.

Apress titles may be purchased in bulk for academic, corporate, or promotional use. eBook versions and licenses are also available for most titles. For more information, reference our Print and eBook Bulk Sales web page at http://www.apress.com/bulk-sales.

Any source code or other supplementary material referenced by the author in this book is available to readers on GitHub via the book's product page, located at www.apress. com/9781484270356. For more detailed information, please visit http://www.apress.com/ source-code.

Printed on acid-free paper

For Lola.

I promised your memory I'd write this book to make sure one good thing came out of 2020.

No doubt you will be murdering tennis balls in dog heaven.

Rest easy, sweetheart.

Contents

x Contents

About the Author

Alexander J. Roxon likes to take complicated subjects and problems, then make them simpler and less intimidating. Alex works for a cyber security consultancy, helping companies implement appropriate cybersecurity strategies and use technology to prepare for the problems of the future. In his spare time, he likes to contribute to the industry with things like phishing awareness blogs full of fish puns, or a deck of playing cards designed to teach people about cybersecurity (The Infosec Deck). Inspired by the *Give Yourself Goosebumps* series, he decided to write his own interactive story in an effort to make information security more accessible. He holds the Systems Security Certified Professional (SSCP) accreditation and is Factor Analysis Information Risk (FAIR) accredited.

About the Technical Reviewer

Sasha Zivojinovic is a part-time security geek and full-time Schnauzer wrangler. During his decade-long adventure in information security, his disclosures have caused countless headaches to project teams in some of the most prestigious organisations in the world. This has included disclosures to Google, McAfee, Redis Labs, Ubuntu and AlienVault products, for which he's received recognition, reprobation and the occasional T-shirt.

When he's not helping make the world more secure, he's busy providing quality assurance on any and every bottle of rum that crosses his path and teaching the various German states how to source and brew a decent cup of tea.

Sasha has donated his portion of proceeds from tech reviewing this book to the Caye Caulker Animal Shelter, on the proviso that this is explicitly mentioned in his bio, while also asking that it not be mentioned that *he* asked for this. I think we can all agree he is a great man.

Acknowledgments

To Isabel, who I am hoping by now is my wife, COVID pandemic allowing, for not questioning me spending large amounts of time working furiously in the bedroom with my laptop. To my editor: Why is this autocorrecting to "working"?

A big thank-you to Andy Compton, the man I told I wanted to be a sponge, octopus and shark rolled into one, and still hired me to my first information security role.

A massive thank-you and apology to Sasha Zivojinovic. Whilst I listened to most of your technical feedback, I ignored some of it, as being succinct sometimes trumped the need for 100% accuracy. Let this section make it clear that anything technically wrong with this book is purely my fault, nobody else's.

More fool you to Andrew Turner, for taking me back into his sales team after an ill-fated attempt at running my own business.

To Susan, Rita and all the hidden people behind the scenes at Apress, let's hope your gamble paid off.

And obviously a big thank-you to my parents, Sara and Gordon, for raising me in a manner where I was educated enough to be able to write, but tortured enough to feel the need to.

Preface

Welcome to my book. I am the author, Alex. I wrote this book with the goal of making information security fun and engaging to learn and interact with. Whether I succeeded or not is up to you.

This book is for people who are interested in learning about information security, either just out of curiosity or because they want to start a career in the industry. Incidentally, please don't be put off if you don't have an in-depth technical background: the book has been written with that possibility in mind. This book puts you in the shoes of a Chief Information Security Officer (CISO) at a company; a fast-moving and in many ways unrealistic pair of shoes, I should add. You'll endure some of the trials and tribulations that come with the role, including responding to a cyberattack. Whether or not the company emerges from the attack unscathed is largely up to you and the choices you make throughout the book.

Note that though the story presented in this book is largely realistic and representative of how things work in the real world, I have taken some creative liberties to keep things interesting. For example, events that could take weeks or months unfurl much more rapidly because I didn't think you'd want to read page after page of not much happening. Also, at some points the technical realities of the world are bent slightly to enhance entertainment and simplicity. This book is written to help you become enthused about information security and to raise your aptitude, but it's not intended to be a masterclass by any means.

There are some opinions scattered around, which, needless to say, are subjective. As for the humour, it's mostly very dry, with a lot of pot shots at some of the mundaneness of corporate employment that we've come to know and ~~love~~ accept.

This book takes you through an interactive adventure. Each section leads you through a scene in the story and directs you to the next section. Do not try to read the book in sequential order! Each section may have multiple exits or pathways depending on the choices you make. Some sections will have a decision point in the middle.

If you're curious as to what this means, go to **Section 153**.

Not all decisions have "right" or "wrong" answers, just as in real life things are often much more nuanced and greyer, rather than black and white. I'd recommend you try reading through the book a few times making the kind of choices you'd be likely to make, but also have a few read-throughs where you go against your instincts completely and see how the story deviates and what lessons you can learn.

The book is divided into a number of phases:

- *Phase one—Prologue: Gives you background on your role and employer.*

- *Phase two—Preparation: A time period where you know how the attackers typically behave and it's up to you to find evidence of their activity or reasons for why they are interested in targeting you.*

- *Phase three—Attack: The cyberattack well and truly begins.*

- *Phase four—Aftermath: A brief period where you can enjoy your success (if you've had any).*

How you do in phase one will determine where you enter phase two, and so on as the story unfolds. Not all stories will make it all the way through the phases; it depends how you play and what happens as a result. I should warn you, the book will not always be as straightforward as you may wish or hope—just like in real life, there is a random element and luck can play its part.

Remember that this is an individual story with individual circumstances and nuances. In the same way, each real-life incident is going to be unique and reactions/responses/ relevant laws and even office politics are going to differ. What I am saying is, this book is a tool to enhance your learning and hopefully to act as a bit of fun, but it is not meant to become your own incident response plan.

As the book is centred around information security and this realm may not be your background, you may want to read the glossary at the back of the book before starting. If you don't fancy reading the whole glossary, just remember, the first time a glossary term is used it will be in **bold**. *For really key topics I will sometimes throw in a quick description for you.*

You may notice this whole preface is in italics, which probably looks weird, but essentially italics means I am talking directly to you, smashing that fourth wall to smithereens. Most of the book is written in the second person (therefore not in italics)—after all, it's your story. But immediately following a decision, I will chime in to offer some feedback on the decision you just made. So remember, italics means I am talking directly to you. Good luck!

Get started and go to **Section 1**.

Life's a Breach

1 Phase One—Prologue

Welcome to Generico McCompany, a global leader in collaboratively reinventing agile products for a nondescript target audience in a competitive marketplace. As well as being an expert in corporate jargon, Generico McCompany is known to sell a wide variety of products and services, including insurance for toupees, shoehorns, smellotape, sausages and a whole lot more. The business operates both online and in retail outlet stores across the world. Generico McCompany is careful to operate in enough geographical regions for nobody to feel singled out and consider legal action against the author.

The company employs 10,000 staff across 24 offices and operates with annual revenues of over 10 billion dollars—what type of dollars is up to you. You are the **Chief Information Security Officer (CISO)**, and you are also the only person in the company who looks after information security full time (good luck). This is now your seventh month in the role, after sailing through your initial probation period. As your boss put it, "I don't know how to measure your success, so I'll go for the innocent until proven guilty approach."

It's Monday morning. After spending an entire 45 minutes inhaling the aromas of a fellow train commuter's armpit, you have a foreboding that today will not be your day. As you walk through the main lobby of the company's shared office building, you tell yourself that a hot drink and half an hour of procrastination will turn things around. You swipe your green security lanyard onto the turnstile as you stroll across the shiny marble reception floor towards the lift.

© Alexander J. Roxon 2021
A. J. Roxon, *Choose Your InfoSec Path*, https://doi.org/10.1007/978-1-4842-7036-3_1

A gentle "ping" indicates that the lift has arrived, and with it an occupant sporting a matching green lanyard. The unfortunate realisation that you now have to engage in conversation dawns on you. You find yourself exchanging typical Monday morning conversation with a co-worker whose name you don't (but probably should) know. The acceptable window for you to ask their name probably closed sometime six months ago.

"How was your weekend?" they ask.

Continue the small talk in **Section 2**.

---

2 Phase One—Prologue

You let your co-worker know your weekend was alright and non-eventful, then with elite-level conversational etiquette you ask them how their weekend was. Clearly, this was a mistake: the short journey in the lift becomes a test of endurance as you feign interest in your colleague's monotonous and overly thorough weekend recap. Eventually the lift doors slide open, and you relish your escape onto the 13th-floor lobby.

The office itself is a futuristic mix of angular furniture and copious amounts of glass, with large meeting rooms stocked with all manner of biscuits and chocolate. You exchange smiles with the receptionist as you head towards the technical wing where your one-person "department" is based. You make an effort to keep the jealousy at bay as you pass by the application developers' trendy office space with bean bags and standing desks a plenty; it always seems to be party time around here. You pass a developer who lies sleeping on one of the bean bags. "This is a whole other world," you think to yourself, as you shake your head and continue to your own area.

Your desk is tucked away in a dark and somehow damp corner of the office, with an intermittently flickering light that can be temporarily fixed by a good old poke with a broom. Maybe it's the lighting, maybe it's your imagination, but your desk seems to be smaller and shabbier than everyone else's in IT, and was plainly a second-hand job—it took you a full day to remove the tapestry of chewing gum that had been attached underneath.

> *Relax, not every company views cybersecurity with the level of disregard Generico McCompany seems to. Information security teams are increasingly being viewed as critical members of the team and given far nicer offices than these.*

You manage to avoid conversation with the people who sit near you by pretending you need to do something urgently. You plug your laptop in and decide to have a scan of your emails.

See what is inside your inbox in **Section 245.**

3 Phase Two—Preparation

"So far, so good," you think to yourself as you watch the perimeter defence software doing its thing. You overhear someone a few desks along breaking up with their partner over the phone, a very brazen thing to do on a Tuesday morning in the middle of an open-plan office. Like a good team player, you listen in; obviously you want to make sure you can support them emotionally. Really, the only thing you're missing is popcorn.

The perimeter defence continues to show nothing interesting. You muse to yourself that Golden Slug might be attacking right now, but their capability is so minimal you can't even notice them.

"If you can't accept both me and Ray as a package, then this isn't going to work."

Great, now you've lost the thread of the conversation just when this ultimatum is getting interesting. A few extra dots representing data packets appear on the screen. Perhaps an application has had an error. You watch the number of dots begin to grow exponentially. Within minutes it becomes plainly obvious that Generico McCompany is under DDoS attack.

Find out if this is just a training exercise in **Section 145.**

4 Phase Two—Preparation

You know Golden Slug are interested in the environment and anything with the word "nuclear" is not exactly the environment's best friend, so this seems a smart choice.

The more you read the plan, the more it sounds like the plot of a bad film. Essentially, the idea is to use depleted uranium to recharge batteries that are acquired from landfill, turning two useless products into charged batteries. Naturally, the "significant" financial gains would have turned a few heads, so surely someone went ahead with it? The only thing is that you can't find any evidence in the folder.

You massage your temples as you ponder what to do next. You can clearly see why this has been flagged as an environmental hazard. You decide to play it safe and get Susan's thoughts. You ping her a message, letting her know you've got a lead on Golden Slug.

"Oh, really?" Susan's attention is piqued.

You outline what you have found so far regarding Project Luminec, and crucially how it supposedly involves nuclear materials.

"Oh, wow. Only supposedly?"

You clarify that whilst the project definitely mentions nuclear material, there isn't any proof that it progressed beyond the planning phase.

"Might be a secret project. You should talk to Rory in operations, he's always drafted into projects like that. Remember he is ex special forces and notoriously tight lipped as a result. I guess as a last resort you could try Guillaume."

This surprises you; Guillaume sits two desks down from you and manages cloud hosting. You ask Susan why Guillaume would know.

"If it went ahead, they'll have needed a network share to store data. Guillaume creates all of those," Susan responds, before disappearing offline. You probably haven't given her the credit she's due, as she's most likely right. Do you want to try your luck with Rory or slide over to Guillaume?

Talk to Rory in **Section 331** or talk to Guillaume in **Section 97.**

---

5 Phase Four—Aftermath

Whilst it was noted that your response to the initial Golden Slug incident was acceptable, the prevailing feeling is that better user awareness training would have led to the store staff knowing that contractors installing cameras out of the blue is suspicious and merits reporting. As much as the annoying member of the National Fraud Office wants you to be fired, Susan rejects the idea that this was all your fault and sends them on their way. Whilst she accepts it wasn't entirely your fault, she does identify the root cause as an ineffective user awareness training programme and looks for ways to prevent this from happening again.

This training involves a lot of coloured Post-It notes and drawing on whiteboards. Generico McCompany receives a fine for the stolen payment card data, which Susan manages to pass over to another department. Allegedly Susan challenged another director to a game of pool with the loser having to pay the fine, but you never verify this.

You remain at Generico McCompany until you get bored, start the process of looking to move and realise you can't be bothered, so instead you stay until…

The End.

*This ending maybe is a little unfair, as you were honest enough to admit you aren't the best at teaching things to other people. Just be conscious that this is something a CISO should be skilled in. Don't worry, though, this ending is relatively tame and it could have been much, much worse. If you feel hard done by, you're free to go back to **Section 249** and see how the story could have played out, but in return prove you are indeed a good teacher of others and help someone out. Anyway, for a completely different challenge, start the book again but when given the choice, try a cup of coffee instead. It'll be a completely different adventure.*

6 Phase Three—Attack

Immediately it is clear that the card details must be coming from your e-commerce transactions: that is the only way they could be being produced at the rate mentioned in the forum post. Generico McCompany runs over 200 e-commerce sites, so essentially you now have 200 haystacks hiding an unidentified number of needles. Things aren't looking great. As you panic internally, your face remains a picture of calm, so much so that a member of the IT helpdesk feels it's safe to approach and ask you for help. A name badge identifies the helpdesk member as Leslie.

"Can you open the email I've sent you?" Leslie asks.

You open your inbox and sit waiting for the email to arrive.

"No, I sent it to you two weeks ago."

Hiding your embarrassment, you look in your deleted items and find Leslie's email. You feel shame course through your soul. The email reads:

"User is reporting blocked popups for Glasshammer website, below are screenshots showing the popups being blocked and the webpage loading correctly after the user manually overrides the popup blocker."

The images outline exactly what has been described, though the Generico McCompany logo looks a little weird in one of the pages: the Latin slogan is usually much more offensive to the eye than that.

Dig a little deeper in **Section 210.**

7 Phase Four—Aftermath

"I received that through the post, Charlotte must have sent it to line up the Golden Slug attack. Head home for the day, you've done good work here. I have some phone calls to make." You gladly obey Susan's command and travel home to put your feet up.

Susan's phone calls prove effective. Charlotte is caught at the border trying to flee the country. The story comes pouring out during her interrogation. Charlotte felt bitter about losing out on the Generico McCompany CISO role and hatched an elaborate plan to extract her revenge. Unluckily for Charlotte, she was a bad actor in both ways. Once she'd come into contact with Golden Slug as part of routine National Fraud Office work, she had the weapon she needed. A combination of knowledge of Generico McCompany's IT infrastructure and the multi-factor authentication code–stealing snow globe were enough ammunition for Golden Slug to happily start a hacking campaign against Generico McCompany.

Charlotte had ensured the attack would happen on a day when she was the only person available to respond, enabling her to come onsite and manage things from the inside. She was in direct contact with Golden Slug using her personal phone.

The planned career and financial repercussions connected to the Golden Slug incident are wiped out, as there was little you could do to stop someone who had infiltrated a government body like that. Whilst Charlotte and Golden Slug have been foiled, you refuse to get complacent, as tomorrow may bring the hack that breaks the camel's back.

The End.

Woo, well done. I'll be frank, you didn't make much progress in phase two and as soon as Charlotte enters the scene there are actually not many good endings available, but you managed to find one. Next time you read through, try to change your early decisions to see if you can be one step ahead of Golden Slug, rather than one behind. If you really fancy something different, try drinking coffee at the beginning of the book instead.

8 Phase Two—Preparation

Tuesdays are a good day, because your favourite bagel pop-up sets up its stand between the train station and Generico McCompany's offices.

You take the first bite out of your delicious salmon and cream cheese bagel and line up a second. Just as you bring the bagel up to your mouth, you feel someone looming over you. You peer through the hole in the middle and see Georgios from the legal team, in an impeccably tailored suit with his arms folded. You lower the bagel slowly, waiting to see what he has to say.

"We are needed in meeting room four in ten minutes, there won't be a calendar invite." He touches his nose in some kind of secret code. You let him know you'll be there and touch your own nose to acknowledge his code, managing to wipe cream cheese on your face in the process. Georgios walks off, having now classified you as an inferior being who is clearly incapable of eating a bagel. You prove him wrong by finishing the bagel and then heading over to meeting room four to see what's going on.

An assortment of people have gathered in the room. As well as Georgios, you can see Michael (COO), Vijaya (IT Backup Manager), Gesa (Project Manager), Cecilia (Public Relations) and Susan (IT Director). Michael seems to be running the meeting and kicks things off.

"Project Degrada, also known as Project Luminec, is an overseas battery recycling plant that uses depleted uranium to recharge dead batteries and then sells them at a huge profit."

Find out why you are needed at all in **Section 40.**

---

9 Phase Four—Aftermath

Whilst I commend your honesty, your employers probably won't.

The next few months pass in a blur. An "anonymous source" leaks to the media that the Golden Slug data is genuine. To your shock, the media, public and stocks seem nonplussed about it, potentially desensitised to large-scale data breaches by now.

Neither Susan nor Petra ever directly asks if the source was you, though they both clearly suspect it. The familiar feeling of being managed out of a business begins to surface, as colleagues start to distance themselves from you, likely with Susan and Petra pulling the strings in the background.

In an attempt to save your Generico McCompany career, you lodge a formal complaint, outlining the conversation that occurred in Susan's office, but they both deny it. It's two directors' word against an employee who hasn't even done a year at the company yet. The investigation is closed in record time.

Rather than save your career at Generico McCompany, the complaint spells its conclusion, as Susan finds a technicality in your employment contract that lets her sack you. Finding new work isn't a problem; the problem is shaking off the feeling in the back of your head that you could have handled the Golden Slug incident better.

The End.

Not the best and not the worst of endings. Most endings in the book are worse than this, so take heart from that. The cold hard truth is that you were in trouble no matter whether you played along with Susan and Petra's plan or not. If you'd been able to stay ahead of Golden Slug, they would never have got access to that data. Try reading through again to see if you can upgrade your ending, or try drinking tea early on instead for a completely different story.

10 Phase Four—Aftermath

Someone has put something inside of the device; you can see a cable that shouldn't be there and the device rattles around when you shake it, which is definitely suspicious. You let Gesa know that unfortunately she's got a brand new company-wide project now to have every single PIN entry device inspected by the manufacturer.

Leaving the store, you rush back to the office and head straight to Susan to deliver the bad news; it seems like this is becoming a regular occurrence. Luckily, Susan doesn't appear too concerned.

"Well, it's typically a bad week for trade in our stores anyway, and we were always planning to close all the stores for a deep clean in the coming months, so I'll just talk to the head of stores and have that brought forward to this week. Can you please line up some contractors to visit each site and fix the PIN entry devices? We should be able to limit the damage on this."

Susan's plan ends up working out pretty much as described: across the country, all 9000 Generico McCompany stores shut down for their deep clean and the PIN entry devices are all inspected and cleaned by the manufacturer. Law enforcement officers are also on hand, inspecting the recovered hardware and looking for any clues that might link them back to Golden Slug. Unfortunately, they are unsuccessful.

> *CCTV footage always seems to be so grainy and rubbish, doesn't it? How can I walk around with a tiny phone that can take a picture with so much detail I can count individual atoms, but CCTV can't see someone's face clearly? Rant over.*

When all is said and done, Golden Slug only managed to steal a relatively low number of payment cards, and because you figured out their plans relatively quickly, it was possible for the cards to be deactivated before a considerable amount of fraud could take place.

Find out the verdict in **Section 127.**

---

11 Phase Four—Aftermath

> *Nice one, unless you're lying. Teaching people is a key skill for a CISO. Knowing a lot is great, but a CISO is one person and the best information security defences are where multiple people take ownership of the information security mission. Everyone can be involved in this mission, even if they aren't technically minded.*

The young man puffs out his chest and replies, "This store has not had communications relating to a Generico McCompany onsite visit today and therefore I will not be able to allow you to inspect any store equipment."

Normally you would be delighted at the shop employee for following procedure so perfectly, but it's typical that this is the one time it would be simpler if they didn't. As luck would have it, Gesa actually has the phone number of the key person in the head office whose job it is to alert the store when staff are coming to handle store equipment. She gives them a quick call, and they promise to put the notification through as soon as possible. You spend a few minutes browsing the shop with Gesa, coming dangerously close to actually buying a shoehorn harmonica, which isn't just a shoehorn, but can also be played as a musical instrument. Eventually, the same store worker who had previously rejected you bustles over, full of smiles.

"We've had word from head office to confirm that you are authorised Generico McCompany employees. What did you want to see again?"

"The PIN entry devices," Gesa tells him.

He leads you to where the PIN entry devices live, which unsurprisingly is at the checkout section of the store. He pats one of the devices fondly, letting you know they've been working faster than ever since they've had their upgrade. You pick up one of the beloved devices and begin to inspect it. The store worker looks horrified as you poke, prod, and rattle; it's almost like you are desecrating a grave. You put the device down and let out a sigh.

Announce your findings in **Section 10.**

12 Phase Three—Attack

"I need a status update. We are having a director's call in ten minutes." You quickly brief Susan on how your conversation with DdoSD went.

"Let me know what that figure is when it comes through." She moves on to ask Guillaume how the cloud environments are coping. Guillaume is not enjoying life at the moment. You decide to go for a quick walk to clear your head and get some water. As you grab a bottle of water from the fridge, you take a moment to think of the poor cleaners. The freshly cleaned kitchen sparkles and smells faintly of lemon, but you know it's just a matter of time before their work is destroyed and the kitchen is in a shambles again.

A single used spoon sits on the counter, an invitation to some people to add a dirty plate or another piece of cutlery. More plates, mugs, and cutlery will eventually add up to a pile of disgusting kitchen mess. You shudder, then head back to your desk to check your inbox.

Tony's email has come through; you scan it but can't immediately see a quote. You reach for the phone to call him and ask him to attach the quote this time, but then realise that what you thought was the telephone number in his email is actually the quote. You send it over to Susan on chat, who simply replies, "Should I push for this?"

Say no in **Section 288** or yes in **Section 52.**

13 Phase Three—Attack

Golden Slug are money motivated, and this application is literally used to move money around, so it seems a reasonable choice.

You announce to Susan that if Golden Slug figure out how to use that payments system, they could start rediverting payments to their own bank accounts. That has to take priority in your view.

"For once I think you are right," Charlotte chimes in. Even when agreeing she manages to slap you in the face. Susan wishes you both luck and scurries off to warn the head of finance of what's going on. You start to perform some diagnostics on the payment processing application, looking at recent activity and focusing on the commands going into the server from Golden Slug's IP address.

Golden Slug are definitely planning something: there is a whole paper trail showing lots of little tweaks and preparation. They've been a bit gung-ho and noisy, so piecing together the clues is easier than it should be. Charlotte starts to drum her fingers on the table in what is somehow the most annoying way possible. You ask her what she wants.

"I'm just signalling that I'm bored and waiting for you to come to the same conclusion I have, but with you needing significantly longer to do so."

Charming. Charlotte has found a large payment scheduled to be sent out in a month's time, Golden Slug were possibly conscious that having it sent during a period when Generico McCompany were on high alert would increase the chances of the payment being identified and caught. You take a copy of the server for future analysis and in case evidence is needed at a later date. Actually deleting the scheduled payment is easy: the application has been designed to make paying out money difficult but deleting payments easy. On top of that, you stop the server from accepting commands from external IP addresses, putting the attack to bed.

Celebrate in **Section 325.**

14 Phase Four—Aftermath

You pick up on a very different atmosphere as you enter the office the next day. Susan's office is packed full of directors, who all look pretty stressed. This in itself isn't unusual, but what is unusual is that everybody in the office has a cup of coffee in their hand (meaning that the stress isn't, as you'd expect, a result of caffeine withdrawal). Also unusual is that the IT office section is made up of mini group huddles, instead of everyone working silently at their desk.

You ask Guillaume and Vijaya why everyone looks like they have lost a winning lottery **ticket**. Guillaume looks around shiftily before beckoning you into their huddle and sharing the big news.

"Apparently some guy in finance paid a fake invoice and lost the company $20 million with just one click of his mouse," Guillaume announces, with the glee of schadenfreude written all over his face.

"They are saying the email came from Petra, at least that's what he claimed," Vijaya chimes in. You ask them both if somebody managed to spoof Petra's email address.

Guillaume wags his finger dramatically. "No, it was genuinely sent from Petra's Generico McCompany address, we had to double-check the **logs** first thing."

As your mind begins to puzzle out the implications of this revelation, Susan appears and beckons you over to join her in her office. Thankfully the crowd has dispersed and it's just Susan in there now.

Walk over and enter in **Section 107.**

---

15 Phase Four—Aftermath

You ask Gesa if she has a minute. She is reclining in her chair looking bored, which suggests she does indeed have a minute, but it's only polite to ask.

"Sure, what's up?"

You tell her it's to do with GMC 4511.

"Look at you throwing around internal project codes like it's nothing! What about it?"

You ask if she recently changed the supplier scheduled for delivering the onsite maintenance.

"No, why?"

You explain your findings to Gesa. She seems not to believe your claims until she **logs** into the Generico McCompany procurement tool and sees the evidence for herself.

"I have never even heard of that vendor," she says.

You ask what the job they were meant to be doing is.

Gesa explains that GMC 4511 is a project with the goal of improving instore shopping experiences by introducing more fun and innovative ways to shop and pay for goods. This particular phase's objective is to upgrade the PIN entry devices where shoppers insert their cards when buying things. These PIN entry device upgrades have been happening up and down the country for the last 24 hours. Golden Slug could have compromised a huge portion of the PIN entry device estate in that time. You ask Gesa to accompany you as you scuttle over to Susan's office to give her the latest news.

Do that mouth-moving thing where words are exchanged in **Section 260.**

---

16 Phase Two—Preparation

The smell of fish lingers in the kitchen, the wispy tendrils of the stink forcing themselves down your nose and throat. Naturally you say nothing. Who knows if the perpetrator is still in the kitchen? Your glass of water seems infinitely less satisfying now it's combined with the smell and taste of fish. You retreat out of the kitchen, tail between your legs.

Susan is outside the kitchen door, her nose unwrinkled. Perhaps it was her fish?

"Good day?" she asks cheerfully—surprisingly cheerfully.

You let her know it's been alright, but you haven't made a huge amount of progress on Golden Slug.

"Did you talk to Guillaume about that project?"

You reply that you haven't yet and that he has gone home for the day.

"Oh, he has?"

Oops, now you've landed Guillaume in trouble. You decide to try to distract Susan before she saves the information into her brain, and quickly outline your proposal to use an overly complicated method so that high environmental risk projects get flagged up before they become a surprise.

"Yup, I've already put a meeting in for that tomorrow morning."

She walks off, clearly the winner in this conversation. You head home to relax, unwind and prepare for that meeting.

See how the meeting goes tomorrow in **Section 8.**

17 Phase Three—Attack

Until you have the full picture of where Golden Slug have infiltrated and what they've been up to, you should be wary of pulling the plug on them. Hackers tend to be as "quiet" as possible once they've got into a company network, hoping to prolong their stay. Once they know they are being kicked out they are likely to become "noisy", setting off a series of plans concurrently to try to make the most of their access whilst they still can. I'm not saying this option was "right", I should add; there wasn't really a "right" option.

Letting out a big sigh, you instruct Galactic Cyber to observe Golden Slug and see if they can learn anything that would be useful. You don't want to risk attempting to purge them before determining how widespread the rot is. To clear your head and also to prevent yourself from backseat driving, you take yourself for a quick walk around the office, grabbing hold of a cup of tea along the way. As you sit down again, Cyberspace Cadet Morgan moonwalks over to your desk.

"Do you have a moment to answer a few questions?"

Naturally you do, so you spend some time helping Cyberspace Cadet Morgan get familiarised with Generico McCompany's network and processes, assisted by Guillaume and Vijaya from the IT team, who couldn't help but eavesdrop. Once the questions are over, Guillaume responds with a question of his own, delivered with the usual tact.

"Why are you called a Cyberspace Cadet? Did you win a job at Galactic Cyber in a box of cereal?"

You presume that Morgan shoots an angry glare at Guillaume, but the tinted visor means you'll never know.

"I didn't win a prize in a cereal box to be here, I just am more junior than Marshal Marshal or Commander Sasha," she replies.

You thank Cyberspace Cadet Morgan and rebuke Guillaume for harassing your support crew.

Find out what Galactic Cyber are able to discover in **Section 357.**

18 Phase Three—Attack

Charlotte seems to be ahead of the curve. It's a risk going against her judgement, but I respect it.

You beckon to Niko and start walking towards Susan's office. Niko's black ball continues to pulse red. Susan's office is closed and the light is off. You feel a little strange going into her office when she's not there, but in your head you have a clear justification. Niko follows you in and stands in the centre of the room. The ball flashes blue.

"Interesting. It will flash faster when it's close to whatever is stealing the two-factor authentication codes," Niko tells you. He walks around the room looking for the source, but the ball continues to pulse gently. It is only when Niko stands over Susan's desk that the ball begins to flash more frequently.

"It's something on or in the desk," Niko announces.

In all honesty your detective skills are honed enough to have come to that conclusion already. You continue to watch as Niko moves the ball closer to various objects on the desk, seeing how it reacts. He reminds you of a waiter offering guests a canapé that he isn't convinced is any good. The stapler, hole punch and Rubik's cube are all innocent. It is only when it approaches a snow globe paperweight that the ball changes from rapid flashes of blue to an all-out disco party.

Niko reaches out to pick it up, but you stop him, and point out it would be better to talk to Susan when she comes back before manhandling her property.

Or you could put it in a Faraday cage, if you happen to have one of those lying around?

Return to your desk to wait for Susan in **Section 53.**

---

19 Phase Three—Attack

With as much grace as you can manage, you stand up and stroll towards the Generico McCompany toilets to work on some hydrotherapy. Along the way you are stopped by a colleague who is clearly unable to read facial expressions. They just wanted to let you know that they really enjoyed the user awareness training video you put together, teaching people how to create a strong password. You thank them and then pause, expecting them to follow up with a request for something, but no request comes. It appears they just wanted to be nice.

You feel a surge of warmth spread through your body. After checking it isn't a stroke, you conclude that it is hope you are feeling. Giving up would be letting your enthusiastic colleague down, so you march back to your desk to fight this breach head on. Do you want to call in your incident response retainer or use your intrusion detection software to pinpoint the thieves?

Pick the incident response retainer in **Section 168.** Try intrusion detection software in **Section 309.**

---

20 Phase Three—Attack

Although your existing DDoS protection supplier claims to filter out a large percentage of malicious data packets, capitalism always ensures that there is an option to pay more for a bigger/better service. Tony is your account manager from DDoS Defence (DdoSD); you take a moment to admire the inspired name. You dig Tony's phone number out from an email he previously sent you (you had never bothered to save him as a contact) and give him a call. You start with a casual good morning, playing it cool.

"Hi, Tony from DdoSD, how can I help you?" It would seem Tony hasn't saved your number either.

After shuffling awkwardly through the exchange of names and you reminding him of the company you work for, Tony gets his head in the game.

"Ah yes, Generico McCompany. Let me pull up your metrics and assess what we are seeing."

The silence that follows feels eternal, like nations rise, flourish and subsequently crumble to dust as you wait for Tony to reply. You check that he is still there and hasn't evaporated.

"Sorry about that, I just had to refresh the console as the numbers looked odd. You seem to have come under massive attack a few hours ago."

He's a perceptive one. You let him know that you expect it to start up again soonish. And that you need to know how much more capacity DdoSD have to take the sting out of the attacks if they increase in size at all.

"I'm going to be honest here." Is he not normally? "This is pretty much at the threshold of your contract. If it gets a lot bigger than this, you'll start to see much more of it slip through."

You ask Tony how much the next level of service costs and the degree of protection it offers. You can see Susan approaching your desk, clearly looking to talk to you, so you hurry things along and request a quote by email before saying some rushed goodbyes. Tony says he'll send the quote through, then calls you by the wrong name and hangs up.

See what Susan has to say in **Section 12.**

---

21 Phase Four—Aftermath

Good news is always received better than bad news, after all.

You tell Susan you have the situation under control. She beams in response, and then delivers her own good news.

"Great, then you can join me in this four-hour meeting. We are planning a collaborative charity event with another company, which, behind the scenes, is just an opportunity to harvest personal data."

You point out that the concept sounds rather evil.

"Yes, the company is Rathervil, how did you know?"

It seems safer just to stay quiet and not admit that you didn't actually guess the company name. You allow Susan to guide you to the meeting room where everyone else has already gathered. The Rathervil representatives look remarkably like a who's who of murderous dictators, which seems fitting. One of them offers you some chocolate, and you feel immediately guilty about jumping to conclusions.

The meeting opens with a detailed overview of the benefits of collecting personal data at a large charity event, which essentially comes down to the fact that it allows many privacy laws to be bypassed. Eventually, it becomes apparent why you have been invited along to the meeting.

"Can you design a mechanism through which we can encrypt and securely store the data collected, but in a way that allows Rathervil to have access too?" Petra, the CEO of Generico McCompany, asks you.

Before you get a chance to answer, a moustache-sporting Rathervil executive jumps in. "Why encrypt the data? It'll just increase computing costs."

I mean... he has a point—and chocolate.

This suggestion is met with enthusiastic nods from all around, except from you. After four hours of discussion you decide that actually, you were right to jump to your initial conclusion. The chocolate was just a distraction. You go home, dust yourself off and go back to work.

Tackle the day in **Section 227**.

22 Phase Two—Preparation

The malicious request sent in by fake Jorge was quite intelligent. You take your non-existent hat off to whoever sent it. If the request had been fulfilled payment card data it would have been processed normally, but with a copy being sent to the malicious IP address each time too. The coincidence that you were present to block the request from being actioned doesn't escape you—it's almost like it was scripted.

After confirming with the National Cyber Security Agency that the IP address was indeed associated with Golden Slug, you open up your to-do list to find something easy to fill the remainder of your afternoon. You begin to work on updating Generico McCompany's **information security policies**.

You didn't think all the other responsibilities of a CISO would disappear just because a few phishing emails were being sent, did you?

The existing policies read like something a lawyer who hates the world would write. You want the policies to be a bit more friendly and written in plainer English.

You decide to replace the line

> Employees will never utilise unauthorised external storage devices or face severe penalties.

with

> Remember to beware of suspicious storage devices and only to use Generico McCompany authorised devices.

The clock strikes five and it's time to go home. You feel satisfied on the commute: Golden Slug have been thwarted and you are the knight in shining armour. Ride your noble steed home and celebrate with a pizza and whatever you do for fun in the evening.

Go back into work in **Section 208**.

23 Phase Three—Attack

"We have identified the methodology which Golden Slug are using to perform their DDoS," Captain Dave announces as you arrive.

"What can we do with this information?" Susan asks, appearing out of the blue.

"Nothing for the minute, but just wanted to give you an update," Captain Dave clarifies.

Susan shoots you a glance and walks off. First Mate Gloria pulls out a flask and takes a swig. She catches your eye and winks. "Apple juice, don't worry."

You are pretty sure it isn't apple juice. You wander back towards your desk and let the Cyber Pirates earn their gold. Once you log back in, you are greeted by a deluge of emails. The one upside of being in incident response mode is knowing that you have a pass to just ignore most of these emails now. You've received a calendar invite for a meeting in half an hour to plan out the PR response to the DDoS attacks; clearly the press have started to catch wind of things.

You glance over at the Pirates and realise that if you want to attend this meeting, you either need to find a colleague to keep an eye on them, or you could possibly take them with you.

Take the pirates in **Section 214,** or if you feel Susan might get too annoyed by them, go to **Section 339.**

---

24 Phase Four—Aftermath

Accusing a member of the National Fraud Office of working with a cyberthreat group? That's a bold move. Let's see if it pays off.

You turn to face Charlotte and accuse her of being an accomplice of Golden Slug. She laughs out loud.

"And what on earth substantiates that claim?" she replies, still laughing. You refer to the device connecting to Golden Slug through the Generico McCompany Wi-Fi.

"Show me."

You show her the connection, and she responds by pulling out her phone.

"So, if your theory is correct, we just need to turn off my phone. If the connection disappears then I am guilty, but if it remains then I am innocent?"

You nod and watch as she powers down her phone. The Golden Slug connection remains. It wasn't Charlotte's phone at all.

"I won't mention this in my final report, but just so you know, based on the levels of inadequacy I've seen here, you may as well start packing up your stuff."

You don't start packing, but in a way wish you had, as Charlotte's report is as damning as her word. Soon you are boxing up your things for good. Getting completely hosed by Golden Slug's payment card-stealing attack was a bad start, but the cherry on top of the icing was accusing a member of the National Fraud Agency of being an inside agent for a global hacking crime group without proper evidence.

The End.

> Sadly, your activities in phase two didn't give you a head start on Golden Slug, which really left you at a disadvantage entering subsequent phases of the story. As annoying as Charlotte is, accusing her without concrete evidence was unlikely to work out well.
>
> Try reading through again but trying some different approaches early on and seeing if that changes your trajectory. Alternatively, for a completely different story try drinking coffee.

25 Phase Three—Attack

You are about to dissect Golden Slug's email when the threat becomes reality. The first round of DDoS attack is like a tsunami crashing into a building made of sugar: the sheer power and fury of the wave send crippling shockwaves throughout the business, taking applications and infrastructure offline.

A procession of department heads come into the room to enquire why everything is "broken". Rather than take the time to explain that hacktivists are targeting the company, the standard line of "we are working on it" is used to placate the masses. As you watch the team's problems pile up on top of each other, it becomes clear that it is time for action.

Scanning the email from Golden Slug doesn't reveal any kind of cryptic clue, though it does remind you of something. You do have their email address, why not email them?

Drop Golden Slug an email in **Section 85.**

26 Phase Three—Attack

"Welcome to Fesrodah's automated customer service line. Your call is important to us, please hold whilst we make you wait an arbitrary amount of time."

You share a look of disbelief with Georgios. The phone still claims to be connected, but no sound is coming out. Georgios begins to drum his fingers on the miniature table; it is clear he has no sense of rhythm. Just as he's about to add whistling into his orchestral mix, the phone starts speaking.

"Thank you for holding. If you are an existing customer or are looking to become a customer of Fesrodah, please press one, otherwise press two."

Press two in **Section 54**; keep reading to press one.

You press one and the voice continues.

"Thank you for showing interest in the Fesrodah empire, home to many acclaimed, accredited and approved cybersecurity defence solutions."

Georgios rolls his eyes. You are suddenly aware of how hot and uncomfortable the room is. The voice on the phone is unaware of your predicament and continues.

"If you are looking to purchase a new service press one, to discuss an existing order press two and for all other enquiries press three."

Press one in **Section 37**, press two in **Section 316**, press three in **Section 194.**

---

27 Phase Two—Preparation

Considering Golden Slug are motivated to retaliate against companies that damage the environment, wasn't the word "nuclear" an interesting enough lead?

Years of smartphone use have drastically shortened your patience and you've reached a point where you get frustrated with anything that takes more than 15 seconds. Project Luminec is definitely not providing you with immediate gratification, so you move your focus to Project Degrada.

By working back from the Project Luminec folder, you manage to navigate over to the Project Degrada folder. It is full of files, all randomly scattered about with what seems to be no rhyme or reason. An image of a country map sits side by side with a quote for laptops, flanked by Word documents with titles such as "1 year Plan v0.6" and "Employment screening process v1.1".

Your job role transcends seamlessly from Chief Information Security Officer to Jigsaw Grandmaster, as you shift and sort through the random collection of documents to try to piece together what Project Degrada was all about.

As far as you can tell, the objective of the project was to open a research and development laboratory in a remote developing country. It's not clear exactly what this lab was supposed to be researching, but it involved a massively exothermic reaction that would require large amounts of water to cool down if things got out of hand. Your high school chemistry teacher's classes clearly did a great job of planting that knowledge deep in your brain. You decide to go onto your teacher's social media profile later and like a few of their statuses as a thank-you.

Back to Degrada. You puzzle over what the major environmental risk could be, but nothing stands out immediately. Large amounts of water boiling would just turn to rain and fall as per usual. Looking at the project team, you see that Project Degrada is overseen by Jennifer, the Director of Finance, and that Recruitment Manager Vlad recruited the team who work at the laboratory site. Both are online on the internal chat.

Message Jennifer in **Section 327** or message Vlad in **Section 63.**

---

28 Phase Two—Preparation

OK, sit down, I have some bad news for you. You just got phished. Don't worry, it can happen to anyone. That second request came from Jorge@ genericomcompany.com. *Notice there should be two cs following the m, as the domain is* genericomccompany.com. *Don't worry, it's not game over, but keep an eye out for these kinds of tricks in both your personal and professional lives.*

Susan asks for a status report as you arrive back at your desk space. You let her know about the line of enquiry so far and she seems happy enough. She then dumps a new project on you. You need to come up with a poster and supporting training material to help defend against **business email compromise**; apparently it's the flavour of the month.

Best of all, she needs this by the end of the week. She discloses that a member of the directorate may have fallen for this recently, but she's not naming names. She then names their name and walks off.

You spend the rest of the day trying to come up with witty taglines to really make your poster stand out. After exhausting popular culture and film references, you draft a shortlist of ten taglines, then bin them all as reading them back over makes you cringe.

You travel back home via your favourite shopping centre and spend time looking at loud and bright clothing, judging those who buy them but secretly wishing you had the courage to wear them yourself. Afterwards you travel home, eat a simple dinner and head to bed, eager to take the fight to Golden Slug tomorrow.

High five tomorrow in the face in **Section 223.**

29 Phase Two—Preparation

Ha, my distractions worked. By the way, the answer to "What are the two whole, positive numbers that have a one-digit answer when multiplied and a two-digit answer when added together?" is 1 and 9. The answer to "What two-digit number equals two times the result of multiplying its digits?" is 36.

Guillaume chides you over your subpar coffee-making skills.

"You been talking to my wife or something? She thinks I should cut the sugar out of my coffee too."

You apologise and offer to get him another coffee. In reply, he opens his desk drawer to reveal his stash of stolen canteen sugar packets.

"Luckily for you, I had a contingency plan against enforced diets." He stirs in his sugar, takes a satisfied sip, then seems to remember why you were there in the first place.

"Oh right, yeah. This thing started seven months ago. The latest files are on your desktop now."

You thank him and slide back over to your desk to scour the files. There is enough evidence to show that the plant has been up and running for the last four months, operating very profitably. There are some technical documents, but you can't really understand them; they could be a recipe for no-bake brownies or the blueprints to a mega death ray for all you can tell. You catch yourself eavesdropping on someone's conversation with their partner as they book a restaurant for dinner. Clearly they have terrible taste and will likely be taking tomorrow off with food poisoning.

As you snap back into the moment, you realise you've hit a roadblock in your investigation. As the day is winding down, it seems like the best course of action is to brief Susan about this nuclear plant tomorrow morning and get her take on things then. As you grab your bag and head home, you notice that Guillaume has now moved to Minesweeper to fulfil his procrastination. You lie awake a bit longer than usual, occupied with the mystery of Golden Slug, but before long you fall asleep, drifting towards the next day.

See if your luck is better tomorrow in **Section 8.**

---

30 Phase Three—Attack

This is sensible. You can't just go about deleting large amounts of data without properly assessing all the different ways it was being used and what knock-on effects there would be. Whilst your job as CISO is partially focused on information security, you also are meant to contribute to the integrity of company data, and deleting a whole load of files isn't good for integrity.

Susan reacts to your news with good grace, and agrees that the telephone payment system needs to be disabled until the call recording properly censors out the card data as intended. Susan confides in you that taking this course of action will definitely ruffle some feathers. "Giuseppa is definitely going to hate you when she hears about this."

You remind her that this is because of Golden Slug, not because of you.

"True, but Golden Slug are a faceless, shapeless entity. You, however, are very much there. She can see you; hating you is much more tangible."

You tell Susan that you are not feeling very reassured.

"Don't worry, it's fine! This is what I'm here for!"

With a spark of hope, you ask if by that she means that she'll accept responsibility for taking the payment option offline.

Susan laughs. "Sort of. I can say that the action was based on your expert advice, but that the decision came from me."

You nod. That's definitely better than having to face Giuseppa's wrath by yourself. Susan shoos you out of her office so she can make a call, and you decide to head straight to lunch. It's early, but you can't be bothered to start something new at your desk right now.

The day's lunch special is soup, which is just about as exciting as finding a worm in your apple. As you settle down with the soup of the day and a roll of soft bread, your mind starts to replay the encounter with Golden Slug. So far you've managed to thwart their attempts to compromise the e-commerce website and have also put a stop to them harvesting the call recordings. You feel invincible.

Finish your meal and go back upstairs to **Section 201.**

---

31 Phase Three—Attack

Well, good for you. I'd never say no to some winning lottery numbers.

You've always been lucky, which is why you didn't study much for the test when gaining certification for the code analysis module. The exam was multiple choice and you managed to scrape a pass by just selecting B on all the questions you didn't know. Thankfully you managed to pick up enough to figure out the attackers have only had their code in the network for four days. This in itself is actually a small victory, as you've read it typically takes over 200 days for a company to even realise they've been hacked.

You tell Charlotte it was only four days. She rolls her eyes, but nods her head and looks bored as she connects her phone to the office Wi-Fi. You look into the malicious code some more and find the **IP** address that the attackers were having the payment card data sent to. You then look back to see if other Generico McCompany servers have communicated directly with this IP address in the past, to give you an idea of whether the attackers had other plans. You are about to smugly announce your findings to Charlotte, but once again she beats you to the draw.

"Presumably by now you've figured out Golden Slug managed to get into your human resources databases. We should kick them out. Before you ask, I've battled them before and recognise the IP address they are sending data to."

You inform Susan that Golden Slug have also been accessing corporate email. You enjoy the pained look on Charlotte's face, as she had clearly missed that.

Feed off that satisfaction in **Section 315.**

---

32 Phase Two—Preparation

Oh no, I felt sure nobody would actually pick this. Erm. Right, give me a second.

You lie and say you're just an admin, not the CISO.

"I am so sorry, I was given the wrong number. Can you please pass on a message to the Chief Information Security Officer that I need to speak to them urgently?"

You tell Ruby you will pass on the message and she hangs up. You continue flicking through emails.

In many months' time when the Golden Slug incident is being reviewed in a post-mortem investigation, this phone call is used as exhibit A of your incompetence. Ultimately HR deems this dereliction of duty sufficient grounds to have you sacked. The events become folklore in the industry, and whenever you interview for a job the first question is "Why did you pretend you weren't the CISO?"

The End.

Telling the truth is a pretty core principle that people are generally looking for in a friend, employee or romantic partner.

Go back and take the call in **Section 139.**

---

33 Phase Three—Attack

As you know Golden Slug are interested in payment card data, the e-commerce website lead is more immediately tangible than a folder full of MP3 files.

Insuremytoupee is Kevin's application. Toupee insurance is actually a highly lucrative industry, much to your amazement. You consider telling Kevin about the alert, but decide to investigate first. He is so defensive of Insuremytoupee you'd find yourself buried under an avalanche of red tape and wigs if you told him there may be something wrong with the application.

The alert turns out to just be a scraper, stealing all the text off the Insuremytoupee website, presumably so a rival can launch their own competitor service at some point. There's nothing you can do really, except let legal know so they can have the impersonating competitor closed down as soon as they crop up. Unless Golden Slug are playing a very, very, very long game, this is unlikely to relate to them.

You are about to turn your attention to the promising alert hidden amongst the MP3 files when your phone rings again. It's Sergeant.

"We are now up to 10,000 fraudulent transactions, all linking back to cards used on Generico McCompany purchases in the last 48 hours. Have you made any progress?"

You inform him you had a lead that ended up being a dead end.

"Well, the fine for all these stolen payment cards is just racking up. I've been advised to suggest you check your **mail order telephone order** payment processes specifically, as a lot of the cards are used by individuals who would normally pay via that channel."

Do so in **Section 191.**

34 Phase Two—Preparation

The fact that Dragarock are a tiny company is a potential red flag. As a tiny company that sell something that is inserted into a much larger company's e-commerce page, they are a valuable target to hackers as they offer a potential route into numerous companies' e-commerce pages.

You line Dragarock up in your crosshairs. They are a micro company that are scarily good at tracking a user's browsing habits and suggesting ways to dynamically change the user's browsing experience to keep their attention and ultimately get them to buy something. They are the trickster of the e-commerce world, ensuring a popup offering a discount appears just before the shopper loses interest, or placing an advert exactly where they know the user is looking on the screen. You haven't dared ask how Dragarock track a user's eye movements, knowing that any answer you get back is not going to improve your mood.

Just researching Dragarock makes you feel slimy. All this tracking is a necessary evil, but as someone who always rejects the cookies on websites you're slightly uneasy about it all. Despite your own reservations, the small team at Dragarock have done a great job and as creepy as their tools are, they are developed securely. You are just about to give the Golden Slug investigation a break when a new message flashes up on the company's internal chat. It's from Jack, the developer.

"Susan tells me you are particularly focused on payment card security at the moment," he messages, teasingly.

You let him know that indeed you are.

"Well, I've found something you are either going to like or not like, depending on your disposition."

Find out what it is in **Section 293.**

35 Phase Three—Attack

The government incident response team arrive, all wearing dark suits and sunglasses, even indoors. They immediately seize control and you are sidelined, now serving as the designated fetcher of coffee. The government incident response team act fast, identifying how Golden Slug are compromising your firewalls and stopping them in their tracks before booting them off. Ultimately, they manage to figure out how Golden Slug were compromising your firewalls and implement fixes.

Time passes, with the Golden Slug incident fading from recent to distant memory, resulting in neither a positive nor a negative dot on your CV, just a beige acknowledgement. You continue to work for Generico McCompany for three years before accepting a job at another firm. Your leaving drinks are one step below reasonably well attended; your leaving gift is most accurately described as "average". You can't help but feel you could have handled the Golden Slug incident differently.

The End.

> *Don't get me wrong, this is a "fair" ending. It could have turned out a lot worse, but it also could have gone a lot better. If you'd stuck to your guns when challenged by Petra, you'd have opened up the possibility for a more thrilling crescendo. But maybe another time, right? You could always read through again, but this time try drinking the tea instead of coffee—that opens up a completely new can of worms for you.*

36 Phase Three—Attack

> *As they say in chess, any plan, even a bad one, is better than no plan. This is definitely true in cybersecurity incident response.*

You slide open your drawer, revealing your printed version of the incident response plan, a paranoid (or more paranoid) past version of yourself worried that if there was a security incident the printers may be offline or controlled by the enemy. Just in case the printers are the source of the incident, you see. The front cover is a blatant Douglas Adams rip-off, simply stating "Don't panic". You have to admit it's pretty good advice. Next, the plan advises you to get a paper of paper to jot down answers to a few simple questions.

First, it asks you to assign an incident manager; you write your own name down. Then, it asks you what is happening.

"We are suffering huge DDoS attacks to the external perimeter," you write.

Next it asks you what negative impact the attack is causing. Looking around at the panic around you isn't helpful, there is too much noise. Each impacted individual in the company is inconvenienced by the individual tasks they can't perform, but at the core of it the DDoS is making some applications run slower than usual, with some being completely offline. You note this down. Now the document wants you to think of ways to mitigate the impact. Well, removing the radiation from the water supply would be good, but that feels slightly flippant for a reply. You go with the more appropriate "Increase **packet filtering** capability and maintain firewall integrity".

To be clear, there are a lot more options than this, but we are keeping it simple for the purpose of maintaining both your and my sanity.

Susan shoots you an exasperated look, questioning why you are just sitting at your desk with a piece of paper at a time like this. You start to get frustrated with the incident response plan. The next question asks what side effects the attack may be having that are invisible. Strange question.

Keep the faith in the incident response plan in **Section 150**. Switch focus in **Section 200**.

---

37 Phase Three—Attack

Good plan. There is no better way to guarantee speaking to an actual person than saying you want to spend money.

Almost instantly the phone is picked up by an extremely enthusiastic salesperson.

"Hi, good morning, bonjour, buenos dias, aloha! How can I help you today?" they say, in one continuous breath.

Georgios takes the reins. "We are looking to halt a live **Stresser** campaign targeting our network."

"Sure, we can do that, but first let me quickly run through this week's special offer. My phone connection is not very good, so I will just mute your side until I am done explaining."

You cry out desperately for the representative to wait, but Georgios shakes his head. It's too late.

"This week's special offer is a showcase of our new fingerprint recreation technology; all you need to do is to send us a picture of your thumb. We can then produce a replica thumb that can be used for unlocking mobile devices. Perfect for those occasions your phone doesn't recognise your own thumb!

Fesrodah would like to add that according to our terms and conditions this should *not* be used on devices that do not belong to your company."

You wonder aloud to Georgios whether that is even legal.

"Let's not get caught up on such issues," the voice on the phone replies.

"I thought we were muted?" Georgios asks.

"You were, then I unmuted you. Please hold for my manager who can help you with your issue. I will forward you on now.

Talk to the manager in **Section 286.**

---

38 Phase Four—Aftermath

You send Susan a message on internal chat; the chats are not saved or stored in any way, so the message will be safe from Golden Slug's prying eyes. You tell her that Golden Slug are monitoring her email right now, and let her know it's time.

"Got it," Susan replies on chat. Seconds later, her email comes through, simply stating:

"I give you my authorisation. Burn the routes Golden Slug are taking to get into the company and make sure you take care of the backdoors too. Come and see me in person once it's done."

The final sentence was your idea, to avoid Golden Slug waiting for you to think you've kicked them out before double-checking their status. You fire up your monitoring tools and wait, looking for the tell-tale signs of a hacker running scared. You picture yourself as a bear camped next to a river, waiting for a salmon to jump into your mouth. Speaking of salmon, what's for lunch?

Your food-inspired daze is cut short by a mix of alerts and messages on your network security console suggesting that Golden Slug are indeed spooked. They've immediately started drafting an email from an internal account they seem to have compromised. In parallel, they've probed one of the Generico McCompany firewalls and revealed that one of the ports that should be closed is in fact open; this must be how they got into the network in the first place. You close the port with a grin. Golden Slug won't be able to get back in now.

Check out the email they are writing in **Section 96.**

---

39 Phase Two—Preparation

Good choice. It was mentioned that Golden Slug tend to work remotely, so this was the more likely attack pathway.

Thankfully your email filter manages to pick up on a lot of the phishing emails that get sent to Generico McCompany, giving you advanced notice of the tactics the hackers are employing against your staff so you can stay ahead of the game. Just for today there are thousands of entries already, mostly the lazy scattergun variety that only the most pliable staff members fall for. You pick out a few examples of attempts that appear to be tailored to Generico McCompany, since Golden Slug are supposedly a sophisticated attacker.

> Dear Sir/Madam,
>
> Post pondering the proposed proposal for purchasing particular products from yourselves, we have pontificated and proclaim: Please provide further proof of price via the attached PDF.

Unsurprisingly, the PDF contained malware. You spend longer than you'd like to admit trying to read the email in one breath without messing up.

The next email reads:

> Good morning Cecilia,
>
> We are running a story on Generico McCompany's successes with your new smellotape product. Our readers are particularly impressed at the range of smells being offered, and we would love to hear your comments. Please see attached our article. Could you provide a comment please?

Upon closer inspection, that one actually seems to be genuine. You release the email to Cecilia from the public relations team and enquire about whether there is a bacon-flavour smellotape.

Continue sifting through the emails in **Section 94.**

40 Phase Two—Preparation

"Well, it was. Until there was an incident yesterday and the factory had a slight meltdown, resulting in uranium leaking into the adjacent water reservoir."

Wait, what?

"Thanks Michael," Cecilia continues. "I am heading up the PR damage limitation side of things. I've invited some friends from IT, as there was some talk somebody was enquiring about something called Golden Snail yesterday."

"Golden Slug." You and Susan both correct her as one.

"OK, Slug it is. Apparently it has something to do with this?"

You give the room a brief rundown of who Golden Slug are and how they operate. Once you are done, the room is thrown into complete meltdown. Susan bravely jumps in front of the madness and excuses you from the meeting so you can check up on the perimeter defence software to see if you are experiencing a DDoS attack.

As tempting as sneaking in a cup of coffee feels, you believe that would be a poor showing after Susan's valiant sacrifice, so you walk straight back to your desk. There are no new emails in your inbox and the perimeter defence software seems fine; nothing stands out. You watch the white pixels float across the screen representing little **data packets**, wondering what they contain. Naturally you could find out, but inspecting random emails/data packets without good reason is a good way to get into trouble. Perhaps Golden Slug don't know about the nuclear incident yet.

Continue to hope this is the case in **Section 3**.

---

41 Phase Four—Aftermath

"You are looking well rested. Was there caffeine in your big bean burrito?" Susan asks wryly.

Before you can put together a response to protect your honour, she waves her hand and continues.

"Don't worry, I think you deserved a snooze anyway. Despite the numerous people complaining to me as I ate, I maintain it was the right call and am happy to stick by that." She commends your ability to identify Golden Slug's initial plan targeting e-commerce website payment card data and places emphasis on your strong leadership when making use of Galactic Cyber's resources. It would seem a shame to spoil her report by pointing out that Galactic Cyber essentially did their own thing.

After a few days, people stop giving you dirty looks over the password resets and life goes back to normal—normal except for the miniscule pay rise that Susan has squeezed out of her budget for you. Miniscule is better than none after all, if not by much.

Somewhere in a clichéd evil lair, Golden Slug lick their wounds after a convincing defeat. Don't feel too bad for them: they'll soon be at it again, but hopefully it won't be Generico McCompany in their crosshairs next time.

The End.

> *Excellent work. You thwarted Golden Slug twice on the same read-through. Save some success for the rest of us! Crucially, you didn't give in to the popular decision at the end, instead putting the business's interests above your own image, as you should. Including Galactic Cyber in your response really ended up paying off. Have you thought about getting involved in genuine incident response at all? There are roles for non-technical people too, you know.*
>
> *Double-check you are cut out for a career in information security by reading through again, but drinking coffee this time—it's an entirely novel experience.*

42 Phase Four—Aftermath

A woman with a slightly nicer suit than her colleagues seems to be in charge and summarises things for you.

"We've received intelligence that the threat actor known as Golden Slug has sold over 400,000 payment card details on various dark web forums in the past month. All of these 400,000 payment card details have been traced back to Generico McCompany. My team will perform a full forensic investigation. Stay out of their way."

The forensic investigation looks back over the original Golden Slug breach, seeking out where things may have gone wrong. After moving through the initial e-commerce and call recording incidents, the timeline reaches the PIN entry device maintenance events.

A team of investigators seize a PIN entry device machine from a Generico McCompany retail outlet and carefully dismantle it, during which they discover that a piece of hardware has been inserted. The hardware is designed to save and transmit the details of any card that is used on the device. The details are then sent over to an IP address, which, needless to say, is the Golden Slug IP address from before. As this is hardware and not software, your attempt to roll back the devices to a previous version did nothing to protect them.

Generico McCompany make a grand show of firing you to try to appease the general public, who are understandably angry at having fraud committed against their payment cards. You learn your lesson and eventually end up at a slightly worse company, on slightly worse pay.

The End.

> *The problem here was you had reason to believe Golden Slug had managed to get their hands on the entire Generico McCompany PIN entry device estate and decided to fix these remotely. Whilst you pushed these devices back to a known safe software version, there was no guarantee that Golden Slug hadn't tampered with the physical hardware itself. This type of attack has historically been quite common in petrol stations, where small inserts are attached to the card machines on pumps that take a copy of each payment card used. The hackers come back after the inserts have been running for a few months and download all the data, ready to sell it on the dark web. Anyway, why not start again, but try having coffee this time instead?*

43 Phase Two—Preparation

> *A more valid choice this time. Golden Slug are known to use DDoS as their modus operandi, so it would be smart to check if there are known **vulnerabilities** in the estate that would make this easier to pull off if they were interested in targeting you. As an added bonus, this work improves the company's overall cyberhygiene and helps protect against other threats.*

Before you review the penetration test report, you decide to drop a line to a friend outside of Generico McCompany. Raul has worked in the industry for decades and you are keen to get his take on Golden Slug. Knowing how hectic Raul's life is, you don't expect a reply anytime soon.

You are a reasonable human being and not a savage, and therefore you find the penetration test report conveniently saved in an appropriately named folder called "External Penetration Test Report". You wince as you read through the report. It was a shrewd move getting this test completed early on so you could appreciate just how mammoth your task is. At the same time, though, it did just produce a huge list of vulnerabilities that you can only ask teams to fix so many times before they murder you.

The seriously bad stuff has been fixed since the test was completed, though two unremediated vulnerabilities jump out as potentially being relevant.

"Application Lockout denial of service"

> *Well, that one has denial of service in its name.*

"**Firewall** set to reboot in weak state"

Weak is bad.

Look at the application lockout vulnerability in **Section 189,** or the firewall-related vulnerability in **Section 173.**

---

44 Phase Three—Attack

You must have paid more attention to your ballet lessons and not your spelling lessons as a child. Are you sure there are two rs in that, by the way?

You spell out "pirrouetter" on your keyboard and hit enter, satisfied that at least you didn't actually feel your fingers leaving the keyboard's top row of letters. Your laptop's cooling fan whirrs noisily as the Golden Slug application hungrily uses up the computer's processing power, comparing the answer you submitted with whatever it deems is acceptable. After a nervous few seconds that feel like hours, the text on the screen changes.

"Before question two, let us explain why we decided to give you this chance to deactivate our surprise."

That would be quite nice actually, how considerate.

"It's because we think you are pathetic."

Oh right, you are going to have to pretend that one doesn't sting and move on as the text on the screen changes again.

"Question two. What never asks a question but always gets answered?"

If you think the word is "Books", go to **Section 77.** If you think the word is "Telephone", go to **Section 340.**

---

45 Phase Three—Attack

Ever heard the expression "you are poking a beehive"?

You nod, letting Susan know that could work, and inform her you'll take the firewall offline next. Susan nods back, then slowly picks up her phone.

"I am going to call one of my government contacts. I need to report the activity relating to nuclear secrets."

You slink out of the room—that doesn't sound like a fun conversation to have. You enlist Guillaume and Vijaya into the plan and proceed to prepare to take the compromised firewall offline. Around you Golden Slug's DDoS continues to rain chaos down on the IT department, but you've got bigger fish to fry now. Preparations are ready, you click your mouse to confirm the changes and Fernando's light blinks out.

Susan rushes into the room. "I know I just told you to, but please tell me you haven't taken the firewall down."

You stare at your hand in horror, as it still grips the guilty mouse. Susan reads her answer off your face.

"My contact warned me they'd realise we were on to them. They are sending trained responders to take over. Do what you can to fend off Golden Slug until they get here."

A quick glance at your perimeter defence software proves Susan's contact right: six firewalls are now compromised and throwing data out of the company network and into Golden Slug's hands.

See how things end up in **Section 35.**

46 Phase Three—Attack

A difficult search is preferable to emailing Golden Slug—what possible reason do they have for providing you any kind of help over email? At least with this route you are making your own luck.

It is now 13:30. Golden Slug's last burst of DDoS attack occurred at 13:00, leaving you not much opportunity to eat lunch. The hunger is clearly getting to you as you eye a colleague's dull green salad with envy. Susan, the mind reader, tells you to go and eat something to recharge your batteries and start fresh afterwards.

The staff canteen's daily special is a stir fry, which you complement with sweet and sour soup and finish off with chocolate sponge. Upon finishing your meal, the realisation hits that you've just eaten essentially a three-course meal in mere minutes and are now attracting stunned looks from those sat near you. After committing the faces to memory so you can hide from them in the future, you make your escape.

Glancing at a clock on the wall tells you it's now 14:05. You brace yourself before walking into the IT room, ready to witness the chaos of the latest DDoS wave.

Oddly enough, the room seems to be calm. After booting up your perimeter defence system, there doesn't appear to be any DDoS attack taking place. You reboot the software just to be sure, but no attack materialises. Theorising that maybe someone went and did something even worse than Generico McCompany, you scroll through the recent news, but apart from some F list celebrities voicing their insignificant views and the world record for the longest fingernails being broken, there is nothing newsworthy. Naturally you check out the fingernails, and they are as gross as you expected.

Another two hours pass without further DDoS attacks.

Tiptoe over to **Section 337.**

47 Phase Three—Attack

"Breaches happen" is the opening statement of the post-Golden Slug fiasco summary report. It goes on to say that reasonable efforts undertaken by members of staff driven by integrity and a risk-based approach are sufficient to handle the majority of less technically advanced incidents.

The rest doesn't make very pleasant reading. After first savaging you for your approach to researching the potential Golden Slug threat, the report continues to lay into you for the "misguided" attempt to subvert the media to paint your failings in a more positive light. *Ouch.* The following day you don't even bother to go into work, knowing that you'd just be escorted out first thing anyway.

In a faraway land, Golden Slug members celebrate their successful campaign against Generico McCompany. The newspaper clippings are used to decorate their offices, in homage to your unintentional assistance in their campaign. They even find your address amongst the data they stole and send you a gift basket, which seems like overkill.

The job market is tough, especially since the very public news stories hang over you for months. Even when you do manage to get an interview, the question is raised of whether you can be trusted to tell the truth in high-pressure situations. As well as you handle the questions, the recruiter always says they'll call back. They never call back.

The End.

> *You didn't think you'd get rewarded for lying, did you? Look, I'll be honest, you didn't have much chance of coming out of this well as you didn't make enough progress in phase two. Try reading through again, but making some different choices to hopefully push you towards a better outcome.*

48 Phase Three—Attack

Lunchtime provides an ideal opportunity to continue thinking about the Golden Slug email. From the murmurings you hear between colleagues, the story has hit the newspapers. Some people shoot you disapproving glances, others put more of a sympathetic feeling into their facial expressions. To avoid conversation on the matter you decide just to get a sandwich from the staff canteen and eat it somewhere quiet.

As you queue at the checkout, you watch a scene play out before you. An elderly man attempts to pay for his food with a payment card, but it gets rejected.

"This card seems to have expired four years ago," the cashier tells the man, who looks astounded at the news and curses technology before paying with cash. He drops a penny from his coin pile and a penny simultaneously drops in your mind.

After paying for your own lunch and rushing back to your desk, you open the Golden Slug email again. You put a call into a contact at a bank where some of the cards were issued from and they confirm that the payment cards in question haven't been active for years. Golden Slug just inserted a load of genuine but old cards into their email to make it look more compelling, but it would appear it was a lie.

You let Cecilia know to backtrack on previous statements and begin to ponder why Golden Slug would bother lying about this.

Find out why in **Section 338.**

---

49 Phase Three—Attack

No sooner is Susan out of eyeshot than the phone rings again, the same number as five seconds ago. Likely Sergeant has forgotten how to use his swanky automatic telephone.

"You've been hacked," he states.

You point out that he told you the cards were nothing to do with you only five seconds ago.

"Forget those, that must have been Golden Slug trying to cause some panic and confusion through misdirection. We've seen fraud patterns that point squarely at you guys now. This is from cards used to make payments for Generico McCompany products in the last 48 hours. I'm counting over 10,000 payment cards and rising."

Sergeant lets you know he will send the details over email, but also that as per his role he will need to make the appropriate authorities aware.

You put the phone down and look at it blankly for a while, just hoping that Sergeant's number flashes up again because he's made a mistake, but it doesn't ring again. You have no idea how or where Golden Slug are taking payment card data out of Generico McCompany, but they are clearly doing so, potentially even right now. Sergeant's email hits your inbox, including details of a sample of 50 payment cards that have been compromised. It's time to call in your incident response **retainer**.

Pick up the phone in **Section 168.**

---

50 Phase Four—Aftermath

Rather than carrying out some kind of elaborate technical hack, Ruben was able to access the internet to message Golden Slug the card details by making some rather simple changes to his browser settings. You commission some **penetration testing** work to check that there are no other simple tricks like that which could be used. When questioned by the police, Ruben confesses that he was approached and enticed over to the dark side by Golden Slug, who promised him cash in his bank account for every payment card he managed to sneak out of the business.

Overall, Generico McCompany are very pleased with your efforts. Thanks to you, the damage was limited to the cards that Ruben had already stolen, and you even exposed the Golden Slug e-commerce attack before it could execute fully. Susan sorts you out with a promotion and a pay rise, and life is good for a year, until Kevin of Insuremytoupee fame falls for an appallingly blatant **phishing** email, which leads to Generico McCompany losing a huge cache of personal data.

The toupee-wearing, insurance-loving general public unite and demand action, and eventually Generico McCompany bow to the media pressure and let you go. It's not all bad news, though: you instantly get a new job at a Generico McCompany affiliate business that pays more anyway.

The End.

> *Excellent work. You have foiled Golden Slug over and over and emerge victorious. I thought you were going to mess up defusing the logic bomb, but what do I know? Why not read through the tea story again, but shake things up early on and see how they play out? Alternatively, why not try coffee this time? You know it's a completely separate story if you do, right?*

51 Phase Three—Attack

"I've found it!" Guillaume announces, pointing to a well-concealed few lines that send copies of all card details that are used on the site through to a Golden Slug **server**. You take a mental note of the **IP** address of their server.

> *This has been known to happen in the real world, with some rumoured instances of the code being smart enough to hide itself when IP addresses linked to security researchers or law enforcement were looking.*

"This is new," Ruby observes, pointing out how much slicker and more refined the Golden Slug code is compared to their usual work. It's unsurprising really: criminal hacking groups still contain "employees" in a sense who will want career development and training opportunities, so it's only natural they improve over time.

Your mind drifts to picturing what the lunch options would be like at an illegal hacking training camp when you get jolted back into the real world. You take a snapshot of the offending code and run a search across all of the Generico McCompany e-commerce estate, finding an instance of the code in every single website. With a huge grin, you hit the "Delete" key and remove Golden Slug's card-stealing payload from the Generico McCompany network.

> *A CISO wouldn't traditionally get this hands-on—this would be a task for the developers.*

You are about to thank Ruby for her input as she packs up to report back to her bosses, when an idea springs to mind. Seeing as you have Golden Slug's IP address, what if you sent a massive load of internet traffic to it as payback?

See what Ruby thinks of that in **Section 266**. If you think it's better not even to ask, go to **Section 104.**

---

52 Phase Three—Attack

> *Susan is approving budget spend. Make the most of it whilst you can!*

You admit that you think it's the best and potentially only option you can think of.

"Get me the contract, I'll try to get approval so I can sign it after this meeting."

The time it takes for an electrical impulse to move from one neuron to another is a tiny fraction of a second, yet somehow that seems slow when compared with the speed with which Tony received your request for a contract and subsequently sent it over to you.

It hardly feels like a minute has passed before you slip a printed version of the contract on Susan's desk. You are tempted to leave a pen with it, but chicken out as that could be taken as patronising. Whilst you wait for Susan's call to finish and for her to sign off on the new contract, you declutter your emails.

You notice that Petra has forwarded you the email she received. Looking at it you notice a curious detail. Golden Slug's email is hello@goldenslug.com. What if you just email them?

Send them an email in **Section 85**.

53 Phase Three—Attack

The space around your desk feels different to how it did mere minutes ago, somehow less evil. You look around and try to figure out why. As your eyes land on the now vacant seat Charlotte occupied, it suddenly makes sense: anywhere would feel different if you removed a cave troll. Standing up to inspect the desk, you notice that it is now completely empty. You ask a nearby colleague, who confirms, "Charlotte packed up and left not long after you and Niko walked off. She looked worried."

That in itself is a victory, right?

You ask if she got a phone call or something, but apparently she just got spooked out of nowhere and left. Fantastic news.

You spend the next few hours checking and double-checking that Golden Slug have been removed from the Generico McCompany network, then triple-checking just for peace of mind. After all of that, you are as confident as you can be that your remediation efforts have been successful.

You spot Petra in your peripheral vision, which must mean the board meeting is finished. You rush to Susan's office to reveal your findings and ask about her snow globe. After hearing your story, Susan's immediate response is to ask you where Charlotte is. You let her know she left in a hurry.

"It's no wonder she disappeared," Susan remarks, as she throws the snow globe up and down. You ask her what she means.

"You didn't look at this thing, did you?" she asks, thrusting it towards you.

You are forced to wait until the snow settles first, then you inspect the globe and finally notice the writing etched inside: "Merry Christmas from the National Fraud Office".

Pick your jaw up from the floor in **Section 7.**

---

54 Phase Three—Attack

The phone hangs up.

> *You laugh, but I remember a company whose actual switchboard had a process exactly like this.*

Call again in **Section 26.**

---

55 Phase Three—Attack

"Yes, and we are very grateful for the professional support from the National Fraud Office," Susan replies. "Will you show Charlotte to a hot desk and bring her up to speed?"

"I don't think there is anything they can bring me up to speed on—you wouldn't even know there was a breach if not for us. But I suppose they can carry my bag. I'll find the hot desks myself. Unlike a certain someone, I have initiative. I will go and set up."

Charlotte makes good on her word and walks out of Susan's door towards the main IT area. You are about to follow obediently, but Susan stops you.

"Wait one second. Let me just set the scene a little regarding Charlotte."

You groan and ask Susan whether you've wronged Charlotte in a previous life.

"Well, actually she thinks you've wronged her in this life. You and Charlotte were the last two in the interview process for CISO. She didn't take losing out on that well and clearly holds a grudge. Luckily for me, it's against you rather than me."

> *Whilst this shouldn't happen, if you know you are down to a final two selection process and then see someone else start the job, you can kind of put two and two together. Best not to divulge those kinds of details, really.*

You agree that it's lucky for her, not so lucky for you, before hefting Charlotte's bag and heading off in search of its owner. You find her talking to your desk neighbours and catch the tail end of their conversation.

"Have they even upgraded the anti**virus** to version six?"

"I don't think so, no."

They immediately drop the conversation upon your arrival and scatter, Charlotte setting up on a hot desk spot opposite your desk. You leave Charlotte's bag on her new, hopefully temporary home.

Wonder why life is kicking you where it hurts in **Section 230.**

56 Phase Two—Preparation

As soon as you start walking towards the bathroom, it becomes an obstacle course. It is always when you are most in need of the toilet that people seem to come out of the woodwork to bother you about things that have nothing to do with you. You put your slippery shoulders to good use, deflecting and diverting responsibility and chitchat as you travel to your destination. You agree with Leanne that the website would look better with less text per web page, but unfortunately that is not something you have any influence on. Does the water pouring out of the water cooler always gurgle and drip so much?

Finally, you manage to escape and enter the toilets. In some ways, you could argue that a company's toilets reflect the company's soul. Generico McCompany's toilets are minimalist but functional, generally clean, and with a soft scent of lemon desperately fighting off other smells. You get on with your business.

Wash your hands in **Section 125.** If you are in too much of a hurry to wash your hands, skip over to **Section 285.**

57 Phase Three—Attack

The majority of cybersecurity professionals would stand by this choice. Paying ransoms is typically viewed dimly by regulators, the public and law enforcement. There is also significant evidence that even companies who pay ransoms end up having their data posted on online forums anyway.

You communicate your reluctance to reward Golden Slug financially, particularly as there is no assurance that they wouldn't just dump the database in any case.

"I will run it by the board just to be sure. Whilst I am getting their opinion, I need Golden Slug off the network or they'll find some way to increase their leverage on us."

You and Ruby exit Susan's office and home in on evicting Golden Slug. To do this you need to figure out how they got onto the network to begin with. As you now know the SCAPI database was stolen, you are able to look through the **logs** relating to the SCAPI database and look for clues on how Golden Slug pulled off their heist.

In your mind you picture some kind of epic hacking montage, potentially involving office stationery that transforms into robots and would then plug in and hack the company during the night. The reality is much more mundane. Golden Slug got hold of the SCAPI database by just asking someone to send it to them. Apparently, no background or cover story was required, they merely brazenly emailed asking for the database and Fernando from the logistics team obliged.

You let Fernando's line manager know about this via internal chat. Their response is simply: "I can't help but feel this is your fault as you are the CISO. It is up to you to prevent this."

You don't even bother replying. You just turn to Ruby and shrug.

> *Some would argue that all security systems should assume the users are either incompetent or outright malicious and work from there.*

Bring those shoulders back down in **Section 348.**

---

58 Phase Three—Attack

"Contact!" Ship Cat Tobias exclaims. "They are using a **zero-day vulnerability** that is targeting **port** 13337."

"Commencing analysis," First Mate Gloria continues.

> *Real-time analysis of a zero-day vulnerability is pretty next level.*

"Shiver me timbers! The honeypot is taking on water, abandon ship."

You ask Captain Dave what he means by abandon ship.

"Nothing, we just have a quota of pirate puns to hit to earn our annual bonuses."

You ask who even tracks that. Instead of a reply, Captain Dave points to Pedro the Parrot and winks. First Mate Gloria's fingers fly over her keyboard at an alarming pace as she deconstructs the **vulnerability** that Golden Slug are using to commandeer your servers.

"Based on my analysis, we can stop them completely by just closing port 13337. If we then reboot the servers they've infected, we'll have removed them from the network—unless they have other **zero day**s up their sleeves," she announces. After running some checks, you conclude that port 13337 wasn't actually being used for anything, so shutting it won't have any adverse effects.

Activity on the screen shows Golden Slug have now moved their attention to a database that contains a treasure trove of personal data and sensitive company secrets. It's a matter of minutes until they have access to all of it. It's time to act: either close the port completely or prevent the IPs that Golden Slug are using from accessing port 13337.

Close port 13337 in **Section 240**. Block Golden Slug's IPs in **Section 366**.

---

59 Phase Three—Attack

Nobody likes having their emails accessed by hackers. It doesn't make shareholders feel good either.

You outline your preference to look into the email server first. Both Charlotte and Susan look at you as if suddenly surprised even to see you there. Charlotte opens her mouth to interject before Susan interrupts, an interaction you enjoy immensely.

"Good idea. I don't want Golden Slug reading our emails. Anyway, I have to attend a board meeting for the next few hours so I won't be contactable, I trust you will retake control of the network."

It isn't clear whether that comment is aimed at you or Charlotte. As Susan is about to leave, she adds, "Good luck." Which you feel is definitely aimed at you.

You race Charlotte to the email server to start investigating what Golden Slug are up to. She wins the race.

In reality you would likely be making a copy of the compromised asset and reviewing that rather than touching the asset itself. You'd also make a copy that is never touched, in case it is needed as evidence during a legal/insurance proceeding.

"It looks like Golden Slug have obtained some administrator credentials from somewhere and are now inside your corporate email. This is not going to make good reading in my report," she comments.

Whilst it's not ideal from an information security perspective, you point out that Charlotte is supposed to be investigating from a purely fraud perspective. She shrugs before letting you know that she won't spare any details in her write-up, even if it's unrelated to fraud, thanks. She whips out what looks like a personal phone and taps away.

You start to triage which administrator account Golden Slug have taken control of, arriving at a surprising conclusion. Golden Slug have got hold of Susan's credentials, including some mechanism for stealing her two-factor authentication code from her mobile phone.

That sounds bad. See if it is in **Section 252.**

60 Phase Four—Aftermath

Guillaume tells a story of how after breaking up with his girlfriend she hid a fish behind a kitchen cupboard as a parting gift, with Guillaume then spending weeks looking for the source of the smell. It's at this point that you connect the dots and realise: what if Golden Slug left a metaphorical fish in your network?

You open up the **logs** and start poring through all the activity from the compromised administrator account over the past month. Whilst the majority of activities look like genuine developer behaviour, you have to spend a lot of time validating these, as that was how Golden Slug snuck their payment card data stealing code in originally. After a very long stretch of work, you filter the suspicious activity down to two events that are potentially worth looking into. Three days ago, at six o'clock in the evening, the administrator account spent half an hour copying user email inboxes into a separate folder. This could be genuine, as sometimes HR need copies of inboxes if people are suspected of breaking corporate policy, but equally it could be dodgy.

As well as this, there is a record of the administrator account making some changes within the procurement tool that Generico McCompany use to purchase hardware. Without a deep dive it's hard to tell what they've changed.

Investigate the email inbox copying in **Section 358**. Look into the changes in the procurement tool in **Section 301.**

61 Phase Four—Aftermath

The next day Susan reveals that Vijaya sang like a canary almost immediately once pressed. She admits to being a member of Golden Slug and acting as an insider agent for them. Bizarrely, she has been disguising tofu as chicken for years to hide the fact she was a devout vegetarian in an over-the-top effort to muddy the waters of her environmental background and interests.

A detailed forensic investigation into her computer activity highlighted she had created numerous **backdoors** throughout the company for Golden Slug or other hackers to use in the future. Those are now closed.

As Susan sips her morning coffee, she reflects on all the tiny choices that led you both to this point and wonders what would have been if your actions hadn't led to uncovering Vijaya's treachery. A full post-Golden Slug investigation does wonders for your career prospects. Generico McCompany thank you for your efforts by paying for an all-inclusive tropical holiday, without a slug in sight.

Upon your return a significant promotion and pay rise await, neatly wrapped up with a garish Generico McCompany signature snot-green bow. You don't get complacent, though. Whilst you won this round against Golden Slug, who knows what threat actors might ruin all that good work tomorrow?

The End.

Wow, you did it. This is pretty much the best ending you can get for the coffee storyline. Not only did you thwart Golden Slug, you also rooted out their malicious insider. That's got to be worth a thumbs-up, maybe even two. Believing in the incident response plan was vital in bringing you to this point. Remember that even a bad plan is better than no plan.

Now the question is: Are you brave enough to read through again, but make some terrible decisions to see how that impacts the story and what you learn along the way?

62 Phase Four—Aftermath

"What on earth is going on?" Susan enquires. Her voice is incredibly calm, considering that Generico McCompany are now approaching 10 minutes of being completely unable to work. As you bring Susan up to speed, her face drops.

"Write down the equation that linked to the kill switch, please," she asks, so you do so. Upon seeing the equation, Susan immediately fires you. Unfortunately, your exit interview can't be scheduled for a few days because of, well, you know, that ransomware you ended up spreading all over the Generico McCompany IT estate.

When you eventually have your exit interview, it is revealed that Susan immediately lost faith in your ability to act in your role upon seeing that you were unable to solve the Golden Slug equation. Susan also points out that your investigation into Golden Slug's activity yielded no usable intelligence.

You spend the next few months mugging up on your maths whilst the Generico McCompany breach rages hot on the news. The NotNotCatya damage ends up being so significant that Susan also loses her job. She immediately gets snapped up into a bigger and better role, but you somehow doubt she'd hire you again.

Generico McCompany eventually recover from the Golden Slug incident and hire a woman named Charlotte to replace you as CISO. You find another job as CISO and manage to last a year, until the company is breached and you are again shown the door. This settles into a comfortable routine of being hired and fired, which ends up being more lucrative than you imagined. But despite that, it's a hollow victory; all you ever wanted was to be a success.

The End.

Remember BODMAS: Brackets, Order, Division, Multiplication, Addition, Subtraction.

Try the maths again in **Section 123**.

---

63 Phase Two—Preparation

It would have been slightly more direct to talk to the person who had oversight of the entire project, as opposed to the person who recruited the staff.

You message Vlad and let him know that you have a small question for him.

"Come to my desk, then, and ask away!"

Of course. How could you forget? Everyone in recruitment always wants to talk face to face. You decide to take the stairs up to floor 14; healthy body, healthy mind and all that. Floor 14 is a mirror of floor 13, which makes navigation easy. You peek into the kitchen on floor 14 to check out the snacks and treats they have on offer. All you see is a fruit basket; that's lame.

As you enter the recruitment room you feel the overwhelming positivity wash over you like an overly pungent aftershave. You catch snippets of recruiter conversation as you walk over to Vlad's desk.

"Yes, our benefits package is very competitive."

"No, we've never had someone quit due to snake bites, where did you hear that?"

"Everybody gets a free puppy when they join, it's true!"

You make a mental note to follow up on that puppy promise, but for the minute focus on maintaining eye contact with Vlad, who is now stood up and beaming at you.

"How are you doing? Long time no see," Vlad says, forgetting that you were in a two-hour meeting together last week.

You let him know you are alright and ask if he has a spare minute.

"Actually no, I don't," he responds. You look at him with a bewildered expression. Why did he tell you to come over in person if he isn't even free?

"Just kidding! What do you need from my team of merry head hunters?"

Inwardly, you roll your eyes. You decide to be direct and try to avoid further mind games. You come straight out and say you need to talk about Project Degrada.

"Oh yeah, I remember that one. The very opposite of chill penguin that was."

Find out why Project Degrada wasn't "chill penguin" in **Section 352.**

---

64 Phase Two—Preparation

What colour was that lanyard again?

You let them know that'll be no problem, reaching out your hand to take the USB and regretting your previous reservations.

"Thanks so much, you've saved me. By the way, plug it into your laptop for a few seconds, it just needs to charge up a little."

They smile, then walk over to reception to chat. You make your getaway back to your desk and plug the USB in to let it charge. You then leave the USB on your desk as a reminder for when Sakura is back. There is an awkward amount of time left before lunch and it's not enough to start anything significant, so instead you spend it browsing pictures of your colleagues' pets.

Feeling thoroughly satisfied, you head towards the canteen on the second floor to take your chances on whatever is being passed off as food for the day. They are serving pasta with a creamy red pepper sauce; your gamble has paid off and it's pretty good. You've not exactly struck gold with the people on your table and the conversation ranges from boring to bland, but years in the corporate world have taught you that lunch is rarely perfect. This one in particular isn't, as you are interrupted by a text message that arrives on your work phone.

"Emergency meeting, my office, five minutes."

It's from Susan. You wolf down your food and move towards Susan's office.

See what the emergency meeting is for in **Section 235.**

---

65 Phase Four—Aftermath

You watch as the Golden Slug DDoS continues to rain down, but with less intensity than before as your existing DDoS defence service provider becomes better equipped at repelling the attacks. The firewall army continue to diligently perform their work, resisting the corrupting influence of Golden Slug thanks to Niko's signature-based packet filtering,

Generico McCompany commend you for your handling of the incident, culminating in a significant pay rise and promotion. They still end up throwing you on the scrapheap a few years down the line when they need a scapegoat, but that's the industry really. You are quickly snapped up to an even better-paying job with a company who let you rollerblade in the corridors and have free cake every single day.

The End.

> *Nice. This is a rather pleasant ending, though it could have been even more pleasant if you'd fought your corner and stood up to Petra when given the chance. Overall, you've done a good job. Enjoy it, as most of the endings in this book are significantly more brutal. Once you've done basking in your glory, why not have another go, but pick tea rather than coffee for a different adventure?*

66 Phase Two—Preparation

> *By doing this you can see just how bad it would be if a large number of these firewalls were forced into crashing and rebooting during a DDoS attack.*

You squeeze in an inane conversation with a passing colleague before inspecting the firewall's factory settings. You lose track of whether you are talking about their child or their pet, but luckily your responses are deemed socially acceptable and they move on, seemingly fulfilled.

The factory settings for the firewall turn out to be pretty bad. In all fairness Burpafence never claimed otherwise and openly recommend their customers to change these settings. A quick peek under the hood shows that the firewall's rules are primitive when running in the factory settings, suitable for preventing non-skilled actors from getting through, but not really doing a lot to prevent someone with a higher degree of sophistication.

There is an obvious fix to this problem: you could simply mass update the firewalls so that if they reboot they start up in the "good" state rather than the "bad" state. You give your sales representative from Burpafence, Greg, a call to see how feasible this is.

"Yeah, that functionality isn't going to be possible at the moment," says Greg. "The mass updater can push out patch updates en masse, but the changes you are talking about need the updater to connect on a one-to-one basis."

Not quite getting it, you ask Greg to explain that again in layperson's terms.

"That won't work, you can only manually update one firewall at a time."

> *This is a case of this being convenient for storytelling rather than fully accurate: most firewalls can be mass updated in parallel.*

You thank Greg and let him know that you're looking forward to paying his huge invoice at the end of the month.

"And I'm looking forward to receiving it."

You hang up the phone. A metaphorical phone rings: nature is calling.

Visit the bathroom in **Section 56.**

---

67 Phase Three—Attack

> *Whilst it is "slower", without you knowing how Golden Slug got their code onto your e-commerce estate there may be no point in deleting it, as they could just put it back. Equally, if Golden Slug were lining up any long-term plans they'd be likely to start them immediately, as they'd be made aware that you are on their trail. By the way, I'm not saying the decision was wrong necessarily. Sometimes all options are just a different tone of grey.*

You outline your plan to work backwards from the changes in the e-commerce website code to find out how Golden Slug got into your network initially.

"What about the payment card data they are stealing? We process thousands of cards per minute. The regulator is going to have a field day," Susan retorts icily.

You agree with Susan, they will have a field day, but if you remove the code first, that gives Golden Slug a heads-up that you are on to them, which might alter their behaviour. Secondly, they could just come back in and change it again. You look to Ruby for affirmation.

"That seems sensible," Ruby replies.

Susan concedes, albeit reluctantly.

> *To be clear, in some situations containment of the issue is so important you'd be better off bringing the business to a complete halt rather than letting things rage on. It is a balancing act. For those who say you should always shut things down immediately, from a security perspective sure, but from a business perspective, good luck making a retailer shut down their e-commerce website in the week leading up to Christmas/peak season.*

"Fine, but make it quick. I need that payment card data to stop leaking ASAP."

The meeting ends there. Susan suggests Ruby stays in the meeting room and uses it as an office for the day if she wishes, which Ruby accepts.

You file out of the room and back to your desk, catching slivers of conversation between Guillaume and Vijaya, including lines like "We got owned by amateurs?" and "Incompetent". You decide to pretend you'd heard nothing.

You talked a good game, but are not really sure where to start with this hunt. You could attempt to track down the user account that changed the code, or you could try to analyse some of the malicious code to identify how it got there.

Look at user accounts in **Section 135** or analyse the code in **Section 156.**

---

68 Phase Four—Aftermath

> *In terms of covering your backside, this is a safe pick.*

Susan is sat on the small sofa in her office, buried in a popular book about leadership. You clear your throat and she notices you waiting at the door. She nods at you to come in, puts the book to one side and asks what you want.

You give her a brief update on the situation and ask if there would be any impact from Golden Slug reading through her last year's worth of email.

"Not much really. Despite what people think, a director's inbox isn't as interesting as you'd think. I'm not emailing any company secrets that would help them with their hacking campaign."

You give Susan two options: you can either try to scare Golden Slug into making a mistake and revealing the method through which they are accessing Generico McCompany's network, or you can focus on getting Golden Slug removed as soon as possible.

"That book tells me that to crush an opponent I first need to know what their plan is. But at the same time, would that just be overcomplicating things by letting Golden Slug persevere on the network longer than need be?"

Lay a trap in **Section 75**. Evict Golden Slug from the network as soon as possible in **Section 332**.

69 Phase Three—Attack

You tell Charlotte that Susan mentioned she was coming and introduce yourself as the Generico McCompany Chief Information Security Officer.

"My name is Charlotte. Please show me to the mess you have allowed to form," she responds.

Charming, you think to yourself as you hand her a red guest pass, resisting the urge to respond to her jab. You lead her to the lifts. As you approach the lift, Charlotte intercepts you and stands next to the control panel.

"What floor?" she demands.

You tell her it's the 13th.

"Excellent," she replies, pressing the button for floor 13 and then immediately beginning to wash her hands with hand sanitiser from a small bottle.

"I press my own buttons," she tells you. You ride up in silence after that, with Charlotte swinging her bag menacingly close to you. Once the lift doors save you from that awkward situation, you walk with her to Susan's office. Strangely, Charlotte seems to know the way already.

When you arrive at Susan's office, Charlotte is suddenly all smiles. "Susan, so good to see you again, though perhaps not in the ideal circumstances," she says, extending an arm to Susan.

A flash of surprise streaks Susan's face before she accepts the handshake and replies, "Good to see you, Charlotte. I see you work for the National Fraud Office now."

Charlotte doesn't correct Susan like she corrected you. "Indeed, I am here to investigate and hopefully guide you through cleaning up a breach that someone has let get out of hand," she says, pointedly looking at you as she speaks.

Oh dear. See what she has to say in **Section 55**.

70 Phase Two—Preparation

Third parties are regularly used as a way in to companies. Typically, company websites will be connected to and supplied with code or data by dozens of third parties. If a hacker can gain access to the third-party company, they can potentially change the code or data that is supplied and make use of the knock-on effects. As an example, a stock-trading platform may set its prices based on financial data that comes into the platform; by changing the data going in, a hacker may then be in a position to buy a stock cheaply or sell stock for above its value. The same premise is true in internet browsers, by the way. There has been a long history of plugins that were useful and used by many that then get bought by someone with a malicious agenda. That individual is essentially acquiring a method of pushing their malicious code down to all the users of that plugin.

You start by opening a document that lists the third-party extensions and code that Generico McCompany's e-commerce websites make use of. There are over 50 entries. You are going to need to start applying some filters to bring that number down.

You see Google appear a few times; needless to say, if something happened to Google you wouldn't be the only company to feel the effects, so you exclude them from your investigation. You remove a few more companies as their code hasn't changed in three years, and some more get sidelined because their names are funny. You split the remaining entries into two lists and discard one list entirely; now you've removed the unlucky third parties.

Three candidates immediately stand out after your thorough filtering process:

- TLK2ME, who provide the interface for online chat on your websites
- Dragarock, a tiny three-person company who provide code that tracks users' browsing habits
- Vatidiva, which seems to provide sound effects to the page during a user's online shopping checkout process

Look into TLK2ME in **Section 198**, explore Dragarock in **Section 34** or review Vatidiva in **Section 98**.

71 Phase Three—Attack

Exactly. Books can't talk, so how could they ever ask a question?

You feed your answer of "Books" in and hit enter, feeling good about things. The screen fades to black before being replaced by a new five-minute countdown, letting you know that that is how long is needed to process your submitted answers. The application then points out it could have had the answers sooner, but it would have consumed all of your RAM. If it weren't for the threat of a devastating logic bomb, you'd be tempted to give this application a good review for user experience.

The five-minute timer is enough time for a bathroom break and to grab a glass of water. You don't feel nervous: the answers came to you so naturally, after all. When you get back from your errands there are still two minutes left on the timer; you'll get a speeding ticket if you keep moving this quickly. You spend the two minutes helping Guillaume with a particularly tricky game of Minesweeper, providing helpful insight such as "I think there may be a bomb here" and "This square is definitely safe".

When the timer approaches zero, you return to your desk to see what happens next. The screen fades to black again and new text appears.

Read it in **Section 167.**

---

72 Phase Three—Attack

"We had the analysts quadruple-check things after last time's false positive, so I can guarantee this is the real deal this time," Ruby informs you after you exchange greetings, crushing the small glimmer of hope that still lived within you that this was just a false alarm. As you approach the barriers you realise you didn't brief reception that you would be bringing in a visitor, but a quick flash of Ruby's government badge is enough to please the receptionist. As you ride the lift up, you hand Ruby a red Generico McCompany guest lanyard.

"At least now when people ask me my name I can point at my red badge," Ruby quips, trying to lighten your mood.

You throw her a half smile: she's earned that at least, but you can't quite shake the feeling that she is about to make your life very difficult. You take Ruby to the meeting room lobby and spot Susan in one of the rooms with an eclectic mix of people. You and Ruby enter the room, making the mix even more eclectic.

After everyone has a seat, it's revealed that Susan has gathered Cecilia from PR, Guillaume and Vijaya from IT and Jennifer, the finance director.

Ruby wastes no time unpacking a laptop from her bag and connecting it to the meeting room's monitor. A presentation flickers onto the screen. Ruby's slides are all black and white: no colour, no pictures, no joy. Which is all fitting, as the news Ruby is presenting isn't exactly much fun.

Get the full story in **Section 221**.

73 Phase Three—Attack

A malicious insider? Someone start some epic music.

Susan's phone rings twice before you realise you are going to need to do this over internal chat anyway, seeing as Vijaya sits two desks down from you. You send Susan an instant message, accusing Vijaya of being a Golden Slug accomplice and requesting approval to override her profile. Three minutes to go.

You are lucky: the missed call you left her was enough excuse for Susan to duck out of the meeting she was in, otherwise she wouldn't have seen the chat message. After approving your requests, Susan says she will start the process of having Vijaya apprehended for questioning.

You screenshot Susan's approval and with the combined help of Guillaume are able to undertake the required changes to prevent Golden Slug's phase two. Security guards storm into the room, homing in on Vijaya. If there was any chance she was innocent, it is swiftly scrubbed away as she scrambles at her keyboard trying to log in to deliver one last crescendo, but her account is now locked.

"You need to come with us," one of the guards says to Vijaya.

Wordlessly, she stands up and follows them out of the room. You and Guillaume share a glance.

"You look awful," Guillaume says, slightly ruining the moment.

"Don't be harsh, Guillaume," Susan retorts, appearing from nowhere. She flashes you a smile and lets you go home early. It's been a stressful day.

Head home, rest and up see what the fallout is in **Section 61**.

74 Phase Two—Preparation

Sorry, you've already admitted to having low levels of attention to detail, so maybe work you commissioned isn't the most reliable source of leads.

A cyberhygiene assessment is quite a standard offering. A consultant goes into a company and looks at how they defend against cybersecurity threats, reviewing people, processes and technology to see where any gaps in the defence may exist and recommending fixes.

The cyberhygiene assessment report in front of you, much like the "pen test" report, stretches the literal use of the English language to new extremes, which is unsurprising as the same company sold you both services. Instead of the expected output, this cyberhygiene assessment provides a detailed insight into the cleanliness of Generico McCompany's laptops, keyboards and mice.

Another entertaining but useless report was generated, and more money than you wish to admit changed hands. Whilst the pen test report was laughed off as an innocent mistake, falling for the same trick with the cyberhygiene assessment led to an intervention. Susan arranged some training, focused on reading and understanding contractual small print, led by the company's legal counsel, Georgios. Looking at your calendar you realise that the next session is scheduled to start in 10 minutes. Golden Slug will have to wait.

You spy Georgios heading over to the booked meeting room with a dejected look on his face. He tries to turn his frown into a smile, but he just ends up looking like someone who has eaten something unpleasant. He dreads these sessions as much as you, it seems.

Get it over with in **Section 187.**

---

75 Phase Four—Aftermath

Laying the trap gives you a chance of finding out where else Golden Slug are lurking in the network so you can clear them out in one strike. As soon as a threat actor knows they are being evicted, they sometimes crank their activity up all the way, making the most of their time before being purged. I'm not saying this is right per se, by the way...

Susan agrees with your thinking. "I've got no idea what Golden Slug are planning and the whole incident with you and Vlad's email is just confusing. I think we'd be better off laying a trap and figuring out their plan, even if it exposes us for a bit longer."

You quickly work out a battle plan with her. First you will create an email exchange that has enough mentions of Golden Slug that it should capture their attention. After building up that fake conversation for a while, Susan will email you telling you to close off Golden Slug's access to the network. The idea is that when they read that, Golden Slug will panic and will double-check that their access pathway and **backdoors** are working. Hopefully, they'll be noisy enough for you to spot them and evict them for real.

Satisfied, you walk back to your desk and start to put the plan into action. Somehow, just in the time it takes you to walk to your desk, Susan has already had time to write and send an essay-length email that mentions Golden Slug in every sentence multiple times. You draft your own reply, with what you would claim are genuine immersion-building spelling mistakes, and hit send. You then move the email thread into the backup folder which Golden Slug are reading from; as far as they are concerned it's merely a backup being saved in the wrong place.

The game of fake email ping-pong has begun. You keep a tab open on the copied email inboxes page, hoping to see some Golden Slug activity that would suggest that they've picked up the scent. You continue your exchanges with Susan for half an hour, escalating to the point where you falsely claim to know exactly how Golden Slug penetrated the network. After hitting send, you notice that Golden Slug have caught wind of the trail.

Spring the trap in **Section 38.**

76 Phase Two—Preparation

The new request is from Giuseppa@genericomccompany.com, who is responsible for the e-commerce estate's revenue. She is asking for an area of one of her websites to be immediately changed from green to blue. Jack is about to allocate it to a member of the team, unless you think this is suspicious.

If you think something is wrong, say so in **Section 79**, otherwise carry on reading.

Jack replies to the email, CCing in a team member who is now tasked with completing the action.

"We don't actually get many requests like this. The big requirements have to go through change control, which you review anyway," Jack informs you. Then as if to spite him, another request hits the inbox. This time it's from Jorge@genericomcompany.com in marketing, asking for the source **IP** address for one of his third-party vendors to be changed to a new one. Again, Jack goes to allocate it to a member of the team. Does he actually carry out any of the actions himself?

If you think something is wrong with this email, say so in **Section 282**, otherwise continue reading.

Jack allocates the request and then frowns at the person sleeping on the bean bag.

"Mind if I just check on them? I should really make sure they are just sleeping."

You tell him to go ahead and thank him for being so helpful. Jack does a strange salute with his hand as he goes to hopefully wake up the sleeping bean bag fan.

Continue your own investigation in **Section 28.**

77 Phase Three—Attack

Right, because books are deep and hold many answers. I like it.

Again, you provide your answer as "Books" and hit enter, with four seconds to spare on the timer. The screen fades to black and then new text appears.

"Thanks for taking part. I will now process your answers and either disarm the logic bomb or unleash hell, depending on your performance. Please do not close the application."

If you want to close the application go to **Section 345**, otherwise head to **Section 167.**

78 Phase Three—Attack

Either a good call or a lucky break.

No matter how urgent Michael thinks it is, Eduard can wait, you have a live incident to deal with. You ask Guillaume what he is seeing, already not looking forward to the answer.

"**Firewall** F42 is doing pretty much the opposite of its job."

"What is it doing?" Vijaya asks for you, wheeling her chair over to have a look. Clearly, whatever it is doing is obvious to someone more technical than you, as she almost falls out of her chair upon seeing Guillaume's screen.

"Who, what, where, how?" Vijaya blurts out in a single breath.

"Exactly," Guillaume replies.

You ask them what they are talking about.

"Oh sorry, let me translate it to cave dweller speak for you. Someone is attempting to steal loads of data from us. Our **data loss prevention** software is blocking the attempts because the **IP** address they are trying to send the data to isn't **allow listed**. It's like they are trying to get into a nightclub, but they aren't on the guest list."

Whilst there is reason for you to be annoyed at Guillaume's condescending tone, there are more important fish to fry. You ask them how you can make sure the transfers keep getting blocked.

Guillaume openly laughs. "As long as nobody is stupid enough to **allow list** their IP address, we will be fine."

Standing up, you start walking towards Susan's office to give her the latest news.

See how that goes in **Section 292.**

79 Phase Two—Preparation

*Good job. Always be wary of **phishing** emails.*

You raise a hand, capturing Jack's attention, and tell him to hold off a second; something doesn't smell right about the request that just came in.

"Yeah?" Jack replies. "Looks fine to me, but I'm probably looking in the wrong places. Should I delete it?"

You confirm it would be safest if he did indeed delete it, and then stroll back to your desk to tackle the pile of emails that have accumulated in your short absence.

Corporate policy regarding phishing emails will differ from place to place. Sometimes the advice is to delete them, sometimes to forward them on to the information security team, or sometimes there is a button available to report the email immediately. Find out what is appropriate based on where you work. Just don't open any attachments or click the links!

You have reached the last email in the queue when you feel someone's eyes on the back of your neck. Turning around in your chair, you find Giuseppa standing with one hand on her hip and looking annoyed.

"Jack told me my request got rejected because of you. I hope you're happy. This is costing us your salary in revenue for every second it's not fixed." She glances at your shabby bag and heavily worn shoes. "Actually, maybe it's more like twice your salary in revenue every second."

You ignore the dig and tell Giuseppa that you genuinely thought her request was a phishing attempt.

"Why?" she asks.

It's a fair question and you realise that you have no reply.

There was nothing wrong with Giuseppa's email.

You wish the earth would swallow you up as you stare blankly at her. She smiles cruelly before walking off.

You spend the rest of the day redoing your own phishing training to prevent this kind of mistake happening again. Go home, dust yourself off and remember that tomorrow is a new day.

Find out if it's a good day or not in **Section 223**.

---

80 Phase Two—Preparation

No right or wrong here. You have nothing to work from other than the project name.

You ask Janet for a link to the Project Luminec documents.

"Yes, OK." She proceeds to send you a link to a graphic of a happy cow running through a field of snow.

"Sorry, that wasn't it." She pastes the correct link and proceeds to drop offline out of shame.

Strangely enough, the Project Luminec folder is mysteriously well put together, containing clearly labelled documents and folders; you are immediately suspicious. Most of these documents seem to have been written by an external company, which makes sense; organisation is not a strong suit for Generico McCompany. As if to prove the point, in the corner of your eye you notice a colleague walk into the middle of the room. They stop, put an empty can in the paper recycling bin and walk away, faux triumph etched on their face.

Shaking your head, you open a file called the "Project Luminec Project Plan"; it probably could have done without the second "project" in that filename. The universal symbol for recycling dominates the front page of the document, which seems counterintuitive if there are supposed environmental risks. You look at the project objective and find the line:

"Luminec is designed to deliver a facility for recycling batteries, using nuclear power."

Life would be simpler if you could just watch the cow running in the field all day.

Drop your enquiry into Project Luminec in favour of Project Degrada in **Section 27**. Go to **Section 4** to continue reading about the nuclear battery plant.

---

81 Phase Two—Preparation

As the lift hurtles up to the 14th floor, you experience that annoying sensation of having something stuck between your teeth. The fancy meeting rooms live on the 14th floor, the ones with the little muffins in place of cheap biscuits— yum. Using your tongue, you finally manage to clear the debris and the world is right again.

Once in the designated room you help yourself to a coffee, partly because you need caffeine to fuel your existence, but also because having a drink is an excellent excuse to pause before you have to reply to any difficult questions raised during the meeting. Susan has booked a large meeting room with spectacular views. You tactically position yourself with a clear vantage point through the impressive window and then start to greet your colleagues.

Susan has assembled a crack squad of misfits, it seems. You can see Michael (COO), Vijaya (IT Backup Manager), Gesa (Project Manager), Cecilia (Public Relations), Georgios (Legal) and Susan (IT Director). After an exchange of pleasantries, Susan kicks matters off.

"First, some things to establish to set the scene. Project Degrada was the prototype that led to Project Luminec. For the purpose of clarity we shall refer to this solely as Project Luminec and avoid the now defunct title Project Degrada."

You all nod.

"Second, Golden Slug are a known cyberthreat adversary who target companies they have deemed to be detrimental to their environmental views. Project Degrada's nuclear spill would definitely meet this definition. Gesa, what is the situation with that?"

"It was confirmed that yesterday at 14:00 our time, 21:00 local time, the Project Luminec site oversaw an incident that culminated in the nuclear source material entering the adjacent water reservoir."

Wow, that doesn't sound good.

"Is the water reservoir only used by the site?" Cecilia asks.

"No, five towns near the site receive drinking water from the reservoir," Michael replies, rubbing his temples.

You gulp; things are looking bad.

See just how bad in **Section 319.**

---

82 Phase Four—Aftermath

You stand up from your desk a bit too quickly and feel slightly faint. It always amazes you that the human body is so robust and well designed, but you can almost break everything just by moving slightly faster than normal. After recovering from your near-death experience, you compose yourself and wander over to the project management area of the office, stopping only to grab a cup of tea from the kitchen on the way. You catch the end of a slightly unsettling game of top trumps between two project managers, where they use project stats like mortality rates and profit margin percentages as their comparisons.

"I've got an ROI rating of seven out of ten, can you better that?" one project manager says to another.

The opponent's shoulders slump in defeat. "Mine is only four out of ten, it was a loss leader," they say, before handing a wad of cash over to the victor.

That project manager tucks the cash away, and then notices you. You approach the competitors and let them know you need to run something by whoever is in charge of the Generico McCompany store maintenance project.

"Ah yes, GMC 4511. That's run by Gesa."

You thank them and head over to Gesa's desk. This has worked out well, as Gesa is one of your allies in the company who actually thinks information security is important. Other than Gesa, you are sort of persona non grata to the project management team.

Companies that don't value information security enough will end up having staff looking to bypass it or keep things in the dark, which goes as well as you'd imagine.

Talk to Gesa in **Section 15.**

83 Phase Three Attack

Susan asks you all to stay alert and not give in to paranoia, before dismissing the groups to continue working on fending off Golden Slug. You aren't paranoid, why would you be paranoid? Paranoia aside, you always had a feeling that Guillaume was up to something and how he walks only confirms it. You see Guillaume flash a suspicion-filled look at Vijaya as he holds a door open for her. It seems he thinks she is the mole. Maybe he'll be distracted and give himself away...

As you sit down, you feel Vijaya's eyes boring into the back of your head. She seems to suspect *you* were the mole. You are dragged out of your paranoid pantomime by an urgent email. There is an Information Security Conference in a month's time and you need to select the food options—critical stuff.

After settling on a starter of a vegetable tart, a baked salmon main and chocolate fondant for dessert, you recognise it's probably a good time to think of a battle plan for Golden Slug. The DDoS attacks continue to hit consistently on the hour, but still only last for ten minutes. Because your DDoS **mitigation** vendor's software learns as it experiences attacks, each attack hurts less than last time, with the most recent barely registering as a tickle. Michael appears by your desk.

See what he wants in **Section 108.**

84 Phase Two—Preparation

I like your honesty.

Reading through the penetration test report makes you regret your lack of attention to detail, as it just serves up a painful reminder of how you got fooled. The "pen test" report was just that, a literal test of the company's pens. A consultant came to the Generico McCompany offices and assessed every pen they could get their hands on, recording the ink levels, colour, pen type and chew status, then returning the pens to where they found them.

The report provides an insight into the different ink colours used across the business, including recommendations of happy hunting grounds for particular ink colours. Other unhelpful findings include the tendency for operations staff to chew their pens and fountain pens only getting used by company directors. Long story short, the pen test was an absolute disaster and made you a laughing stock; the only saving grace was that it was cheap.

You force the pen test nightmare out of your mind and return to the present. Naturally, the pen test report is not going to help in thwarting Golden Slug if they target you. Thinking back, you also commissioned that company to perform a cyberhygiene assessment; that might be a better lead. Alternatively, you could abandon this train of thought and speak to a friend who you know has faced Golden Slug in the past.

Look into the cyberhygiene assessment in **Section 74** or phone a friend in **Section 312**.

---

85 Phase Three—Attack

Getting into direct contact with hackers who are in the middle of an attack isn't unheard of, but it's something more traditionally mediated by a government cybersecurity agency.

Writing an email to a **hacktivist** group is harder than you thought it'd be. Getting the tone right is challenging. You want to ask a question without sounding too aggressive, passive or stupid.

"Hi…" You delete the line, saving "hi" for menial small talk, not negotiation with cyberenvironmentalists.

"Good morning." Again, no. For one, you don't even know what time zone they operate in; it could be afternoon or evening for all you know.

"Hello." Bingo.

You draft an email asking simply what Generico McCompany need to do to get the DDoS attacks to stop. You play the sympathy card, outlining your plight as just a pawn thrown into the deep end by their overlords. After hitting send, you attend Susan's standing meeting to ascertain the damage so far.

"Actually, it's not looking so bad. We have had some things go down, but we are battling hard to bring them back online," Vijaya informs Susan.

Guillaume flashes you a rapid thumbs-up. Susan dismisses the team and reminds you to update her if anything happens. You see the notification pop up on your laptop screen: Golden Slug have replied.

Read their reply in **Section 188**.

---

86 Phase Four—Aftermath

You manoeuvre the curry around your plate, hoping that the process will bend reality and improve the flavour. Lifting the fork to your mouth confirms that your experiment was a failure. You abandon all hope and resign yourself to a lunch of plain rice. From where you are sat you begin to eavesdrop on a nearby conversation, at first unintentionally and then intentionally.

"Yeah, I got an email with an urgent invoice to pay from Petra the CEO. So weird, but I guess I'm doing my job well enough to make it onto her radar."

"Dude, there are over 20 people whose job it is to pay invoices just in this office. Unless you provide a box of chocolates or a mug of coffee whenever you pay an invoice, I doubt she even knows you exist."

"Harsh, man."

"Hey, it's possible, though. Just before coming to lunch I got an urgent invoice request from Michael over in operations and he spelled my name correctly. He usually refers to people in finance as thieves. Maybe the world is finally starting to notice us."

You interrupt the conversation to confirm that both of them received urgent invoice requests out of the blue from two company directors. They confirm that is true and proudly let you know they paid the invoices immediately. You start running, and you don't stop running until you get to your desk.

Catch your breath in **Section 106.**

---

87 Phase Two—Preparation

Good call. Her lanyard was blue and nobody at Generico McCompany is supposed to have a blue lanyard.

You apologise, but let the woman know you can't take ownership of a USB drive of which nobody from the company gave you prior notice. She seems to be very surprised by this.

"Oh, OK then. By the way, have you heard much about a cyberthreat group called Golden Slug?"

This seems very suspicious. You shrug and let her know that perhaps you do and ask why she is interested.

"No reason. Just saw them in the news and wondered if they were relevant to Generico McCompany."

You let her know you aren't open to speculation and walk away from the lift area, not failing to notice that instead of walking to a desk your mysterious lift friend gets back into the lift and goes back down to the lobby. Strange. A cup of coffee shakes the events from your mind and you are able to reset yourself. Susan is at your desk, looking very glum.

"Emergency meeting in Petra's office, in five," she tells you.

The emergency meeting seems to have a lot of people present, and even Petra the CEO seems unnerved, which is unusual. Once everyone is assembled, she displays her screen on a large monitor on the wall.

> Dear Petra,
>
> We are Golden Slug. We are going to take your computer systems offline. You know what you did. To make it stop, clean the water.

Catch your breath in **Section 25.**

88 Phase Three—Attack

The same attendees who were present at the morning session gather, though Petra also tags along. The first wave of DDoS has died down, but you know it is only a temporary respite.

Vijaya provides a situation report on the firewall estate, noting that thankfully only 15% were taken offline, and those were able to restart. Cecilia shares the bad news that local media have picked up on the story and it's only a matter of time until the international press gets involved.

Susan asks for an update from a security perspective. You let the team know that the DDoS attacks themselves are annoying, but not particularly damaging as things stand, and add that the business is still able to transact and comply with relevant laws and contractual SLAs.

Everyone looks pleased.

As you open your mouth to continue speaking, everyone stops looking pleased. You continue that it would be prudent to assume the DDoS is just stage one, with stage two being more tailored attacks through the weakened, rebooted firewalls.

Some creative licence here, this is vastly oversimplified. You can put down your pitchforks…

"What if there is no stage two?" Petra asks, perhaps hopefully.

You reply that your damage limitation efforts end up being unnecessary, but at least the company is covered either way.

She doesn't seem convinced. "But what if they just ramp up the scale of their DDoS attack instead? We should be putting emphasis on stopping that rather than preventing something that might not happen."

Do you want to challenge Petra and stand by your stance on preparing for stage 2?

Challenge Petra in **Section 205**, or continue reading.

Petra pounces on your momentary pause like a starved lion, using the opportunity to double down on her position. "Susan, I want your team to prioritise deescalating the effects of the DDoS as a priority."

Susan nods, and you get to work.

Do as you are told in **Section 20**.

---

89 Phase Four—Aftermath

A few weeks later, just as you are putting the finishing touches to your report into the Golden Slug cyberattacks, an email lands in your inbox. It's from hello@goldenslug.com and contains a link to an article outlining the variety of ways you can change a device's IP address. It seems weird that Golden Slug would be trying to better prepare you for your next duel with them, but you reply thanking them and submit your report to Susan.

Two minutes later you can see her familiar figure approaching your desk. She must be a very quick reader to have finished your report already. You are about to ask her what she thought of your font choice, but she seems to have other things on her mind.

"Golden Slug have just sent a ransom email to Petra. They've got all our corporate secrets and intellectual property."

You let her know that can't be true, you blocked their IP addresses.

"Yes, they mentioned you'd say something like that. They sent me a helpful link showing me exactly how they evaded your block of their IPs."

Oh.

Susan isn't mad, just disappointed. The board members, on the other hand, are livid, with more than one call for an on-the-spot execution. Susan talks them out of this on the grounds of illegality. Besides, it'd be easier just to fire you, which she does.

The End.

> *Closing the **port** was a much more robust solution. IP addresses are relatively trivial to change, so Golden Slug merely had to wait until the heat died down and go straight back in. Ah well, better for things to play out like this in a book rather than real life, right? Why not have another read through, but pick tea at the beginning instead?*

90 Phase Two—Preparation

> *This was potentially the least effective of the three options presented, as the other two made direct reference to things going wrong with either payment card data itself, or on the area of the network where you know payment card data is collected. Maybe you will luck out and find a promising lead anyway.*

You decide to investigate the user awareness training angle and focus in on the audit findings. Generico McCompany run a variety of cybersecurity training. On top of the weekly new starter induction you run yourself (admittedly with mixed results), there are posters, effective (but poorly attended) online training resources, and even free information security playing card decks scattered around the office. What more do people want?

> *Genuine question. If you would appreciate different content to help you learn about information security, you should let someone in your company or school know, as they probably would be more than happy to help.*

Despite your offerings, the results of the **phishing** tests carried out by an external company every few months always make painful reading. The percentage of click-through and **malware** downloads seems to be impervious to any corrective actions you try to take. You think back wistfully to your proposal to slap someone in the face with a fish every time they fell for a phishing email. Predictably, the idea was rejected by HR, but you are pretty sure that would have been more effective at changing your colleagues' behaviour.

> *I should point out that a situation where corrective actions are having no effect really shouldn't be happening. If it does come to that, then the security team will just have to assume all phishing emails will be successful and either work on preventing the phishing emails from hitting inboxes, or design things in such a way that even if someone falls for a phish, there can't be a negative outcome. Both options are virtually impossible, though!*

As you continue reading you notice that you've repeatedly flagged the developers' willingness to insert vulnerable code into company products, including the e-commerce websites.

Delve deeper into the developer angle in **Section 303**, or focus on more general user awareness training blind spots in **Section 215**.

---

91 Phase Four—Aftermath

The old switcheroo? Bold, I like it.

You decide to go along with Golden Slug's plan, but only so you can gain their trust just to double-cross them later. Your bank account swells the next day, and you decide to treat yourself to a new TV to crown your first successfully defended cyberattack. Nothing much happens in the immediate future. The Golden Slug attack is condemned to the history books and life carries on, one meeting that could have been an email at a time.

Many months later, the police knock on your door and place you under arrest on suspicion of being a Golden Slug accomplice. This is no problem: you'd planned for this eventuality and inform your arresting officer that they just need to ask Generico McCompany for a copy of the Golden Slug email as you outline your double-cross plan.

The officer leaves the interrogation room for a few hours. When he comes back in, he is shaking his head. There is no record of your Generico McCompany email account receiving the message that your defence hinges on, even the offline copy you saved on your company laptop. The testimonial and character statements made by your colleagues and peers count for nothing when the verdict comes in. You are tried, found guilty and serve two years in prison for being an accomplice to a cyberhacktivist group.

The End.

Snatching a defeat from the jaws of victory there. You had done so well to stick to the incident response plan and stand up for your approach against Petra, but one lapse and boom, prison.

*How could the evidence of that email have been scrubbed from existence. Could there potentially have been a **malicious insider** within Generico McCompany? Have another read through to find out, or alternatively try drinking tea this time for a completely different story.*

92 Phase Two—Preparation

I respect your ability to push where you feel is appropriate, though be warned that not everyone will feel the same.

You look Michael squarely in the eye. He has the eyes of an assassin and maintaining eye contact is challenging, but you persevere. You ask Michael to categorically confirm that the project was cancelled.

He takes another drink of water, sizing you up. "Yes, but the board vote was very close. It wouldn't surprise me if someone else decided to restart it under the radar. The money to be made was astronomical."

The words "Project Luminec" leave your mouth before you can help yourself.

At this Michael stands up, walks over to his office door and presses a button on the wall, which shuts the blinds across all four walls of the cube. He then returns to his desk, opens the drawer and pulls out a gun. Not really—but you were expecting him to. Instead, he pulls out two glasses and a bottle of scotch. He pours two glasses and offers you one.

"Well done, you've sussed it out." He congratulates you, but in a way that makes you feel more nervous than jovial. He sips from his glass and continues. "It was always going to come to light anyway I suppose, what with the recent events and such."

You ask him what recent events he is referring to.

"Oh… I presumed that's why you were asking. The spill. It's only a matter of time before that hits the news, but we can throw PR at it…"

You ask Michael what spill he is talking about.

"The radioactive spill into the water reservoir."

You announce that it's probably time for you to go.

Michael flicks his wrist as a send-off, before sinking his glass and reaching for your own, untouched whisky.

You open the door, and it's only once you stride out into the operations office that the reality hits you. Golden Slug target companies based on their environmental impact and Generico McCompany have apparently just poisoned a water reservoir with radioactive waste.

Head back to your desk in **Section 132.**

---

93 Phase Two—Preparation

In response to your question about what caused the firewalls to get taken offline, one David writes an incredibly long statement explaining that **servers** and firewalls go offline all the time, and that usually the root cause is so random and chaotic you are better off just rebooting them and getting on with things rather than obsessing. The other David reiterates this, in significantly fewer words. You would continue your interrogation, but a Generico McCompany staff member has reported 107 emails as **phishing** attempts, all in one go.

Now you are forced to go through every single one, checking, double-checking and then triple-checking whether they are real or not. For the malicious phishing emails you reward the staff member with a virtual cookie and a thanks from the CISO, and for the emails that are actually genuine you reply with the reasons you believe the email to be genuine. All 107 emails turn out to be genuine emails, not phishing. You look on your internal chat and see that both Davids have fled and are now offline. You resign yourself to having to pick up the trail again tomorrow.

The rest of the day is filled with boring tasks, more coffee and some daydreaming. As the clock hits five you slide out of your chair, go through the door and walk off into the sunset, feeling semi-fulfilled.

Your evening is stellar: a hearty meal, an excellent session at the gym and some top-quality television. Paranoia combined with the never-ending need to be respected by your colleagues forces you to check your work phone before bed, but there is nothing urgent sitting in the inbox. Life is good.

Find out what tomorrow holds in **Section 100.**

94 Phase Two—Preparation

The next email says:

> Igor, I had an idea for your weekly quiz round. Check this link out—it's got a list of 10 obscure animals which you can just copy and paste into the quiz.
>
> Thank me later.

In fairness, that was actually a decent attempt: Igor does indeed run a weekly quiz, which you stopped joining after finishing either last or joint last a few too many times. Whoever wrote this phishing email needed insider knowledge that Igor runs a quiz and must have taken the time to actually put together a list of 10 obscure animals, or Igor might have suspected something was up.

This is why it is recommended to be careful what you share on social media. The more you give away, the more people can accurately impersonate you, or trick you by delivering phishing emails that are heavily linked either to things you like or to companies you genuinely get emails from.

Actually, come to think of it, why was this email blocked? Closer inspection reveals the email came from a spoofed domain, made to resemble Generico McCompany's, but the **payload** on the link leads to a download for a bitcoin miner **trojan**. Seeing as Golden Slug are interested in payment card data, this seems unlikely to be their work.

You spend the next few hours flicking through more of these emails, looking for anything where the malware targets payment card data, but nothing suits the description. You decide to call it a day there. You haven't really made any progress.

Tomorrow is a new day in **Section 223.**

---

95 Phase Two—Preparation

Cecilia fills you in on the details, then later forwards you the email that Golden Slug have shared with news outlets. The email even contains some of the payment card data they are claiming to have stolen from Generico McCompany.

Susan catches wind of the story before long. "I thought you said you stopped Golden Slug yesterday!" she asks, appearing by the side of your desk out of nowhere.

You point out that you thought you had too.

"So what is this email all about?"

You concede that you don't know, remarking that it seems a bit strange for Golden Slug to have put Generico McCompany on high alert if they already had a working method for stealing payment card data from the business.

"Could it be real, though? Could that payment card data be linked back to us?"

You admit that it potentially could. Even if the breach was unrelated to you, there would likely be Generico McCompany transactions linked to every single payment card in circulation, due to the company being a multinational goliath.

For this reason, it's generally left to the card schemes and banks to identify suspicious patterns suggesting a breach, rather than instantly trusting a random email from a hacking group.

Cecilia left you with a decision to make and you are running out of time to make it. Do you want the PR team to deny the card data originates from Generico McCompany or ask them to admit it could be your customer's payment card data?

Deny in **Section 328**. Admit a possible link in **Section 114**.

96 Phase Four—Aftermath

Golden Slug have taken over the email account of Jennifer, the finance director. The email they are drafting so far reads:

> Tamara, I'm in a meeting for the next four hours. Pay
> the below invoice ASAP.

Underneath you can see Golden Slug writing out a fake email conversation between Jennifer and some made-up company. Looks like Golden Slug have given up on stealing more Generico McCompany payment card data and are instead looking for a **business email compromise** payday. To be fair to them, on a different day it might have worked. But before they are able to send the email, you get Tamara on the phone and inform her that she is about to receive a message from Jennifer relating to an invoice that needs paying, but that she should not, under any circumstances, pay it.

"What, you're asking me to intentionally not do my job?"

You tell her that the email will be fake.

"Like, it won't come from Jennifer's email address?"

You let her know that it will come from Jennifer's genuine email, but that it is not Jennifer who has written the email. This is met with hostility. You have to spend a few minutes bringing Tamara onside, first by outlining how you have nothing to gain from getting her sacked, and explaining a little about how business email compromise attacks work.

You let Golden Slug send the email, and then wipe them off the network for good. You spend the next few hours glued to your screen, waiting to see if you missed anything. So that you don't have to leave your desk, you order in a pizza delivery. That by itself isn't weird, but the fact you make reception bring the pizza direct to your desk draws a mix of strange and some jealous looks from your colleagues, but you don't care. You can't look away from the screen. You've poured salt on Golden Slug, but you need to make sure you finish the job.

See if your pizza also needs salt in **Section 129**.

97 Phase Two—Preparation

Whilst your colleague Guillaume potentially set up a network share for files to be stored for the project, Rory was almost certainly working actively on the project, so may have been a slightly stronger avenue of enquiry.

You decide to give your feet a break and roll across the room on your chair, coming to a rest behind Guillaume's computer. On one screen he has a cloud hosting management console, on the other a game of Solitaire. He closes the game of Solitaire so fast his mouse leaves a smoke trail behind it. He then spins around in his chair, sees it's you and looks annoyed. You've probably cost him what looked like a winning game.

"Yes?"

You apologise and let him know you need to ask about a project you are researching for Susan. This is a good plan: whilst he may be annoyed at you, he is line-managed by Susan.

He sighs, conceding to your excellent tactical play. "The only project I manage is stopping everything from burning. If you want me to help you with your fire, you'll need to get Susan to approve it."

You tell Guillaume that all you need to know is whether he was ever asked to make a file share for Project Luminec and if it is being used or not.

"Fine, fine, but you have to get me a coffee. No milk and one sugar." He waves you away as he starts flicking around his management console.

Walk over to the kitchen in **Section 213**.

---

98 Phase Two—Preparation

Starting here is wise. Payment cards are provided during an online checkout page, so any third-party functionality that is active during checkout is a huge risk.

You can't help but groan as you familiarise yourself with the Vatidiva **third-party** code, a ground-breaking, essential program that plays a happy jingle after a customer puts an order in, with the jingle changing depending on the value of the order. You remember being astonished that code like this was allowed on a payment page, and even more astonished at the pushback you faced when you suggested it should be removed. It goes without saying that you lost that battle. Watching Vatidiva in action, all your feelings of despair bubble back up to the surface; code that only launches during a user checkout experience is very bad news for a CISO.

And actually, it would more typically be something someone who reports to a CISO would be looking into, rather than the CISO themselves. But seeing as you are the only full-time information security employee, it's all yours.

Listening to the jingles adds further insult to injury; it's not like they are even good. You decide to be fair and browse to Vatidiva's website to let the poor software defend itself from your onslaught of negativity.

Vatidiva claim to "offer next-generation checkout affirmation software solutions". You browse to see what products they have to achieve this, but their only offering is the checkout sound effect. Can they really get away with calling that next generation? You aren't the marketing regulations authority, so you leave judging that to them. Suppressing the feelings of annoyance, you open up the hood to have a look at the Vatidiva code.

Find out what is hidden within the code in **Section 207.**

---

99 Phase Four—Aftermath

The next morning, the manufacturer sends an engineer named Earl to inspect the slightly suspicious PIN entry device. You set him up on the desk next to you.

Earl is a hungry man. He's just eaten two bacon sandwiches for breakfast, and he's constantly reaching into his pocket to pull out a sausage and nibble on Pork pasty. You also notice that he takes a pork pie from his toolbox to munch on whenever he accomplishes something. In this case it is to reward himself for popping off the casing of the PIN entry device.

Don't try this at home in the off chance you have one of those lying around— it'll likely trip a switch and fry the circuitry if you do it wrong.

He spots you watching. "That's tricky, you know; if you mess it up you could easily set off a bomb within the device." He rewards himself with another bite of pie.

You wheel your chair slightly away from the desk Earl is working at.

"Not that kind of bomb," he scoffs. "A memory bomb. It wipes the device's storage memory completely if it believes the device is being tampered with."

You nod and Earl gets back to work. You watch the sweat begin to drip down the back of his head. Based on his diet, you reckon that the sweat must be at least 50% meat.

Finally, Earl brings his head up from his work again to give you an update. "You like golf?" he asks.

You say you suppose so and ask why.

Earl holds up a golf tee. "This was inside the device. Just some jokester having a laugh when it was first assembled, I would bet."

Earl can't find any evidence of foul play and hands back the reassembled PIN entry device so that it can return to work in the store. He finishes off his pork pie and sausage and leaves, probably in pursuit of more meat.

Continue on to **Section 110.**

---

100 Phase Two—Preparation

As the train nears your stop, you discover that you've filled in a wrong number somewhere in your newspaper's sudoku and the puzzle is now unsolvable. You give a quick glance around and sneakily fill in random numbers to give the appearance to the people in the carriage that you have successfully completed it, and then dispose of the evidence. Your morning coffee doesn't judge you for the sudoku incident and tastes just fine.

You navigate your way from the station to the office via the labyrinth of passageways to avoid the unexpected deluge of rain. Although yesterday's investigation didn't yield much, you've got some fresh leads and ideas to pursue, which makes you feel somewhat optimistic. Once you reach your desk, the first thing you do is to load up the perimeter defence software. Although Golden Slug are known for DDoS, you don't see traffic levels resembling a DDoS.

Susan walks in, dripping wet and (based on her facial expression) clearly not happy. You instinctively open your desk drawer to locate your umbrella for later, but only find an umbrella sleeve, as if the umbrella had shed its skin and moved on to a new owner.

"Tell me you've got some good news on Golden Slug," she fires at you.

You let her know that so far you haven't found anything to suggest Golden Slug would be targeting Generico McCompany, and no reason that they'd be interested in the business at all.

"That sounds like no news, but in this case I'll take it as good news," Susan remarks, heading off to sort out her soggy hair.

Vijaya from IT continues the interrogation. "They do DDoS attacks, right? My team haven't seen anything that resembles that at all." She smiles reassuringly at you, but looks as if she's expecting an answer.

You let her know you haven't seen any either, but will keep her posted.

"Good plan. By the way, you have a package waiting downstairs in the lobby. Reception asked me to let you know."

Go down to reception to pick up the package in **Section 144.**

101 Phase Four—Aftermath

The Cyber Pirates spend the next couple of days confirming that Golden Slug have been properly evicted from the network and haven't left themselves any **backdoors** to stroll back in. That evening, Susan takes everyone out for a meal to celebrate, The Cyber Pirates regale the table with tales of previous incidents they've responded to and, after a few pints of grog, treat you to some shanties. The other patrons in the restaurant want to murder you by this point.

The next day Susan's mood is only slightly dampened when she receives the final bill for the Cyber Pirates, noting that Pedro the Parrot was counted as a billable resource. She signs it off anyway; they did undeniably prove their worth.

Ultimately, whilst the Cyber Pirates did most of the heavy lifting, your role in the incident is recognised, resulting in a juicy pay rise and your own parking spot. You don't ever drive to work, but it was a nice touch. When thinking back over the Golden Slug incident, you can't shake the feeling that you missed something—something food related? You don't lose much sleep over it though.

The End.

> *Pretty good going. Your work in phase two allowed you the option of calling in an incident response company and you let them do their thing without impeding them, all of which has worked out nicely. Trust me, there aren't many better endings than this, though they do exist if you are feeling brave…*

102 Phase Three—Attack

The best of two bad choices.

You don't bother calling the NotNotCatya helpline; it would likely just rub the whole incident in your face anyway. Instead, you calmly walk into Susan's office and explain what has happened.

Susan hears you out and then nods her head. She calls in an external information security incident response company to handle things from here, and apologises for putting you into a situation where you were potentially out of your depth.

The incident response team come in, wipe Golden Slug completely from the company's network and walk off into the sunset. Susan demotes you and hires a more experienced CISO, who promises to mentor you during your time working together.

Over the coming years the new CISO helps raise your proficiency to the point where you feel that you'd have handled the Golden Slug incident completely differently. Just as you are about to really press on in your Generico McCompany career, you are used as the scapegoat after a minor data leak occurs and are thrown on the scrapheap. After dusting yourself off, you get yourself onto a job board to start the cycle all over again.

The End.

> *Oh dear, it looks like your incorrect answer unleashed NotNotCatya on the company network. Remember BODMAS: Brackets, Order, Division, Multiplication, Addition, Subtraction. Perform the maths in **Section 123** in that order to find the right answer.*

103 Phase Three—Attack

It's happening: the company is under a full-scale attack. Your fancy network traffic software now resembles an old-school bullet hell arcade game as an avalanche of data **packet**s hits your corporate network over and over again.

Vijaya isn't taking it well. "Those animals are hitting the **firewall** estate hard. I am never going to maintain the uptime service level agreement at this rate."

You almost commend Vijaya for being able to think like a bureaucrat at a time of crisis. Soon there isn't much point watching the network traffic software anyway. You can tell what service is offline or running slowly based on the verbal, email and phone **ticket**s that are raining down on the IT team.

Susan sets up temporary residence in the hot desking spot adjacent to your desk, as she fields a seemingly endless stream of directors who come to complain. It's become blatantly clear that it's time to step up your game. You think back to the recommendation you made to Generico McCompany before you even joined. One option was to sign up to an incident response **retainer** company.

> *A company who provide technical experts either remotely or onsite within a given time period to assist with combating cybersecurity incidents.*

Alternatively, it was to develop Generico McCompany's own **incident response plan** (developing is perhaps an overly generous term; creating might be more appropriate).

> *An information security incident response plan is a list of instructions, processes and procedures to work through when a company is undergoing a cyberattack.*

Which recommendation did you make?

_____

If you suggested Generico McCompany enlist a retainer company, go to **Section 148.** If you preferred to develop the incident response plan, turn to **Section 36.**

_____

104 Phase Four—Aftermath

Some say that victory tastes sweet, or in a situation where victory is not very satisfying it may even be bitter. In your case, victory definitely tastes of umami as you sip on a mug of tea, which probably shouldn't taste of umami. The blueberry muffin you have paired with your tea tastes like a gym membership would be a good idea, but the prevailing taste in your mouth is still victory. You browse pictures of celebrities reimagined as dogs to savour the moment.

Behind the scenes Golden Slug have reinserted their malicious code into all of the Generico McCompany e-commerce websites, stealing thousands of payment card details all over again, but this time in a manner that the National Cyber Security Agency don't detect. Months later the breach is discovered and Generico McCompany is issued with a massive fine. Your handling of the Golden Slug incident is scrutinised in a forensic investigation, which criticises you for considering the case as closed after removing Golden Slug's code since you had no idea how it got there in the first place, allowing Golden Slug just to stroll back in and redeploy it.

Susan is forced to readjust the budget to account for the massive fine. Spending hours in Excel to accomplish this annoys her enough to decide it's time for a new CISO and the business lets you go.

The End.

> *Yup, pretty much what the forensic investigation said, really. Golden Slug weren't going to go away just because you deleted their code. It's the equivalent of someone breaking your door down and knocking over your milk. Sure, you can clean the milk up, but the door is still broken and not doing its job. It appears you didn't make much progress looking into Golden Slug in phase two. Why not read through again, but change your early decisions to see how that impacts the story? If you want something completely different, try drinking coffee at the beginning instead of tea.*

105 Phase Two—Preparation

A CISO needs to be capable of ruffling feathers where appropriate.

Using the tried-and-tested method of rocking his chair back and forth, you manage to wake Rory up. As he comes to, he sizes you up; if you were a junior, he'd probably have snapped your neck there and then. You are spared death, but not guilt as he yawns loudly, stretching his arms out dramatically. He works a "Hello" into his yawn, so it seems apt to get to the matter at hand.

You ask Rory about Project Luminec. His dramatic performance continues with an extravagant sigh. "Isn't it always?"

You wait for him to elaborate. When he doesn't, you take the lead, asking whether the project is live. The question seems to snap Rory back into wakefulness; you can almost hear the cogs in his brain whirring.

"No, it's been put on standby, most likely indefinitely."

Curious, you press him for the reason.

"Can't say." He glances at his phone, frowns and continues, "It looks like I might need to fly back there soon to wrap things up. Can I get back to sleep?"

Keep pressing Rory in **Section 159** or slink over to the kitchen to grab some water in **Section 16.**

106 Phase Four—Aftermath

It becomes apparent very quickly that Golden Slug did indeed manage to get access to at least one director's email; in fact, they got access to all of them. Knowing that their way back into the network is now shut off, they've sent invoice requests from every director to random members of the finance team, always claiming the request is urgent and always having the money paid into the same account.

By the time you communicate this eventuality to Jennifer, the head of finance, over $30 million has already been filtered out of the business. Jennifer imposes some additional emergency measures, including requiring verbal approval prior to paying invoices, but the damage is done.

When the Golden Slug incident is dissected, your initial efforts are lauded, as you were able to neutralise Golden Slug's initial e-commerce attack before it even began. The decision not to force a password reset on all Generico McCompany users is viewed as a calamitous mistake; hindsight makes everyone a master tactician, after all. Whilst you are not initially sacked, Jennifer seethes with rage every time she sees you from then on, until both sides accept that it's probably best you left.

The End.

It was worth annoying everyone to ensure you had performed a thorough clean-up. The CISO role isn't a popularity contest, after all. Good work up to that point, though; trust me, there are a lot worse endings than this. Why not have another play through, but switch up your decisions and see where things take you?

107 Phase Four—Aftermath

Susan reveals the **business email compromise** fraud that you had already been told about. You feign surprise masterfully; the B you got for drama at school definitely should have been an A. Fingers were being pointed at her, as the National Fraud Office have confirmed that the address where the $20 million was sent belongs to Golden Slug, implying that Golden Slug were the ones who sent the email from Petra's account.

The board came to the conclusion that Susan's budget for the year will decrease by $20 million to make up for the loss. Susan confides to you that she can easily make that money back for the department by having the support team charge staff for laptop and phone screen repairs, so she isn't too fussed.

The End.

Golden Slug got away with $20 million, but you managed to keep your job, so is this a victory or a defeat? On the one hand, you did quite well in phase two, so to finish with a "meh"-feeling ending is potentially bad. But equally, so many endings in this book result in you losing your job, so maybe it's a win?

Tell you what, why don't you read through again, but pick coffee instead of tea early on and see how that changes things?

108 Phase Three—Attack

"How are we doing on this Golden Slug thing, then? I'd really like this whole fiasco to disappear."

You reply that Golden Slug are currently launching DDoS attacks against the company, but so far you've been able to fend them off relatively comfortably.

"So, you nerds beat them?"

You state that you wouldn't go that far.

"Well, I expect you to apply the knockout blow soon. By the way, Eduard from my team has some software he needs your approval to run. It's important." He finishes and walks off. For a man who is almost entirely to blame, he seems to have an incredible knack of somehow making this feel like your fault.

You continue to curse Michael under your breath. A support **ticket** request for enabling a document's **macro**s comes in from Eduard@genericomccomany.com wanting your approval.

Guillaume waves his hands above his head. "I've found something."

Better see what he's got. Want to quickly approve the request first or do it later? Michael did mention it was urgent.

Approve it in **Section 334** or do it later in **Section 78.**

---

109 Phase Three—Attack

"Brace for ignition," Sasha tells his team, before Galactic Cyber and Generico McCompany jointly prepare to send Golden Slug out of the network. Cyberspace Cadet Morgan begins to feed you, Guillaume and Vijaya a list of users who have had their login credentials compromised by Golden Slug. The list is worryingly long. As a team you begin to force password resets and terminate live sessions, resulting in a flurry of support **ticket**s from disgruntled users.

"Commander!" Marshal Marshal exclaims, waving his hands above his head.

"Yes?" Sasha replies from his seat. When you are wearing a huge heavy space suit, it's quite sensible not to get out of your chair for every social interaction.

"I've found a Golden Slug **backdoor**, sir."

That is sufficient rocket fuel to get Sasha out of his seat and peering over Marshal Marshal's shoulder.

Marshal Marshal explains the setup to Sasha, who then hurries over to pass it on to you.

"Golden Slug have set up a blockchain-enabled quantum tunnel using nanotechnology and artificial intelligence. This is how they intended to get back into the network after our efforts at removing them."

That's not a real thing, except for being a marketing buzzword haven.

You ask Sasha if he can delete it. He scoffs, then remembers he is on paid consultancy time and gives you a proper reply.

"We could throw some flux into the dark matter region of the tunnel and make it implode, yes."

> *Again, not a real thing. When you create an imaginary problem, you can fix it with an imaginary solution. To be clear, backdoors are real, but to go into an example of how one works seemed like it would risk straying into overly technical territory. If you are interested in reading about backdoors, the Open Web Application Security Project (OWASP) community have produced a top 10 list of the most commonly exploited backdoors that is freely available.*

You tell them both that so far this sounds like enough impressive words to be satisfied, and give them the green light to fire the flux.

See how the flux works out in **Section 134**.

110 Phase Four—Aftermath

After returning the PIN entry device to its home at the Northallerton Street store, you sit at your desk with a nice cup of tea and begin to ponder. Why would Golden Slug hack a procurement system to get their own people's hands on the payment card processing devices, only to leave them as they were? You think about it for a good two minutes before giving up and moving on with your life.

Months later, a monumental cache of payment card data is sold on the dark web, leading to significant levels of fraud against customers. There is a long investigation by the National Fraud Agency.

> *It would be more likely to be Generico McCompany's acquiring bank in tandem with a Payment Card Industry Security Standards Council member, but let's keep it simple.*

A common link is found: all the cards had been used at a Generico McCompany store recently. The accusation is thrown your way, but you push back against the report and provide the evidence from Earl showing that the PIN entry devices were clean.

Feeling content, you wait for the National Fraud Agency staff to back down and leave, but they don't. Instead, they produce evidence showing that when the contractors went into the stores, instead of tampering with the PIN entry devices they installed cameras to capture the card numbers and PINs when people paid for goods in store. One member of the National Fraud Agency delivers this evidence with particular gusto, verging on unprofessionalism really, but nobody else seems to care about their conduct.

See how things play out in **Section 5**.

111 Phase Three—Attack

The morning newspapers run stories about a potential data breach at Generico McCompany. You decide it would be wise to keep your work pass hidden until you get to the office building. Once there, you are greeted by a swarm of press flowing around the lobby in unison looking for insight, intrigue and updates. You overhear that the reporters mainly want confirmation that Golden Slug's claims of stealing personal data from Generico McCompany are genuine, as apparently it's a claim they've falsely made numerous times in the past.

You manage to get through the turnstiles, into the lift and up to your desk without the gathered press noticing you are the Chief Information Security Officer. The file that Susan has sent you does not look good. It takes you mere minutes to conclude that the information has indeed been stolen directly from Generico McCompany; no doubt about it.

There are two pieces of good news, the first being that Guillaume has figured out how Golden Slug got into the internal network to activate the firewall DDoS and has already applied the appropriate fixes. The second is that your DDoS protection vendor has upped their game and now Golden Slug's external DDoS attacks are like an ant trying to break open a tank.

Reflecting on what you overheard in the building lobby, it seems clear that the media would believe Generico McCompany if you claimed the data was false, and Golden Slug are now evicted in any case.

Admit the leak is real in **Section 279** or say it's fake in **Section 298**.

112 Phase Four—Aftermath

Obviously, the good times don't last. Golden Slug sell the personal details they stole from Generico McCompany to a criminal group. The criminal group start using the details in the database to commit fraud against the individuals listed. The levels of fraud reach such heights that the public demand a government investigation.

The investigation opens up a question regarding the authenticity of the data Golden Slug shared with the media. An independent forensics team concludes that the data was indeed genuine and labels your inability to identify this as "gross negligence". You are sacked, with a black mark against your CV for ever.

The End.

You probably shouldn't be surprised that lying doesn't end well. It would have helped if you'd taken the network offline for a brief period and had some time to think; fighting a fire continuously is exhausting. Anyway, believe it or not there are worse endings, so don't feel too bad. Why not read through again, but try drinking tea instead of coffee for a completely different story?

113 Phase Four—Aftermath

Within seconds of arriving, Susan's forensics team pick up a strange signal, which they trace to a USB sitting on your desk. It's the USB you were holding onto for Sakura. They break it open to reveal a listening device. It was activated when you plugged it into your laptop to "charge" it. Looking back over the security tapes, they identify that the mysterious stranger you took it from was wearing a blue lanyard. Generico McCompany only issue red, yellow and green passes.

As for the firewall rule, the ticket you approved came from Eduard@ genericomccomany.com, but Generico McCompany emails come from @genericomccompany.com.

And sorry, the p is not silent.

The listening device clearly let Golden Slug overhear your conversation with Michael and spoof the incoming service desk request from the real Eduard.

Golden Slug make use of the data they stole to disgrace Generico McCompany, badly damaging the company's reputation, share price and image in the industry for years to come. Suspicions that you were an insider for Golden Slug are dismissed, with the leadership team instead deciding you are too incompetent to have played such an intricate role. Eventually you are yet again tricked, this time into blindly signing a document releasing you from employment at Generico McCompany.

In a distant country, Golden Slug celebrate their great victory and laugh at how they never even needed to deploy their trump card.

The End.

*If it makes you feel any better, even if you hadn't fallen for the **phishing** email you weren't on a path to victory—you needed to have made more progress in phase two. I wonder what Golden Slug's trump card was. Read the book through again making some different choices and maybe you'll find out.*

114 Phase Three—Attack

I know this option sucks, but it's safer. You can't be certain that card data belongs to Generico McCompany, but openly denying it would risk you ending up with egg on your face if the cards were indeed proved to originate from you.

You tell Cecilia to work on the assumption that it is genuine. She goes offline, probably to focus on the mountain of work you've just dumped on her. You spend the next hour rechecking your workings from the previous day, looking for something you may have missed, but with no success. As much as you want to continue to throw yourself as the Golden Slug email mystery, an 11:00 meeting reminder beeps at you. Not just any old meeting, it's a product evaluation meeting.

Prior to you joining it, Generico McCompany had a long history of the company's business units buying all kinds of software services at a frankly ludicrous rate. These would then get stitched together into some kind of Lovecraftian horror, which on the surface looked like a reasonable product, but looking under the bonnet would reveal a hellish abomination. The majority of these abominations are an information security nightmare. To combat the creation of more abominations, you persuaded the procurement team to give you one meeting to discuss new software that is being considered for purchase so you can sanity check it.

This is a relatively common practice nowadays.

The purpose of today's meeting is to assess Evictionnoticed software. Evictionnoticed software tracks employee behaviour and pinpoints the exact moment they are about to start job hunting based on changes in their computer usage. Evictionnoticed then lets HR teams decide whether to consider attempting to retain the staff member, or alternatively "randomly" to allocate the employee to training that will help them pass an interview so they can be moved on, out of the company. You were convinced this would be a train wreck, but as morally questionable as the software is, from a security angle there is nothing wrong, so it gets your approval. All of this has made you hungry.

Head to lunch in **Section 48.**

115 Phase Three—Attack

"Fesrodah, John speaking. How may I help you?"

Forgetting the small meeting room, both you and Georgios lean forward and almost clash heads. Georgios points at you, prompting you to talk. You let John know you are calling from Generico McCompany.

"Oh hello. Fesrodah is very grateful for your platinum-level Stresser service purchase, I hope this is progressing well. Just to confirm, is the email for the invoice still hello@goldenslug.com?"

You take a note of the email before replying. You let them know that there is a problem, as you never requested this service and are looking to take legal steps to halt the Stresser activity. You introduce Georgios, who then takes command.

"Georgios here. May I take your surname, John?" Georgios asks, in a way that comes across as a command rather than a question. You really need to learn how to do that sometime.

"Sure, it's Doe. I don't handle legal requests, my colleague Jane is in charge of that."

"What is her surname?" Georgios continues, again with his mind tricks.

"Also Doe, not related. I will forward your call to her now."

Hold music blares out of the conference phone, and you instinctively mute the console before taking stock with Georgios. It's clear that this whole company is dodgy, and for all you know the guy might keep you on hold forever.

Stay on the line in **Section 186** or try emailing Golden Slug in **Section 85.**

---

116 Phase Two—Preparation

It's just a Stupid Pointless Annoying Message (SPAM) text trying to trick you into clicking a link and downloading **malware** onto your work phone. You pass the details on to the IT team so they can stop messages from the same number from hitting your colleagues' work phones. No doubt some people will click the link before the IT team can get the block in place. It's baffling how many people can be tricked into claiming the prize money for competitions they never entered...

Your friend Raul replies to your message from hours ago. He hasn't had any dealings with Golden Slug before, but he has had experience mitigating the damage of DDoS attacks. Raul sends you the contact details for a few vendors, most of which you've already had budget denied for.

Looking back on the day, it seems you haven't made a huge amount of progress researching Golden Slug so far. Perhaps tomorrow will be more fruitful. You wrap up for the day and head home. On the commute you pretend not to eavesdrop on the passengers next to you, who seem to work somewhere that sounds more like a TV show than real life. They get off before you, so you'll never find out whether Clara got fired or not.

You arrive home and cook a dinner that, despite promising ingredients, ends up leaving you feeling less than satisfied. The hours flit away and before you know it, it's time to sleep, wake up and go into work all over again.

See if the next day has better things in store for you in **Section 100.**

---

117 Phase Two—Preparation

It was your only lead, so there's not much commentary I can offer, really.

You walk over to the operations area of the office, and as always, you wonder at the bizarre layout. The room is a large square filled with open-plan desk space, except for the single-cubicle office that sits bang in the middle, surrounded by glass walls on all four sides. The office belongs to Michael, the Chief Operations Officer.

As you knock on the glass door, you can clearly see Michael inside, not looking particularly busy. Awkward seconds pass, during which Michael can clearly see you and you can clearly see that he sees you, but you still wait to be invited in. Michael pretends to look at some papers on his desk before finally stepping up and opening the door.

"Oh, I didn't see you there. Come in, come in and take a seat." He gestures towards two chairs; one is clearly Michael's chair and you give that a wide berth. The chair you select is shockingly uncomfortable: it doesn't allow you to sit up straight or even lean back, so you end up perching on it in a stress position you believed was outlawed by the Geneva Convention.

Michael lowers himself onto his throne, which is no doubt infinitely more comfortable than your chair. He then proceeds to talk for two minutes about nothing, before asking, "So what can I do for you?"

You respond that you have a few questions you need to ask about Project Degrada.

"Oh, that was a silly little project that got disbanded. What do you need to know?"

You ask Michael when the project was disbanded and why it was given a critical risk rating for environmental impact.

Michael's face is unchanged, but his eyes suddenly narrow.

Find out why Michael's eyes narrowed in **Section 289.**

118 Phase Four—Aftermath

You find Julia in the west wing installing a computer cable. She accepts the envelope with glee, revealing that the contents are a gift card voucher as a thanks for doing a favour for Susan. You decide to ignore the fact that Susan has just rewarded your sterling efforts by making you deliver internal post.

In the months that follow, you never get a gift card from Susan, despite the excellent job you did in handling Golden Slug. But to be fair, you do end up with a promotion and a nice pay rise, which is most likely the better option.

Before long you find yourself back in the fray: another sophisticated hacking group wants to have a go at hacking Generico McCompany. The thrill of the battle is what keeps you alive; that and your cardiovascular functions. Eventually some giant whale hacking group will come along and prove too much, but until then you strap yourself in and get ready for war.

The End.

Well done, you managed to keep Golden Slug at bay and avoided the trap right at the end. If you aren't already working in information security, maybe you might want to be? If you'd like to test yourself in a completely different scenario, try reading through again, but go for coffee early on rather than tea.

119 Phase Three—Attack

The Cyber Pirates begin work on deploying their honeypot; the fact that they had one sitting ready to go that merely needed minor tweaks is encouraging, as at least they aren't completely winging it. Your technical skills are mediocre, so instead your excellent memory is utilised as you collect a hot drinks order for the Cyber Pirates.

Susan inspects the ongoing work as she makes her way around the office and seems satisfied, perhaps even impressed, although she'd never say so.

Before long the plan is ready to execute. Captain Dave reminds everyone of their duties.

"Ship Cat Tobias, you are in the crow's nest on lookout duty, let us know as soon as you see the Golden Slug galleon on the horizon. First Mate Gloria, I need you on the cannons, prime them ready to fire, we need to be able to stop Golden Slug in their tracks. As for me…" He stops, dramatically. Very dramatically.

"Well, er, I'll also be in the crow's nest."

So much for the build-up. The honeypot gets deployed.

A quarter of an hour passes. Ship Cat Tobias puts his finger in the air and you all snap your heads towards him. He sneezes. You throw him a sympathy "bless you", but deep down wish he'd not got your hopes up like that and hope his sneeze hurt.

Minutes pass without incident, until the weekly fire alarm test suddenly pierces through the room. A healthy group of people start making their way towards the emergency exit, clearly newbies working their first week and unaware that it's a drill. The Cyber Pirates are either following your lead of ignoring the alarm, or simply aren't afraid of fire.

Don't ignore fire alarms, even during a cyberattack.

Continue to **Section 58.**

---

120 Phase Three—Attack

Walk the plank—puns are fun. Bad news for you: writing the entire arc again but without nautical puns would make the book too big, so you'll just have to put up with the puns or start again.

Go back to **Section 267**, or of course simply return to **Section 1** to begin again.

---

121 Phase Two—Preparation

It was mentioned that Golden Slug are known to operate remotely, so the likelihood of them starting things off by sending someone onsite is slim. In general, physically breaking into a head office is something a military or government-backed operation would do; criminals tend to work remotely (often hiding behind their country's local extradition laws).

As you prowl the office, it becomes apparent just how defensive your presence makes some of your colleagues. Some immediately snatch up the nearest phone, even if it's not theirs, and pretend to be engrossed in conversation.

Others suddenly remember important meetings they have on the other side of the building or a different floor. Worst of all though are those who pretend to be transfixed by mundane objects like paperclips or staples to avoid your gaze.

It's clearly a professional fear, as these are the same people you get on well with at work socials, but because information security often is delivering bad news you are made to feel like the big bad CISO wolf. Shoving aside the feelings of persecution, you scan your surroundings and spot two offenders without lanyards and one with a white lanyard. As you remind the guilty parties of the rules, it becomes clear that perhaps the defensive attitudes are merited.

Your hunt continues for longer than you envisioned, producing a fair few findings, but all in staff who you recognise and are legitimately employed by Generico McCompany. Before you can turn your attention elsewhere in the Golden Slug inquiry, you are reminded you have a meeting you need to attend. One of those meetings where Generico McCompany show off they have a CISO but don't actually want you to talk, this ends up taking up the rest of the day.

Pick things up tomorrow in **Section 165.**

---

122 Phase Two—Preparation

"Project Degrada? You know that doesn't exist any more, right?" Jennifer asks you.

Before you can reply that you had no way of knowing as she wouldn't answer a question over chat, your conversation is interrupted as another brave soul faces Jennifer's gatekeeping gauntlet.

"What do you need Jennifer for?" the first line of defence asks the newcomer.

"It's urgent," the challenger declares. The first line of defence turns away, satisfied.

Before the challenger has even taken a step, the second line of defence swivels around and confronts the invader. "Why is it urgent?"

The challenger is about to reply, but they look up and right before doing so, a classic giveaway of someone about to lie.

The second line of defence catches this subtle tell, raises a palm and tells the challenger to be on their way. With the challenger now slinking away, you turn back to Jennifer.

"Wait, why do you care about environmental issues again?" she asks.

You explain that a threat group you are currently researching are environmentalists. She raises her hand to stop you.

"I'll brief Susan after this. She'll set up a task force meeting for tomorrow morning. I guess you are part of the task force now. Cecilia from public relations will collect you."

You take that as a dismissal and slink away to your desk. The rest of the day feels slightly surreal. You've never been part of a task force before. You've mentally designed the uniform you'd want the task force to wear when the clock strikes five, telling you to go home. Go home, go to bed and let's see what tomorrow has in store for you.

Find out what being in a task force entails in **Section 323.**

123 Phase Three—Attack

Golden Slug seem to have included a mechanism through which their operation within Generico McCompany can cannibalise itself, a virtual **kill switch**. You'd need to fire a particular number of **data packets** with a certain length at one of the compromised **server ports**. If done correctly and Golden Slug's code were present, this would force the server to restart, but with all trace of Golden Slug activity removed entirely. This failsafe mechanism allows Golden Slug to remove any trace of their activity if they suspect their hacking victims have discovered them.

The kill switch itself is an incredible mess, resembling a bored child's random scribbles, either intentionally designed with confusion in mind or perhaps cybercriminal developers aren't paid particularly well. After an hour of trying to make sense of things, you manage to boil it down to a simple maths equation:

$$X = (50 - 5 * 4) + 55 * 2$$

You are just about to start firing packet guesses at the application when Niko, the reformed hacker working as short-term apprentice at Generico McCompany, passes your desk and comments, "Be careful with that. Get it wrong and the NotNotCatya virus will encrypt our systems quicker than I can finish this can."

He proceeds to down the last of his soft drink can to emphasise his point.

NotNotCatya is an incredibly potent piece of **ransomware** technology. It seems Golden Slug included this to punish people who tried to disarm their code. Solve the maths equation and move to the section you think is the answer to X.

Head to **Section 140, Section 170** or **Section 290**, depending on what your maths gives you.

124 Phase Two—Preparation

You greet Cecilia, taking the lead in the conversation because she looks at you vacantly.

"Actually, maybe a meeting room would be more appropriate," she eventually replies. "Can you find one and I'll join you in a second? I just need to grab a coffee."

You oblige, strolling over to the meeting room area, holding your cup of tea like a beacon of light in front of you. There is only one meeting room free at this early hour, even though you know that the majority of the rooms are being used to gossip in rather than work. As you walk into the vacant room, it becomes clear why: it smells like a scientist has devoted their life to concentrating the scent of the human backside and, after perfecting the recipe, has unleashed it into the room.

You turn around to flee, but Cecilia is already standing in the doorway, her nose wrinkled and a grimace on her face. You tell Cecilia that it wasn't you. She waves her hand as if dismissing the idea, or simply wafting away the smell, you can't be sure.

"Have you heard of a group called Golden Slug?" she asks.

You concede that you have, as they were targeting Generico McCompany only yesterday.

"They claim to have hacked us and stolen payment card data. They've sent the details to the media."

Pick yourself up from that sucker punch in **Section 95.**

125 Phase Two—Preparation

I'm not going to applaud you for washing your hands.

You wash your hands thoroughly and reflect on your day so far. You have now concluded a reasonable investigation into Golden Slug and have identified a piece of work that, if completed, would reduce the company's exposure. Tomorrow you consider having a quick look through your address book and reaching out to anyone who might have first-hand experience of facing Golden Slug so you can pick their brain. As you return to the real world, you realise you have now washed your hands so thoroughly you fear you've scrubbed down to the bone.

The stroll back to your desk feels good. The only thing that could take the spring out of your step would be to have to deal with some tedious but necessary tasks. As if on cue, you log in and notice 12 new emails in your inbox. Five of these are requests for annoying, tedious but necessary tasks. You let out a long sigh and power through the emails.

As the day winds down, you ping a meeting into Susan's diary for the following morning to give her a status update and run by your idea for improving the firewall estate. The evening commute home is disrupted by buskers murdering songs that you once enjoyed. Your evening meal is disrupted by an unexpected pie filling. Your night's sleep is disrupted by owls hooting. The sun rises on the next day and you head to work full of hope.

You may or may not have that hope crushed in **Section 278.**

126 Phase Three—Attack

Georgios leaves to go and write up his notes from the call. Once again you return to your desk and do the single most important thing anyone with an office job ever can do: answer emails. The first stage of answering an email is always to decipher whether the email even requires an answer. Many of the messages waiting in your inbox fall foul of this first screen and are flung into the deleted box, much to your satisfaction. Those that do require answering can then be assessed based on whether you are likely to get into immediate trouble for sitting on a reply. This leaves a priority list to work through. You lose yourself in repetitive music and the satisfying feeling of purging your inbox. Hours pass.

Crucially, hours pass and no further DDoS attacks hit Generico McCompany during that time. Susan manages to slink her way behind you and catches you observing the normal-looking results on your perimeter defence software.

"What's happened? Things seem a lot calmer than a few hours ago."

You triumphantly reveal that you and Georgios got in touch and issued a cease and desist.

"Hacking groups listen to those?" she asks incredulously.

You fill her in on how you sent the cease and desist to the company they were using to stage the DDoS attack, not Golden Slug themselves.

"Great. So is it over with, then?"

You certainly hope so, but let Susan know you are going to look for evidence of any nasty surprises that Golden Slug might have tried to leave behind. She gives you a thumbs-up that smells of a pay rise and glides away.

Check for hidden surprises in the **logs** in **Section 337.**

---

127 Phase Four—Aftermath

Unfortunately, it's not all good news. A lone dissenting voice from within the National Fraud Office attempts to throw you under a bus. Luckily, the view from the regulators is that you dealt with the Golden Slug attack professionally and within a reasonable timeframe, so that lone dissenting voice gets muffled pretty quickly. Susan even manages to wrangle you a pay rise, which is considerably better than a kick in the teeth.

In an ideal world you'd celebrate your newfound minor riches, but in a sudden turn of events a pandemic sweeps the nation, and the public's refusal to wear face masks results in a four-month lockdown.

The End.

> *Excellent work. I know a minor pay rise may not seem like you've secured a huge win, but trust me, this is a pretty good ending. Not the best, but 8/10 for sure. If you fancy a completely new adventure, see how well you fare if you pick coffee at the beginning of the story.*

128 Phase Two—Preparation

The Generico McCompany canteen is very much like the school canteens you remember from your childhood, but whilst the food may be slightly better, the table manners on display are definitely worse. You have to stop yourself from watching in horror as someone eats a slice of pizza using a spoon. What an animal!

Spoongate has put you off the idea of pizza. Instead you opt for a grilled chicken and pesto salad, which ends up hitting the spot. Looking at the people sat around you, you see you are definitely in the minority, with pizza reigning supreme. Conversation at the table follows a predictable rhythm, with the one extrovert doing all the talking and the rest of the table providing enough of a reply not to appear rude, whilst deep down wishing the extrovert would just let them eat in peace as they daydream about quitting their jobs.

Once lunch is taken care of, you return to your desk in high spirits, ready to continue your investigation. The two vulnerabilities are still waiting, circled on your notepad, ready to reveal their secrets.

Before you can begin your research, a calendar reminder pops up letting you know you are running a new starter cybersecurity induction training session in 20 minutes. This training session is going to take until the end of the day. It looks like you only are going to have time to look into one of those two vulnerabilities.

Research "cross-site scripting" in **Section 269.** Or research "administrative console exposed" in **Section 353.**

---

129 Phase Four—Aftermath

The pizza tastes good, and is made even better by the taste of victory once you are able to confirm that Golden Slug have been banished to the shadow realm. You write up a detailed report outlining the timeline of the Golden Slug cyberattacks; Susan thanks you for it, but it never actually gets read.

Generico McCompany make contact with the regulator to inform them of the payment card data breach. As with any breach, the regulator is impressed that you are bringing the news to them and the resulting ruling is favourable. The fine that they end up having to pay is small, at least to a company the size of Generico McCompany, and so they happily put the Golden Slug story to bed.

Susan is impressed with your handling of the situation and sorts you out not only with a pay raise but also a new desk, one that is clear of chewing gum. Despite this victory, you know that you can't celebrate for too long. Golden Slug came, had a go and were thwarted, but there will always be an endless queue of cybercriminals eying up Generico McCompany and waiting for their opportunity to strike.

The End.

Well done: an ending where you keep your job and eat pizza is pretty good going. Extra impressive as you flirted with catastrophe a few times. Crucially, you took your time and made sure you had a complete picture of Golden Slug's movements before striking, giving the remediation process the best chance of success.

There are multiple other endings and story pathways to explore. Why not start again and see where things go if you make different choices?

130 Phase Three—Attack

The telephone on your desk rings. It's Reginald, who works in the fraud department for a major payment card brand. After years serving in the military, Reginald prefers to go by his old title, which you oblige him with though it makes you feel a little silly. You let Sergeant know it is good to hear from him.

"You won't be saying that when I tell you why I am calling."

You laugh and ask if he is referring to the fake Golden Slug claims.

"I'm looking at the data right now, there is nothing fake about it. I've got roughly 200 payment cards that have been used to buy Generico McCompany services flagging up for fraudulent transactions all over the globe. Each of those cards was used on your websites in the last 48 hours."

Golden Slug were just diverting your attention... A sound emerges from your mouth, somewhere between a grunt, a sigh and a moan.

"Pardon?" Sergeant replies, not fluent in strange noises.

You tell him it was nothing and ask him to share the details so you can start working on locking things down. Sergeant pings the details over by email.

Someone is in the network and stealing payment card data from under your nose. It's time to retaliate. Do you want to call in your incident response **retainer**, or attempt to pinpoint the thieves with your intrusion detection software? Alternatively, you could just hide in the toilets and cry.

Call the retainer in **Section 168.** Try intrusion detection software in **Section 309.** Cry in **Section 19.**

---

131 Phase Three—Attack

"Pretty clever macro you just sent me," Niko says, taking a seat on your desk.

You'd tell him off if you didn't need his insight quite so badly. Instead, you ask him what the macro does.

"Well, it's designed to make the user who executes it travel to a particular firewall."

"Firewall F42?" Guillaume interrupts.

Niko nods before continuing. "Yes, Firewall F42, and if the user has high enough privileges it will then make them add 15 IP addresses to the firewall's allow list. If they aren't high enough privilege, it just autodeletes itself to hide the trail."

As you digest this information, Niko decides to finish off his analysis. "Anyway, it looks like someone fell for the **phishing** attack, because those IP addresses have been added to the allow list."

You, Guillaume and Vijaya stare at Niko.

"Why didn't you tell us that from the start?!" Guillaume exclaims.

"Hey, I am just meant to analyse **malware**, don't shoot the messenger," Niko retorts, walking off. You'll probably need to bribe him with energy drinks before asking him for help in the future.

Guillaume removes Golden Slug's IP addresses from the allow list whilst you get the macro added to the archive of banned attachments. That should put an end to the phishing attempts for now, but what did Golden Slug accomplish in the time the rules were live?

Find out in **Section 222.**

---

132 Phase Two—Preparation

There are no critical emails in your inbox and network traffic levels are looking normal. You schedule a meeting first thing tomorrow with Susan to give her a status update fuelled by your latest discoveries. She adds a string of colleagues to your invite, booking a swanky meeting room.

Your afternoon is hijacked by an induction session for new starters. It seems unfair that some departments have headcounts in the thousands and information security is still just you, on your own. Ideally you would just record the induction presentation so it can be played as a video each month rather than requiring an hour of your time, but HR said that felt "impersonal". One of the new starters knocking over their glass of water turns out to be the highlight of the hour.

Once you get back to your desk, a set of unread emails greets you. One of your colleagues is requesting your input on how the company can word a reply that gives the impression they have a bigger and more comprehensive information security function than… well, just you. You've got the reply to this one saved in your favourites: vague wording such as "support from world-class third parties" and "a mindset where all staff are part of the information security mission" effectively obscures the truth and ticks the box.

Whilst I'd like to say things like that never happen, they do. Sales teams will often attempt to be creative with the truth. It's the job of the information security team at the customer to perform proper due diligence on Generico McCompany, not your role.

Before you know it, it's time to pack up and you head home, feeling satisfied with your day's efforts. The commute is calm, and you lounge on the couch watching mindless TV where C list celebrities degrade themselves in the latest format of reality television. Sleep comes easy when it's time to go to bed. You head into work the following day with a clear plan.

Start day two in **Section 81**.

133 Phase Three—Attack

"Greetings. We knew you'd discover this eventually, but don't think deleting it will be easy. You are now at the mercy of Golden Slug. Get a question wrong and you will set off our **logic bomb**, **encrypt**ing all of your data and throwing away the key."

You start to drag your mouse towards the top right of the screen to close the application, but the application is clearly tracking your mouse movement, as the text changes.

"Not so fast. You've started this, so now you'll have to see it through. Closing the tab will cause the Golden Slug logic bomb to detonate immediately."

Still want to close the tab?

Close the tab anyway in **Section 345**; otherwise continue reading.

After a few seconds the text changes again.

"Very good, time for the first question. Type your answer with your keyboard and hit enter when you've made your decision. You have 15 seconds to answer each question after it's appeared."

You look around the office for someone who might be helpful in this kind of high-octane environment. You can see one colleague who has a pen stuck up their nose and is attempting to casually remove it. It appears you are in this alone.

The text changes once more and a 15-second timer appears.

"First question. What is the longest word you can write using only the top row of characters on a standard QWERTY keyboard?"

If you think the word is "typewriter", go to **Section 149**. If you think the word is "repertoires", go to **Section 273**. If you think the word is "pirrouetter", go to **Section 44**.

134 Phase Three—Attack

"Fire the flux cannon," Commander Sasha orders.

Cyberspace Cadet Morgan clicks her mouse, which you have to assume is how a flux cannon is fired.

> *To clarify, flux cannons don't exist. They're just launching a script.*

"Direct hit," Marshal Marshal confirms. "The virtual black hole has been formed."

You voice your concerns to Sasha about having a "virtual black hole" on the Generico McCompany asset register, but he lets you know that it'll envelop itself soon and be erased entirely. You'd feel reassured if you weren't so confused.

The three-way team of yourself, Vijaya and Guillaume reach the end of the compromised email list and simultaneously come to the same conclusion. All of the users who are known to have had their email compromised are relatively junior. Commander Sasha comes over to let you know that the operation was completed successfully, Golden Slug have been removed from the network, as far as Galactic Cyber can tell. You ask Sasha for his opinion on the relatively junior pool of compromised emails.

"Are your senior staff more information security aware?" he asks.

You laugh for 10 minutes straight before replying that no, they are not.

"There is a possibility that it's simply that none of the senior staff clicked any phishing links. You could be safe and just reset all user accounts."

Guillaume winces. "Last time we did that there was almost a riot," he lets you know.

Do you want to risk a riot and force a password reset on all users, or do you let things play out?

Push out the password reset in **Section 218**. See if you can get away without one in **Section 195**.

---

135 Phase Three—Attack

> *Looking for the user account that changed the code is sensible, as it can pinpoint the user who has been hacked (or has gone rogue) and give you a timeline of when the changes to the code were first implemented.*

Searching through the version histories of the various Generico McCompany online assets showcases just how dynamic they are, with most websites getting multiple updates per day, ranging from minor tweaks to full facelifts. Only one user has made a change to every single e-commerce website in the previous week and that is an administrator helpfully called "Test". "Test" seems to have been made a year ago and after interrogating the developers, you discover it's the account people use to deploy code when the developer can't be bothered to use their own account as they are in the middle of something else.

You ask the question that needs asking and get the answer you don't want, but expect. First you ask what the username and password combination are for the account in question.

"Well, we wanted to make sure it was easy to remember, so the username is Test and the password is too."

You ask him if he means the number two.

"No, the password is Test."

You point out that he said the username was Test and he nods. Oh, great. It must have taken Golden Slug's top brains years to crack that password. You inform Susan of this issue and she tasks the support team with decommissioning the account and approving your existing project plan to enforce stronger password complexity rules. In your head you feel disappointed rather than angry: you keep reading stories on the internet about people setting passwords like hello or welcome or password, or even username admin password admin, it just seems surreal for it to have actually happened at Generico McCompany.

Google "most used passwords" to see for yourself.

Now that Golden Slug's way in has been closed, it's time to purge the e-commerce pages of their malicious code.

Do just that in **Section 162.**

---

136 Phase Four—Aftermath

"I'm sorry, but this does not make good reading," Susan comments.

You ask her what she means, as Charlotte was there from the minute the initial e-commerce attack was discovered and the fire was suppressed before it could get out of control.

"That's what I thought, but she has spent most of this report outlining a long list of reasons why this attack was easier to pull off than it should have been due to missing **controls** and what she describes as poorly configured security tools."

You look at Susan and ask her what that means.

"The report is signed off by the National Fraud Office's CEO and has had the regulator's eyes on it. Even if what they claim isn't completely true, we don't have enough evidence to disprove it."

You mentally start packing your bags—and you start packing them for real when Susan confirms she is going to have to let you go, implying that the regulator will be more lenient with the fine if a new CISO is put in place.

> *Probably more than a regulator would ever demand, but who knows what happens behind closed doors or in COVID times closed virtual meeting rooms?*

As you walk out of Generico McCompany for the last time, you notice a familiar face sitting in reception. Typical: Charlotte isn't even waiting for your seat to get cold. She flashes you a nasty grin as the door hits you on the way out.

The End.

> *The damage was done in phase two really: not finding any clear leads in the initial section left you chasing shadows. If it's any consolation, there were very few ways of emerging unscathed once that initial damage was done. Why not read through again, but mix up your decisions early on and see if this allows you to get the jump on Golden Slug? Alternatively, you could start again and pick coffee as your drink rather than tea, which will give you a completely different adventure.*

137 Phase Two—Preparation

> *Something's not quite right, is it? It would be safer to refuse the USB, though, because you have no idea what it contains.*

"This USB is completely empty," Niko says.

That was the last thing you expected him to say. You let him know that can't be true.

He looks at you dismissively; you have to concede this is much more his domain than yours. "OK, pedant, there is an Excel file in there, but it's completely clean." He hands you the USB.

"Maybe it genuinely is something Sakura wants?" he finishes, opening a crossword to reward himself for his 20 seconds of effort.

You can't believe it, but you can't really challenge Niko's findings, so you take the USB back to your desk and store it in your drawer, to reunite it with Sakura once she's back from leave. A feeling of annoyance ripples over you:

you were so sure the person in the lift was dodgy and the USB was a trap. Susan walks over and turns your annoyance to panic.

"Our CEO has just received a ransom note via email. Golden Slug claim one of Michael's projects has poisoned a country's water supply. In retaliation they are going to start firing DDoS attacks at us in five minutes, unless we pay them $20 million."

You sit with your mouth open, although Susan seems to be expecting a reply. You let out a gurgle; that doesn't seem to be the reply she expected. It looks like it's all hands on deck.

See what the fallout is in **Section 270.**

138 Phase Four—Aftermath

Over the following weeks Vijaya is forced to redo the entire anti-**phishing** training, but she doesn't seem to mind; if anything she seems ecstatic as she watches the corny cartoons all over again.

You successfully defended against the Golden Slug attack and tell the tale as your party piece for years to come. You earn a pay rise and promotion out of the whole ordeal, you even get budget to hire your own member of staff. The interview process reveals that the budget provided is only enough to hire someone with no hobbies, mortgage or rent, but it's still better than nothing.

> *It's hard to write jokes about people not being paid much money. Anyway, don't worry, many people earn a very good living in the industry. I hope to be one some day!*

Generico McCompany put more stringent **controls** in place to prevent nuclear programs popping up out of nowhere. As you sail into the sunset, just know one thing: Golden Slug are not defeated.

The End.

> *Well done, a fine ending indeed. You were rewarded for following through with the incident response plan and standing up for what you thought was the correct course of action when challenged by Petra. Here's an idea: why not read through again but make intentionally bad decisions and see where things go. You might end up learning something completely different.*

139 Phase Two—Preparation

You pick up the receiver and ask the caller to identify themselves.

"Good morning, this is detective Ruby Romero from the National Cyber Security Agency. Am I speaking with the Generico McCompany Chief Information Security Officer?"

The national body interested in protecting the country's private sector from cyberattacks naturally has a different name depending on the country. The National Cyber Security Agency itself doesn't seem to exist.

Reply "no" in **Section 32**, continue reading to reply "yes".

You confirm your name and job title.

"I am sorry to call in such circumstances, but as part of our countrywide monitoring we have strong reason to believe the Generico McCompany network has been compromised."

Oh.

"This may come as a shock, I appreciate. In normal procedure I would come onsite to your office to show you the evidence and begin planning a response. Will that be appropriate?"

You provide Ruby with the office address and she lets you know she'll be there in half an hour. Your tea still sits on the coaster on your desk, suddenly much less appealing than it was a little while ago. Dazed, you spend the next few minutes staring into space, not really present in the moment. The cup of tea moves from optimum temperature to lukewarm; what a waste. From where you are sat you see the light flicker on in Susan's office and decide to walk over to give her the bad news before waiting for Ruby in reception.

Susan takes the news well. This has happened before, apparently, and it turned out to be a false alarm. She says she'll book a meeting room. You ride the lift down to reception, hoping that it's another false alarm.

Keep those fingers crossed in **Section 72**.

---

140 Phase Three—Attack

Nice. Core math skills are useful over a wide range of career choices, including information security.

You carefully untangle Golden Slug's kill switch, then fire a message containing 140 packets into the application's port. In your mind you were visualising a really intense scene where you get visual confirmation of the code being deleted, perhaps accompanied by some epic music, but in the real world when code runs it's often quite dull.

You manually confirm the code has been deleted, then investigate how the code got into the e-commerce pages in the first place. Unsurprisingly, the root cause of the problem is laziness: someone in development created an administrator account with the username and password both set as "Admin".

Please tell me you don't do this. Just to elaborate, this is one of the first combinations a hacker will try, as it used to be the default setting when applications were launched. It's also worth adding that technically setting a corporate password policy would fall under a CISO's remit, so this is kind of a self-burn.

That sort of sloppiness was too tempting a carrot for Golden Slug to pass up. You force a password reset on the account and write a very annoyed email to the perpetrator, CCing in Susan. You also put a reminder in to work on the corporate password policy.

Upon reading your email, Susan drops by for the full story. "Is that weak password account linked to the dark web forum posting thing?"

You inform her she is correct. Using the administrator account Golden Slug were able to plant their malicious code into Generico McCompany e-commerce websites and steal payment card details. However, you conclude that this is now over.

"Well, that seems like a decent outcome really," Susan replies, before looking at her watch. "It's getting late and you've had a long day. We can open dialogue with the regulators tomorrow. Not much is going to be achieved right now."

Suddenly realising how tired you are, you head home to rest. You wake up refreshed and go back into work the next morning.

See what the day holds in **Section 248.**

141 Phase One—Prologue

You select hot water, just hot water. The machine seems confused as it clicks, whirrs and beeps, perhaps horrified at what you have asked it to do. The jovial chat behind you is silenced instantly and people slowly creep towards the door. Boiling hot water flows out of the nozzle, like the tears of the innocent. The mug itself appears to quiver in fear as the water fills it. The machine beeps sadly to let you know it's finished dispensing your "drink".

You reach out, grab the mug and lift it slowly towards your mouth to take a sip. A woman from the sales team has established eye contact with you and now seems to be struggling to look away. You maintain the eye contact as you take another sip. The sound of sirens reverberates in the background, though that's potentially unrelated.

As you step towards the door, the remaining onlookers swiftly clear a path, two people are crying, and one seems to be hyperventilating.

You feel a sense of doom and reconsider your choice. You dump your mug of hot water in the sink and face the beverage machine again. The universe sighs in relief.

Get some coffee in **Section 250** or brew some tea in **Section 161**.

142 Phase Three—Attack

Sasha points a giant gloved finger to some red characters on his screen and states, "We've found UHOs in this section of your network."

You ask him what a UHO is.

"Unidentified hacking object."

This isn't a real term, by the way, for anyone who is taking notes.

The UHOs are inside the database where recorded phone calls are kept, specifically the calls where customers pay for their purchase over the phone. Sasha pulls up a recording that has been listened to and hits play.

You hear a nervous woman buying colourless nail polish, interacting with a hyperactive call centre clerk. The process reaches the stage where the clerk hands the customer off to the automated payment process where the customer says their card number, expiration date and secret code, and then the call is handed back to the clerk. In theory the call shouldn't record any of the payment details, so this section of the recording should be empty, but in practice...

"Eight, zero, zero, eight, five." Sasha ends the recording. He shows you that Golden Slug have already listened to 2000 call details and are going through an additional 500 per hour. Each call is resulting in a stolen payment card. This isn't good.

"This is obviously less than ideal. We could strike now if you are confident they are only interested in payment card data, but we may miss other plans they've initiated," Sasha concludes.

Do you want to attempt to kick Golden Slug off the network immediately, or observe their behaviour for another few hours to see what you can learn about their activity?

Kick them out in **Section 233**. Observe them in **Section 17**.

---

143 Phase Three—Attack

Oh no, I'm not sure we can be friends now.

You leave your food on the table and swagger out of the canteen. Cleaners get paid to clean, right? If you didn't leave a messy table, they'd have no work to do and they would become redundant. By not picking up after yourself you are single-handedly creating jobs. Really there should be statues made in your honour.

The lift breaks as you ride it back up. You stand in the dark for hours reflecting on how bad a human being you are. When the lift finally starts working again, you change course and go to the ground floor. Scanning your badge, you walk through the turnstile and out of the door. Once you get home you resign from your position and enjoy the limited benefits of unemployment.

Someone else can clean Golden Slug up, right?

The End.

*Ah, I was hoping you didn't reach this ending, I am now judging you as a human being. Go to **Section 291** if you have learned from the error of your ways and want to clean up after yourself.*

144 Phase Two—Preparation

The lift pings to confirm you've reached the ground floor and opens to reveal the vast lobby. You vaguely know the building's lobby staff by appearance and typically give them a head nod as you pass. You've convinced yourself this is a polite alternative to speaking to them. As you greet them and ask about a package that has been left for you, you notice their surprise at actually hearing you speak.

The receptionist's name tag is at least two font sizes too small for you to be able to make out his name, but luckily his voice comes across loud and clear. He flicks open a folder and looks through the listings. "No, I am sorry, but I've got nothing arriving for your floor today."

You look at him gormlessly, unsure how to proceed with the conversation. As you stand there puzzled, the receptionist sits and waits for your next move. In this game of conversational tennis, the ball is in your court. You let him know you'll be leaving now. You cringe internally as the conversation replays in your head and retreat to the safety of the lift.

You are joined by an immaculately dressed colleague, who has successfully managed to match their blue scarf with their lanyard. They flash you a smile as they pack away their umbrella and make small talk.

Ride the lift up in **Section 229**.

---

145 Phase Three—Attack

Nope, sorry, it's the real deal.

The DDoS attack starts to bring its first casualties as firewalls, **server**s and applications succumb. You can tell what has fallen even before it's reported to IT based on the phone calls and **ticket**s that come into the support team who sit within earshot.

Chaos fuels further chaos as knock-on effects from the first casualties lead to collateral damage. Kevin, who heads up the insurance branch of the company, comes over in person to complain.

"Insuremytoupee is offline," he tells you. "Do you know how much revenue Insuremytoupee brings this company?"

Despite only having been at the company for months, you do know: it's all Kevin ever talks about. "13%," you reply.

"14% now, actually, they let us include the revenue from Insuremywig too, despite them being completely unrelated. Anyway, why have you taken it offline?"

Kevin seems to think you are someone on the support desk who hasn't fixed his issue. Susan appears and clarifies things.

"Nothing to do with them, Kevin, support is over there." She points towards support, who watch her forsake them with horror in their eyes. Kevin retreats to harass support, leaving Susan free to harass you.

"It's Golden Slug, isn't it? What do you plan to do?"

Curling up in a ball and crying doesn't seem to be the answer she wants, so you come up with some options more likely to appeal to Susan.

Move to **Section 148** if you want to call an incident response retainer company, or take the fight back to Golden Slug in **Section 321**.

---

146 Phase Three—Attack

As Susan slinks away, Guillaume points at something on his screen and beckons you over wordlessly. Perhaps realising that you are unable to translate what his monitor is displaying into anything tangible, he provides a helpful summary.

"Golden Slug stole this entire database. The logic bomb was just a red herring."

You don't know what is more surprising, the news itself or Guillaume using a term like "red herring". You ask him what was in the database, dreading the reply.

"Erm, let's see." He opens up the database. "Personal data relating to our customers, it seems."

Rather than ask him how much, you watch him scroll down continuously, hoping that the mouse will hit the bottom row soon. It doesn't.

"Well over a million records, it looks like." Guillaume looks around, then lowers his voice. "That's pretty bad, right?"

Releasing an exasperated sigh, you drag yourself to Susan's office to share the bad news. You wait outside because Susan is talking to Petra, the CEO, but she beckons you in.

See what they want in **Section 272**.

---

147 Phase Three—Attack

You've already stood up to the CEO today, what's a few more executives?

For the second time today, you put your neck on the line and demand the extra time. Susan's face says it all: if this doesn't work, she won't be able to save you. The horde of directors leaves, potentially to peel out of their skins and reassume lizard form. Guillaume is hard at work. You ask him if you can help and he just laughs.

You decide to repay the favour by grabbing him a coffee. In the kitchen you run into Kevin, who runs the Insuremytoupee application. Kevin lets you know that the application is doing better than ever and even drops a teaser that soon he'll be launching a new product, "Insuremydentures". You decide this is an appropriate time to leave.

After you fuel Guillaume with coffee and nervously wait for him to finish the task, he spins round in his chair and beckons you over. Pointing at his screen, he asks, "See that?"

You let him know that you can't.

"Exactly, those crafty guys left themselves a **backdoor**. If we hadn't taken our time they'd have been back in here in a week or two to start it all over again."

You let Guillaume know you'll owe him positive feedback in the next appraisal cycle.

"That, and perhaps coffee delivery for a few months."

Accept his terms in **Section 234.**

148 Phase Three—Attack

An incident response retainer is rarely a bad choice. The technical know-how and experience combine into a more than capable ally.

You slide open your drawer and pull out a fancy business card. The logo is of a skull and crossbones made up using 1s and 0s, with the tagline underneath "Send the hackers overboard". Not your ideal kind of company to keep on retainer, but somebody signed these guys up before you even started. You ring the number and an automated answering service picks up. You state your company name.

"Was that Generic Company?" the automated voice asks.

You laugh to yourself. Generico McCompany sounds nothing like that, so you try again.

"Was that Generico McCompany?"

You confirm that yes, it was.

"Thank you, a Cyber Pirate will call you back ASAP."

You die a little inside. True to their word, though, a Cyber Pirate does call back and identifies himself as Captain Dave, which doesn't sound as piratey as you were expecting. You give Captain Dave some background on what is going on.

"Golden Slug are unchartered seas for us, but DDoS attacks are common foes on the seven seas."

You admit you've not read the full contract and ask how quickly they can get someone over.

"We can have an all hands on deck call within 24 hours, as per your SLA. But I will send a message in a bottle calendar invite for four o'clock today to start our voyage together."

Do you want to ask Captain Dave to drop the nautical puns?

Ask for an end to the puns in **Section 120**, or let the puns stay and continue on to the four o'clock call in **Section 267**.

149 Phase Three—Attack

If you looked at your keyboard before writing that, shame on you.

You write out "typewriter" and hit the enter key. The text on screen is replaced by an hourglass, with sand dripping down from the top to the lower half. Seemingly satisfied with your answer, the text changes again.

"Before question two, it may have struck you as peculiar that we would give you a chance to deactivate the logic bomb."

You find yourself nodding your head in response, it does seem weird.

"We would compare you to a Spartan who cannot raise their shield. It would benefit us more if you were to keep your job so we can just hack Generico McCompany again in the future."

Your hands clench into fists. Now Golden Slug have made this personal.

"Question two. What never asks a question but always gets answered?"

If you think the word is "Books", go to **Section 184.** If you think the word is "Telephone", go to **Section 236.**

150 Phase Three—Attack

Good on you: believe in the plan.

You plough forward. This incident response plan was written for a reason and cost money to produce, so it must be going somewhere. You reread the question: "What side effects may the attack be having that are invisible?"

Then it clicks. Time slows to a standstill despite the ongoing chaos surrounding you; reality repackages and presents itself in black and white before converting to binary and then back to normal. Suddenly, everything makes sense.

The invisible side effects are all those firewalls being knocked over, then rebooting in their weak state. You ask Vijaya to remind you what happens when the firewalls get forced to reset.

She looks worried for a split second before answering. "They reboot, but in a state that allows some more basic attacks to get through."

You thank her and then contemplate. Could Golden Slug continue their DDoS purely as a distraction, whilst lining something up that is far more impactful using those weakened firewalls?

> *Just to point out, this is a little bit fanciful, but to avoid dragging things down into the technical dirt let's just run with it.*

You turn to Susan and let her know that you need to get a dashboard up and running to display the firewalls that have been knocked offline in the past 24 hours, and haven't had an update patched to them since.

She looks at you quizzically, but delegates the task to someone in the IT team. You are not going to be popular. In your state of ultra-sensory perfection you wince as you sense an IT helpdesk member take a sip of their coffee, despite it being one and a half degrees hotter than optimal. This is confirmed when they put the mug down sharply, offended by the overly hot contents.

You coordinate with Gesa to set up an incident response update meeting and head on in.

Attend the meeting in **Section 88.**

---

151 Phase Two—Preparation

As you leave Michael's office, you catch Gesa's eye. She gives you a knowing look and then goes back to pretending to work. She has really mastered that art: the way her fingers move across the keyboard combined with a few glances at a printed document on her desk really make for a convincing performance.

As you wander back to the IT area, you muse about how everything is starting to feel more mysterious. You waste 10 minutes having a conversation with one of your colleagues who has clearly mistaken you for someone else. Despite realising this pretty early in the conversation, you are too polite to point out the mistake. Lucky for you, the conversational topics are fairly vague and broad and you somehow get away with it. Whoever this person thinks you are will have a surprise on Saturday, as you agree plans to meet up for a meal and some paintballing and then slip away.

You spend the remaining hours of the day making unnecessary changes to documents and resubmitting them for legal review. They were rejected initially, but you know with some persistence you can get them through eventually. The trick is to make subtle changes and then hope that they can sneak through the approval process. This never works, but you do it anyway. Once the clock signals the end of the day you make your way home, feeling satisfied with your work.

At home, you find yourself engrossed in a film centred around a nuclear submarine; considering your newfound subject matter expertise in all things nuclear, this seems appropriate. Before you know it, it's bedtime. The next morning, you undergo your routine and work starts.

See what the day holds in store for you in **Section 81.**

152 Phase Three—Attack

A bit of a lose–lose situation really, but in general blatant lies are likely to come back to haunt you, so this is the safer but less comfortable option.

You confirm to Cecilia that the email did indeed come from you.

"OK, thanks. Also, Susan asked if you can pop into her office." Cecilia disappears offline before you can enquire further.

You shuffle over to Susan's office, ready to face her wrath. After offering you a seat, she unleashes pity rather than wrath, which if anything is worse.

"I believe I have misjudged the situation. I took you on from a relatively inexperienced position and expected you to deal with a sophisticated attacker like Golden Slug all on your own. Clearly, this is a job better suited to a team rather than one individual, so I am bringing in a second information security person to help moving forwards."

You ask what will happen to the current Golden Slug situation.

"Don't worry about that, I've got some government contacts who are willing to send a clean-up crew to sort this out."

True to her word, a government clean-up crew eradicates Golden Slug from your network in a matter of hours, and Susan begins the hiring process for a new information security manager to join you. Eventually she hires someone called Andy, who has similar experience to yourself, although it takes him four days to demonstrate that he is more educated and talented than you. Susan jumps on this by making Andy your boss. His first act as your manager is to fire you, his last line being: "Not that you were competition, but this frees up wage budget."

The End.

I'll be honest, you were doomed whether you lied about the email or not. Because you made slow progress in phase two, there really was not much wiggle room once the attack started. Why not read through again and see if you can change your fate with some different choices?

153 Phase One—Prologue

Well done. Sometimes a page will give you a midway option for making a decision.

And so the story continues, with different outcomes depending on the choices you make as the reader.

Anyway, enough chat. When you are ready to begin, jump back to the Prologue or go straight into the story on **Section 1** *to start the adventure. Good luck.*

154 Phase Four—Aftermath

It would have been safer to involve Susan in the problem. That way you are covering yourself more.

You are particularly interested in the Vlad lead, so you decide to pursue it. You get up and walk over to operations, knowing there is no point messaging recruitment on internal chat; for some reason that team always want to meet in person. Guilt forces you to take the stairs up to the 14th floor, where you spot Vlad. He is leaning against a wall, gazing into nothingness. You observe him for a few seconds to make sure he is breathing (which he is) and then walk over.

When you greet Vlad he continues starting into space, oblivious to your presence. You wave your hand in front of his face and try again. He shakes his head, snapping out from his trance, and then turns to you.

"Yes?" he says, completely skipping over the reason he was asleep against a wall.

You inform him you have evidence that a hacker group has been looking through his emails from the past year. You pause, letting that sink in. Vlad looks like he'd rather go back to sleep and pretend this was a bad dream, so you carry on in an attempt to stop him from returning to the land of nod.

You ask if he can think of any email threads that a hacker might find interesting; potentially something that could be useful for blackmail. Vlad's eyes glaze a little again, this time because he's doing a deep search within his brain to see if he can think of anything particularly juicy for Golden Slug to find. He gulps.

Find out why in **Section 193.**

155 Phase Two—Preparation

Very indecisive of you.

You decide to leave Project Degrada for the minute and shift your attention to Project Luminec. You browse to Project Luminec's project page yourself, knowing that Janet will likely put in a complaint about you if you try to engage her in conversation again. There are more files in the Project Luminec folder, but most of them are the company's template files with no changes at all. You sigh. If only more people knew that simply changing a document name from "Project Plan Template" to "Project Plan Template – Luminec" doesn't magically populate the document.

In contrast, whoever completed the **risk register** for the project clearly didn't take any half measures: each entry is followed by an avalanche of words that threatens to engulf anyone foolish enough to try to read them all. You filter down to environmental risks and find an interesting line: "Small chance of complete destruction of local water supply."

You whistle to yourself: that definitely could be described as a "critical" risk. Unfortunately, the document author decided there was no need to provide any additional information on this risk, leaving you unsure how exactly this could happen.

You flick to the version history section and find that the document was created by Gesa, one of the project managers. Gesa is actually in your good books as she frequently puts her foot down and says no to people when they try to bypass information security. Seeing as she only works down the hall in the operations office, it seems sensible to stretch your legs, drop by and pick her brain in person.

Walk over to Gesa in **Section 203.**

156 Phase Three—Attack

*It's a good idea if you are an absolute specialist in **malware** reverse engineering. As a CISO you are more likely to be an all-rounder, but as I've made it ambiguous what skill set your character has, you won't be penalised for that choice, don't worry.*

It doesn't take long to discover Golden Slug's code now you know where to find it and what to look for. The idea is to analyse the inner workings of the malicious code so that it can reveal how Golden Slug got it onto the network in the first place. Two things become apparent almost as soon as your investigation begins. Firstly, your chair setup is not conducive for working on code as you develop immediate backache; secondly, there are absolutely no clues relating to how the code was first injected into the e-commerce page.

You run a Google search to confirm your suspicion, and also to quickly scan the local news in the hope of finding some uplifting stories to raise morale. You find a heart-warming tale about a cat who opened their own doughnut shop, which brings a smile to your face, though it's balanced by also reading that your approach of analysing the code to determine how it got there is a waste of time.

"What, you think hackers are going to draw a map or something, lol?" says one post on a forum thread started by someone who was likely in a similar situation to you. At least they got to close the thread by saying: "Turns out it was just a cryptocurrency miner."

Oh, how you wish Golden Slug were just **cryptomining**. It's time to change focus to the user accounts to hopefully stop you fumbling in the dark.

See if there is light in **Section 135.**

157 Phase Two—Preparation

Whilst talking to people is great, and a lot of problems could be avoided if people communicated better, given the frequency with which third parties are used as the way in to companies, this direction is less clear.

The Generico McCompany e-commerce estate is run by Giuseppa, known to operate with an iron fist and not to have much time for anything that isn't related to her precious money-making websites. Approaching her desk, you take in a brief exchange between Giuseppa and some poor sod who must have brought news that displeased her, since he almost bumps into you as he makes his escape, his vision clearly impacted by the tears waterfalling down his face.

With a gulp, you enter the lion's den and say hello to Giuseppa.

She turns to acknowledge you and smirks. "Great, the data police are here, probably to try to get us to stop recording people's eye colour when they browse."

You let her know your visit is much more innocent then that, though you point out the eye colour thing does sound like something you will need to look into.

She deflects with a nonchalant flick of the wrist before continuing. "We have nothing to hide here. What do you want?"

You let her know you are researching a cyberthreat group who target payment card data. That certainly gets her attention.

Giuseppa's back straightens and she cracks her knuckles. "Then they'll be coming after my babies."

Rather than pounce on that weird revelation you press on, stating that is precisely why you thought to go to her.

Suddenly Giuseppa seems a lot more helpful now she knows you are defending her "babies" and are not a threat.

See what you can find out in **Section 257.**

---

158 Phase Three—Attack

"Any idea what is happening here?" she asks, peering into your soul.

You admit you have no idea, except you do know you didn't change any firewall rule.

She looks unconvinced, but moves on out of necessity. "Make sure that firewall isn't sending out more data. I'll get a forensics team in to understand what happened to the firewall rule once we have the situation in hand."

You all start to move towards the door, but Susan stops you. "One last thing."

You freeze, fearing the worst.

"Can you action the ticket for Michael's team member? He's bugging me about it."

You let her know that you've done it already.

"He messaged me just before you came in that it's outstanding, can you double-check?" She then puts her headset on, as clear a dismissal as any.

Oddly enough, she appears to be right, as Eduard's ticket has reappeared in your inbox. You approve the request from Eduard@genericomccompany.com and he drops you an internal chat message thanking you. Strange.

Another email sits in your inbox. It's from hello@goldenslug.com and all it says is "Thanks!" For some reason Golden Slug are mocking you, but it looks like you'll have the last laugh, as the Golden Slug DDoS attacks are now negligible and the firewall rule has been fixed. Susan's forensics team are coming in tomorrow. They'll clear your name and let you chalk up Golden Slug as a big career win.

Get the good news in **Section 113**.

---

159 Phase Two—Preparation

You may as well continue. The other option didn't really have any potential for breakthroughs.

You decide to change tack with Rory, and instead tell him why you are asking about this project, outlining Golden Slug and their environmentally based agenda.

Rory replies simply, "Look, I can't talk about this project, but let me put it this way. If I knew I had a potential problem with a Golden Slug, I'd forget this project and just focus on having enough salt in storage."

That makes a lot of sense actually. Whether Golden Slug are interested in targeting Generico McCompany or not, you could always look to get in contact with someone who has dealt with a Golden Slug attack previously and see how they coped.

You thank Rory, who is already snoring, and walk back to your desk to make a phone call. You privately ask some of your information security industry brethren if they have faced Golden Slug in combat before, with one person confirming they have and providing you with their number. You punch in the number, the phone rings and the cold fear of talking to a stranger grips you.

"Sonal's phone."

You ask if you are speaking to Sonal, someone answering the phone on behalf of Sonal, or perhaps the phone itself?

"Very funny, I am Sonal. We swapped a message a few seconds ago. Yeah, I've had a run-in with Golden Slug before. It didn't go well."

You ask Sonal how it didn't go well.

"Well, they put my old employer out of business with one of their DDoS attacks."

You could certainly describe that as "not well".

If you want to rub it in, go to **Section 324.** Hear Sonal out in **Section 360.**

---

160 Phase Three—Attack

You set up Galactic Cyber on the available hot desk seats. Thankfully they seem to have brought modified laptops that they are able to use freely, even through their space suits. Sasha declines your offer of a drink on behalf of the group, stating, "We can't lower our visors when on a foreign body. We drink from a pre-installed flask connected to our visor."

It would perhaps be safer not to ask him about their toilet arrangements. Galactic Cyber may look a little strange, but you decide they seem to know what they are doing. You are barely able to start a game of Minesweeper when you feel Marshal Marshal's gloved hand tap your shoulder.

"Sorry to intrude, but the commander needs to speak to you."

You follow Marshal the four steps to where Sasha is sat. You ask the commander what he has found, and he responds by raising his gloved palm in the "just a second" gesture. Sasha then makes a call on his radio and states, "Euston, we have a problem."

You ask Sasha who he is talking to.

"Oh nobody, I called our head office in Euston Square. It's the only way to be guaranteed of getting that line in."

You ask Sasha what happens if the call needs to occur at a time when that office is closed. He points out there are many places called Euston or Houston in the world and Galactic Cyber have an office in each.

Find out what problem he has found in **Section 142.**

---

161 Phase One—Prologue

You select a tea bag from the jar, fill a mug with boiling water, and move away from the sacred hot drink machine, allowing another colleague to take your place at the drink altar. You set the mug on the counter and attempt to throw the tea bag into your mug, basketball style. It misses. You try again. It misses. You try again. You score. Rewarding yourself with an internal fist bump, you watch the infusion work its magic. The colour swirls around the mug hypnotically, but not hypnotically enough to fight off your urge to stir the tea impatiently, forcing the brewing process along. Sure, coffee drinkers don't have to suffer this tedious process, but you are comfortable with your life choices. Removing the tea bag, you add a generous dash of milk and finish stirring, then quickly wash your spoon and leave it in the drying rack.

Tea in hand, you walk back to your desk. You're relieved to see that Susan has drifted away from her previous spot, but her comments continue to prick away at the back of your mind, until you give in and do some research into Golden Slug.

A swift Google search shows that Golden Slug seem to be money-motivated criminals who specialise in remotely stealing payment card data and then selling the information on the **dark web**. The only places you know of where Generico McCompany processes payment cards are on the retail **e-commerce** websites and high street stores.

> *Quick recap. Payment cards are debit and credit cards. e-Commerce websites are online shops, like Amazon, where you can buy things and pay using a payment card.*

As Golden Slug is known to work remotely, you decide to focus more on the e-commerce angle.

> *Hackers are generally more likely to try remote attacks, as they can hide behind the extradition laws of whatever country they live in. Also, attributing a cyberattack is much harder than attributing an attack where the person is physically present at an office or shop.*

Your calendar is looking relatively empty for the morning, so it might be worth doing some poking to make sure Golden Slug isn't wreaking havoc on your network. Where to start, though? You could look into the latest **vulnerability scan** results, or you could read the most recent information security **internal audit** report.

Turn to **Section 304** for the vulnerability scan results. Turn to **Section 261** if you'd like to read the audit report.

---

162 Phase Three—Attack

The morning descends into a game of whack-a-mole as you manually plunge into each e-commerce website's code, pinpoint Golden Slug's work and whack it with a hammer. You could write a script to do this, but decide you want to feel the satisfaction of ripping Golden Slug out root and stem yourself, no matter how long it takes.

Something a CISO wouldn't be doing themselves normally, but then I couldn't use that nice whack-a-mole line.

With convenient timing, your stomach begins to rumble just as you whack the last mole and purge Golden Slug from the e-commerce estate. This will make lunch taste that extra bit better. You collect Ruby from her temporary office before making your way to the staff canteen. Offering to pay for Ruby's lunch is an easy karma win as you are going to expense it anyway.

As you sit and update her on your progress, she begins to talk about her previous run-ins with Golden Slug.

"I can't name who the company that got breached were," Ruby says, before providing a description of their business that narrows it down to only one possible option. She continues to explain how Golden Slug played the same trick with the e-commerce website code insertion, but managed to evade detection for months.

Before you get on your high horse, you remember that if it weren't for Ruby's intervention, you'd have had no clue Golden Slug were in the network and likely would have been rinsed just as badly. You finish your food. Do you want to clear your table?

Clear your table space in **Section 291**. Leave it to someone else in **Section 143**.

---

163 Phase Two—Preparation

There's no right or wrong here, you have nothing to go off other than the project name.

You ask Janet for a link to the Project Degrada documents and she links you to an internal folder. You manage to thank her before she promptly sets her status to 'offline'. Clearly, Janet isn't a fan of interacting over chat either.

You begin to browse through the folder and open up the business plan, which seems to be the logical place to start. Except for the project name and the project risk ratings table, the document is incredibly lacking in detail. The only text talks vaguely about "novel methodology for enhancing synthesis protocols" and "expanded opportunities for elongated sensor reading windows", whatever that means. You find some image files, but all they showcase are some silver boxes that resemble washing machines.

The sight of the "washing machines" painfully reminds you that your own washing machine needs replacing. Of course, it broke the day after the warranty expired. You waste some time browsing the website of the manufacturer of your deceased washing machine before reverting to the task at hand. You click through into a document that appears to have been written by an artificial intelligence that was playing cheesy marketing bingo with every sentence, but you still have no clear view of what the project entails.

Finally, you stumble upon a set of meeting minutes; the minutes themselves provide no insight, but they do contain the names of the four people who attended the meeting, who presumably know more. Three of the team members have since left, but you have a lead at least in Michael, who is now the Chief Operations Officer.

This looks and smells like the kind of project that is going to need some deeper diving. You hear Narinder telling Mark off for farting; maybe that's what the smell is.

Pursue Project Degrada via Michael in **Section 117**. Switch attention to Project Luminec in **Section 155**.

---

164 Phase Four—Aftermath

You survive the Golden Slug incident and spend four more months working at Generico McCompany, but seeing your influence decrease gradually, which is impressive as you didn't feel you had much influence to begin with. This starts out small, with people involving you less in their projects, perhaps fearful that you are a bad-luck charm. Vijaya is the only person who doesn't shun you; if anything, she is nicer to you than before.

Eventually you make a miniscule administrative mistake and the company decides to sack you over it. It turns out your employment contract was written by a sadist and there is no room for any kind of legal challenge at all, in fact because of the nature of your dismissal you even have to pay a small fine.

As you job hunt, you ask Susan for a reference. She is willing to go as far as stating that you "oversaw" the Golden Slug incident, but is unwilling to add any adjective that implies you were competent, calm or even average. It doesn't seem to make a difference, as you get snapped up by a company that recently disposed of their own CISO following a data breach. During the interview process you are asked what you would have done differently in the Golden Slug case and you reply honestly: a lot.

The End.

Before you get too annoyed, this is actually a solid 6/10 ending. It can be much worse, trust me. You did well not bothering to lie about the data Golden Slug leaked, but things would have been much simpler if you'd taken the network down when prompted. It's those kinds of painful decisions that can make or break a breach scenario. Anyway, dust yourself off and try reading through again, but drinking tea this time instead for a completely different adventure.

165 Phase Two—Preparation

The next morning, the marble floors of the Generico McCompany lobby must have been cleaned overnight, as you swear you can see up your own nose in the reflection as you make your way to the lift. Making a hopefully unrelated mental note to buy some hair trimmers, you punch in your floor number and wait, as usual hoping nobody joins you. In a rare victory, the doors close and you get to ride the lift alone.

Brashly, you decide to get your cup of tea before even sitting down at your desk this morning; you live life on the edge, after all. The kitchen is full of bleary-eyed co-workers, although whether their eyes are bleary due to doing all-nighters or attending Matt from sales's pub crawl last night is open to interpretation. The hot water machine doesn't know or care about your backstory: it has one job and it dedicates itself to it entirely.

Steaming mug of tea in hand, you leave the kitchen and its atmosphere of regret to move instead to your desk in the IT section, which has its own atmosphere. You wouldn't describe it quite as regret, more of longing to win the lottery and never come to work again; standard.

After you boot up your laptop, you reflect that your email inbox is disappointing more than anything: the spam is low quality and lacking in imagination and the daily deluge of **phishing** emails you receive is equally substandard. Where is your random email showering you in riches?

Probably in that junk folder. If it sounds too good to be true, it probably is.

The clock strikes nine and your phone rings immediately.

Pick up the phone in **Section 139.**

166 Phase Three—Attack

A sensible move. Down time is bad, but you just can't risk that problem growing and spreading.

There is no choice, you conclude. Things have reached the point where keeping the network online will only increase the collateral damage. Golden Slug are running rampant and need to be stopped. With the help of Guillaume and Vijaya, you take the entire Generico McCompany offline temporarily. In a parallel universe, people greet this action with cheers and praise.

In your own universe, the uproar begins immediately. Because internal chat is down, people come to complain in person, first directing their attention to the support desk, but once your meat shield of support desk staff gives you away, the fury is swiftly redirected. It becomes easier to make a list of bad things that aren't your fault, as the list of things that are your fault appears to be never-ending. Somehow the kitchen being out of chocolate muffins is also your fault; supposedly IT being down meant a replacement order didn't go in.

Other than racking up complaints, the decision to take the network offline does serve a purpose. Guillaume identifies how Golden Slug were able to get into the network and plant a **logic bomb**. He disables their access route, kicking them out of your systems.

Susan walks over, looking stressed. "Please tell me there is an upside to taking everything offline like that."

Guillaume gives her the good news, whilst bringing everything back online again.

Susan seems satisfied with that: her 1000-yard stare is downgraded to a mere 900 yards.

Move over to **Section 146.**

167 Phase Three—Attack

"You have failed the quiz, the logic bomb has now been detonated. Thank you for choosing Golden Slug as your preferred hacking partner," the message mocks you, whilst you watch in horror as the threat is made reality. The laptops and desktops around you all flicker to show the same screen, where a giant picture of a padlock is displayed announcing the device is now encrypted.

A trickle of colleagues arriving to vent their annoyance at you turns into a deluge. Now seems to be a good time to find Susan and fess up.

As you approach Susan's office, you can see that the ransomware has reached her devices too, and the giant screen above the table now displays the familiar padlock. Susan has clicked the link provided to see what the ransom figure is. Golden Slug know that they have Generico McCompany over a barrel and are demanding an enormous amount of money to provide the encryption keys needed to get everyone back to work.

"What has happened?" she asks you, resignation in her voice.

Before you can reply, Petra the CEO storms into the office and asks the same question, only with some colourful language inserted.

You explain the order of events to both Susan and Petra and watch their faces sink as they come to terms with just how bad the situation is.

Petra seems to have the answer, though. "Susan, call the government incident response helpline and get in whoever they recommend. Cost is no option," she says decisively. She turns and hands you a company credit card.

Find out why in **Section 295.**

---

168 Phase Three—Attack

Good call. Incident response crews deal with breaches on an almost daily basis and their expertise can be invaluable. They may have come up against your adversary before, giving you insight into the tools, techniques and tactics they are likely to be employing.

You reach into your desk drawer and pull out a business card for Galactic Cyber. The card's design is sleek and minimalist, with a white body and subtle black lines outlining the portrait of an astronaut. The company's tag line sits at the bottom: "One small buffer for man, one giant remote code execution for mankind." You call the number. A friendly voice lets you know your call is important to Galactic Cyber; fast-paced epic music then acts as hold music whilst you wait for a Cyber astronaut to answer.

"Commander Sasha reporting for duty, how can I be of assistance?"

You provide Sasha with the background.

"Understood. We will deploy an incident response team to your location immediately. Can you confirm your coordinates?"

You try to piece together what he is asking for.

Sensing your confusion, Sasha rephrases it. "Your office address."

You provide Sasha with your office address and he confirms he will have a team with you within the hour.

After you take time to reserve hot desking seats and sort out guest passes, your phone rings. It's an internal number. Your heart races, fearing that Susan has interrupted her board meeting to chastise you, but it's reception downstairs informing you your guests have arrived.

Greet Galactic Cyber in **Section 362.**

---

169 Phase Three—Attack

Bicarbonate of soda, vinegar and soapy water all fail to tackle the stain. You resign yourself to the fact it's here to stay. You spot Susan making her way towards you, no doubt looking for a status update on Golden Slug and the alleged breach. Seeing as you have nothing to give her, you are grateful for your phone's good timing in deciding to ring. It's Sergeant.

"Your boys have been lazy," Sergeant announces in place of a greeting.

You ask him who your boys are.

"Golden Slug."

You point out they aren't your boys at all.

"Yes, yes, you know what I mean. Those payment cards they are circulating are old, they come from a breach on some petrol station card machines from six or so months ago."

You conclude that the cards had nothing to do with Generico McCompany. Susan, who was walking away, picks up on this and comes to stand next to you, clearly wanting the inside scoop.

Sergeant confirms it was indeed nothing to do with Generico McCompany and lets you know he's contacting the appropriate media to clear the company's name.

Susan is delighted by this. She was about to go into a three-hour board meeting and having that hanging over her head would have been a real pain. You half expect her to give you a dog treat before leaving, but she doesn't.

Get over your disappointment at missing out on that dog treat in **Section 49.**

---

170 Phase Three—Attack

That seems to have worked.

You fire off a message containing 170 packets and are rewarded with a satisfying scene where you can almost picture the code deleting itself across the company estate. Rather than relaxing, now is the time to pinpoint how Golden Slug managed to get their code into your websites in the first place so you can stop them from reentering the network in the future.

As an information security professional, your job is to make it hard for hackers to get into the company's network, but people who create administrator accounts with the username: admin and password: admin may as well leave a fruit basket out for the hackers they are inviting in. You can see suspicious login activity on the administrator account that correlates directly to when Golden Slug first started harvesting payment card data from the company. You force a password reset on the user and email the culpable colleague, warning them against using such a weak password in the future.

As if by magic, Susan appears. "Please tell me you've got to the bottom of that weird dark web image."

You state that Golden Slug had inserted code into the Generico McCompany e-commerce estate to harvest card data. Susan frowns. You continue, letting her know you just deleted every instance of it and closed off the access point Golden Slug used to get into the network in the first place. Susan smiles. Finally, you concede that you lost a few thousand payment card details, so there will be a call from the regulator in the near future.

Susan waves her hand, letting you know the fine will be small fry, and congratulates you on your good work.

Wrap things up in **Section 263**.

171 Phase Three—Attack

Perhaps it's your own fault for not predicting it, but the Cyber Pirates are not only waiting in the company lobby at 08:00 the next day, they are all in costume dressed as pirates. Captain Dave even has a real parrot on his shoulder, who is apparently called Pedro. It also turns out that Ship Cat Tobias is actually a human, much to your disappointment, though probably better for Pedro's life expectancy. You greet them, hand them their red temporary passes and take them to the IT hot desking space.

"Now that we are boarded and have connectivity, we will inspect the rigging and report back with arrrrrr findings." Captain Dave seems particularly pleased with himself for slipping in an arrrrrr.

Now that they are underway, you move to your own desk and see where things are at. It looks like Golden Slug have been hitting the company with waves of DDoS every two hours or so, but the business's defences are faring quite well so far.

As you get started on your own tasks, colleagues start to drift into work, filling up the empty desk spaces and, understandably, doing double or triple takes at your pirate ensemble. You read the damage report that Vijaya has just written and hear the flutter of wings. Pedro the Parrot approaches, gliding smoothly over your head and releasing his payload, which you are grateful is a piece of paper and not poop.

"We have spotted buried treasure" it reads. You decide to ignore that the Cyber Pirates sent a parrot courier to deliver a message when they are sat three metres from you.

Shuffle over to see what they've found in **Section 23.**

---

172 Phase Three—Attack

As things stand you didn't have substantial proof that the connection belonged to Charlotte, so gathering more evidence first was a shrewd move.

Charlotte is a Teflon woman: no accusations will stick to her unless they are accompanied by irrefutable evidence. You start to inspect the traffic travelling from Golden Slug's IP address through the Generico McCompany wireless network. There are chat **logs** between the device and Golden Slug, but nothing that could be linked directly to Charlotte.

In truth you'd be able to see that her phone was communicating with Golden Slug and maybe what communication protocol was being used, but to actually view the messages is approaching the realm of sci-fi.

Charlotte looks up from her keyboard to ask what you are doing, as she wants to make sure her report is accurate. This is your chance. You tell her you've encountered a whole cache of un**encrypt**ed payment card data in a project folder, but will start the process of cleaning it up after lunch.

"What project folder?" Charlotte asks.

You tell her the project is called Titan, and purposely neglect to mention that the project Titan folder is in fact empty. You yawn and pretend to go for lunch, seemingly leaving the poor payment card data undefended. You glance back as you leave the room: Charlotte is texting on her phone, hopefully incriminating herself.

You wait in the office lobby for a few minutes to let the evidence build up, attracting strange looks from people who don't know if you are waiting for a lift or not. When your patience runs out, you head back to your desk and immediately check the chat logs.

Charlotte makes a throwaway comment about eating too fast and getting indigestion, but smugly you think to yourself that soon she'll be the one with her stomach tied up in knots.

Enjoy that little play on words in **Section 335.**

---

173 Phase Two—Preparation

*Firewalls serve as the first line of defence when facing attacks from outside of your network, such as DDoS. Looking at **vulnerabilities** within the firewall estate is a shrewd move.*

The firewall estate for Generico McCompany is surprisingly consistent: the vast majority are Burpafence Model 10 devices. These little beauties spend their time beeping and booping, letting through safe traffic and slapping unsafe internet traffic down before it can wreak havoc on your internal IT systems. Spread across the entire planet, your army of firewalls work around the clock to keep your perimeter safe, but they aren't perfect.

Snapping back into reality, you reread the vulnerability title: "Firewall set to reboot in weak state". Perusing the details, you find that the firewalls are all configured well, but when they reboot they default to their weaker factory settings as opposed to their normal status.

Factory settings are just the settings a device has installed when it is manufactured, like how your home Wi-Fi has a generic password and you can change it to something else.

The firewalls remain in this weakened state until the midnight update push, which reverts any that were downgraded to their enhanced status. Given that over the last year only five firewalls rebooted outside of the planned schedules, the business decided to accept this risk.

Your thoughts are interrupted by a member of the sales team, who calls you to tell you she has an information security questionnaire that needs submitting by the end of the day. Upon opening the document, you are irked to see that the questionnaire was sent through a month ago.

Don't be that person.

Luckily, it is a standard questionnaire and you are able to send it back to her in just one hour. Regaining your line of thought, what are you going to do regarding the firewalls?

Review the Burpafance Model 10 firewall's factory settings in **Section 66, or** look into the five firewalls that went offline last year in **Section 326.**

---

174 Phase Three—Attack

At this point you are in so deep there are no good choices, only different flavours of bad.

You end up having to dial the NotNotCatya number from your mobile phone, as your landline has an internet connection and therefore is also now locked down with ransomware.

A cheerful voice answers. "Hello and welcome to the NotNotCatya support line, please provide your customer reference number."

You reply that you are a NotNotCatya victim, not a customer.

"Well, we would consider that to be a customer. You can find your customer reference number located just above the cheeseburger."

Glancing at your laptop screen, you notice that the number 15 is indeed written in a small font, hidden in the burger bun. You provide this number to the helpdesk.

"Ah, Generico McCompany. I have it written down here in our notes that you only would have launched this **malware** as a result of being bad at maths. How would you rate the effects of the NotNotCatya malware?"

Looking around, you watch the office descend into chaos as colleagues are unable to access their laptops, or even get a coffee. You give the voice an honest five out of five and two enthusiastic thumbs-up, then ask how to get the malware removed.

"Thank you for your excellent review, we will be sure to include this feedback in our next marketing brochure. To deactivate NotNotCatya you must pay the ransom. Do you need help accessing bitcoin?"

You look around and see Susan approaching with a face like thunder. You hang up.

Face the storm in **Section 62.**

---

175 Phase Three—Attack

Slow and steady wins the cyber race. Sometimes.

You explain your reasoning. If you let Golden Slug know you are aware of them, they may crank things up to 10 and go nuclear, and since you don't know how they got in, you'd have no guarantee you could stop them getting in all over again.

"What do you propose, then?"

You suggest trying to figure out how Golden Slug are taking control of the firewalls first. If that can be done in time, Generico McCompany can kick them off for good.

"Make it so," Susan commands as she stands up to pace around her office.

Your rush back to your desk is stalled by someone travelling in the opposite direction carrying a mug. You step to your left, they step to their right. You correct the situation by stepping to the other side, but they also had the same plan. You decide to stay still, letting them move over. They have the identical idea. The situation is resolved when you both sheepishly apologise profusely and slowly navigate around each other.

When you arrive back at your desk, the enormity of the task dawns on you. You've got to figure out how a sophisticated attacker is exploiting your firewalls before they steal every scrap of data from Generico McCompany.

Crack your knuckles and have a look in **Section 284.**

---

176 Phase Three—Attack

Susan's email contains a screenshot of what appears to be a dark web forum. A user by the name of Allyourshellsarebelongtous is selling "High quality card dumps". You read the product description.

> Best of day to you.
>
> AYSABTU here, I am selling details for payment cards that are active and used in the last 7 days. Selling in blocks of 10,000 first come, first served. Generico McCompany will find me eventually, so act fast!

Surprisingly aligned to reality: these are just like any normal forum really, only with more crime.

The advert proceeds to list the vendor's average rating, an impressive 4.6 out of 5 with over 600 reviews. You can't fail but notice the most recent review, which reads: "Loving these Generico cards, long live the slug."

"Allyourshellsarebelongtous is apparently a known Golden Slug alias," Susan says from behind you, making you jump in your seat. "I got sent that by a contact in law enforcement. If it's true then you were too late encrypting the call recordings."

You click over to your script to check on its progress. So far it has encrypted 8000 out of 15,000 files. Afterwards you inform Susan that Generico McCompany only store call recordings for three months and even with the last three months, there are no more than 15,000 in total. For Golden Slug to be selling in blocks of 10,000, they must be getting them from somewhere else.

Susan's face moves from being cool, calm and collected to frenzied in an instant, before recovering again.

"Find it, fix it," she instructs before marching off.

Do as the lady says in **Section 6.**

---

177 Phase Three—Attack

Whilst it's tempting to strike at the heart of the problem immediately, remember that it can backfire. Because you don't know how Golden Slug put the code there in the first place, they could simply put it back. On top of that, by deleting the code you are alerting Golden Slug that you are aware of their presence. I'm not saying this was the wrong decision, by the way—this is one of those grey areas.

You announce dramatically that first things first you have e-commerce websites that are funnelling payment card data out of the company and that tap needs to be turned off. You crack your knuckles.

"And how will you do that if you didn't even know how they did this?" Susan asks, a dagger to your heart.

Time stops momentarily, allowing you to miraculously prepare a strategy from scratch. Time resumes and you share your strategy with Susan. You will compare known clean versions of the website's code with the malicious code that is running now, identify the differences and use that to find Golden Slug's **payload**, which can then be removed.

Susan seems happy enough with your plan and tasks Guillaume and Vijaya to help you bring it to life, or possibly she believes you need supervision. A tap on the meeting room glass tells you that you've overrun your time slot, as all meetings do. You sheepishly apologise as you leave the room before heading to your desk to begin work, Ruby in tow to offer support.

The walk from the meeting room to the desk is that perfectly awkward distance, not long enough for a proper conversation but too far to walk in silence. You pretend to be furiously reading emails on your work phone, angling the screen to hide the fact the battery is dead. Finally, you reach your desk.

Get to work in **Section 206.**

178 Phase Four—Aftermath

This protects against any malicious software that might have been pushed down to the PIN entry devices, but what about physical tampering?

You conclude that you should make use of the technology that's available and roll back the PIN entry devices from here. Just the thought of having to do additional walking is making your feet hurt.

It's only after making this decision that Gesa reveals that although she is aware the remote update option exists, she has no idea how to actually perform the action. As a result, you have to spend time researching how to issue the command yourself. Like a child on a long car trip, Susan spams your instant messenger with numerous chat messages asking if you are nearly there yet. Luckily, she isn't around to notice your rapidly increasing frustration, which you vent through exasperated sighs and increasingly forceful typing of the word "No". After a good hour and a half, the update is ready to be deployed to all 9000 stores at the touch of an enter key.

You decide to let your drinking-bird desk toy do the honours and position it to deliver the telling blow. Mindful of health and safety, you move the water well out of the way. As the bird's beak comes crashing down on the enter key, the world hardly seems to change at all. Yet behind the scenes, every single Generico McCompany PIN entry device moves back from version 11.1 to version 11.0, a magical feat.

You allow the drinking bird one more moment of glory and set it up to send Susan and Gesa a confirmation over the internal messenger chat that the reset is complete.

Start to tie up the final loose ends in **Section 192**.

179 Phase Three—Attack

"In my opinion pineapple should be nowhere near a pizza." You overhear this as you walk the floor back to the IT department, and it reminds you that whilst it's the biggest day ever for you right now, it's just Tuesday for everyone else. You ask the IT team for their view on the matter as you sit down.

"Definitely no to pineapple on pizza," Guillaume chips in.

"Pineapple is fine, but no ham for me," Vijaya counters.

The general consensus is that ham is welcome on pizza, but pineapple is not. If you manage to get through this Golden Slug incident unscathed, at least you now know what to serve at the victory party. The next step is to figure out what phase two of Golden Slug's attack could be. Seeing as you've essentially gone all-in on this decision, you conclude it's better not to think about what'll happen if you are wrong and Petra was right. Pizzas may still be relevant, except in that timeline perhaps you'll be delivering them.

You pull up the dashboard showing all of the firewalls that were forced to reboot by the DDoS attacks. At a quick glance, the devices are working smoothly. You check to see whether new **IP** addresses have been added to any of the **allow lists**, but find none. If Golden Slug are planning to sabotage these firewalls further, they are hiding it well. You lick your lips nervously; you could really do with a breakthrough.

See if a breakthrough comes in **Section 307**.

180 Phase Three—Attack

First you make changes to Petra's email so that even administrators can't send emails on her behalf, and then turn on two-factor authentication for all of her email applications. Whilst that'll annoy her, it'll prevent Golden Slug from following through with their plan and that seems like a worthwhile trade-off.

Charlotte asks what progress you've made. You lie and pretend you are still trying to figure out Golden Slug's intentions. She flashes you an eerie grin before returning to her phone.

Rewarding yourself with a sip of water, you look at the network traffic and are pleased to see you've cut Golden Slug off from the Generico McCompany network for now. Only one connection remains, still that one going through the office Wi-Fi. You drop your water as the realisation hits, the glass shattering when it hits the ground.

"I suppose someone on your wage doesn't care about the cleaners of this world," Charlotte sneers, as a red overall-wearing cleaner rushes over to take care of the broken glass.

You don't even bother replying to Charlotte, but instead sit in a daze, processing what your brain has pieced together. Could it really be Charlotte's phone that is communicating with Golden Slug?

Confront Charlotte in **Section 24** or lay a trap in **Section 172**.

---

181 Phase Four—Aftermath

"My refunds team have alerted me to the fact that all of our call recording data is suddenly gone. Disappeared. Seeing as you were asking me about this only a few minutes ago, I can't help but feel that this has something to do with you."

You explain the situation in full to Giuseppa. If you were expecting understanding or sympathy, she is not dishing it out. Instead, she gives you new problems to contend with.

"It wasn't just the call recordings from people paying for things in that folder, you've also deleted all of the recordings from the annual customer feedback survey, as well as all of the complaints submitted to the company's public mailbox. The board made a public promise to review that mailbox once per year."

Your decision to delete the folder immediately without first checking what else was in there, or considering what the ramifications might be, means that you've either accidently or intentionally put information security and compliance ahead of Generico McCompany's other business units. Although you successfully reduced the fine from any regulator for losing card data, the lost revenue and time from having to redo all of those calls make it a pyrrhic victory.

The End.

Yup, deleting a load of data can come back to bite you like that. Besides, how were Golden Slug gaining access to that folder in the first place?

182 Phase Three—Attack

"Mission accomplished," Sasha reports. Galactic Cyber have managed to purge Golden Slug from the Generico McCompany call centre database completely and, after performing a thorough sweep, found no evidence of any **backdoors**. From tracking Golden Slug's movements, the total count for stolen payment cards is 2308, which will earn the company a slap on the wrist and a **PCI DSS** fine, but it could have been much worse. You thank Galactic Cyber for their excellent work. All three Galactic Cyber members nod their comically huge helmets in acknowledgement.

"We must prepare for re-entry," Cyberspace Cadet Morgan informs you, before busying herself packing up equipment.

Within moments, Galactic Cyber's gear is all neatly tucked away and you cram back into a lift together as you escort them to reception again. You wave them off and watch as they struggle to shuffle out of the revolving doors, their space suits catching on the handles.

You spend the rest of the day writing up a summary for Susan to present to the board and to the regulator. The report is well received; stories with happy endings always are well received. Tedious tasks fill the dregs of the working day, the kind of things you can do with 5% of your brain power. Eventually five o'clock comes and you are finally able to go home and gorge yourself on food to reward yourself for a tough few hours.

Finish things up in **Section 322.**

183 Phase Three—Attack

Come on, you didn't really.

Now go to **Section 305.**

184 Phase Three—Attack

That's some next-level problem solving. Books, of course, never ask questions and are full of answers...

You type your answer "Books" on your keyboard and hit enter, except the word remains on the screen; your enter button appears to have broken. You watch the time drip slowly out of the little hourglass icon as you hammer on the enter key, willing it suddenly to have fixed itself. The final second ticks away, and you watch in despair as the last hope for the Generico McCompany network disappears. The screen fades to black.

A troll face appears on the screen, letting you know that your answer of "Books" was received, they were just messing with you. The caption underneath the trollface asks "u mad?" Indeed you are. The troll face then lets you know it is calculating whether you got the answers correct and will tell you shortly.

Looking up from your keyboard, you realise your enter key assault has drawn some attention. You cover by explaining you were wasting time playing an online game. Everyone seems happy enough with that and goes back to their business.

This seems like an opportune time for a bathroom break and for a refill of tea. Then you come back to your desk to discover your fate.

Head to the big reveal in **Section 167.**

---

185 Phase Three—Attack

Whilst that may halt the flow of payment card details reaching Golden Slug, just deleting a ton of data can have knock-on effects if other people in the business need it.

You wipe the call recordings folder completely, releasing many gigabytes of storage. The call recordings will trickle back in, but at least for now Golden Slug won't be able to harvest the previous day's call recording data, and are instead limited to 5000 new card details per day. You call the provider of your call recording software to start the process of getting things fixed.

"Hello, this is Laurel from tech support. Did you know, as well as being tech support I am also a psychic? I will answer your next question rather than the question you ask."

You ask her if that approach generally works out well.

"Um, it's usually terrible."

You laugh, and admit that you definitely believe that, but respect her ambition regardless. You give her an overview of the situation with your call recordings and ask her whether that is better or worse than the standard performance of the software.

"I don't like the sound of that at all."

You reply that you don't either, but then remember she wasn't actually answering the question you just asked. This is confusing. You ask her what she thinks of you just hanging up?

"Money you shouldn't give to dogs," Laurel lets you know.

You put the phone down and make a note to ask for a non-psychic team member next time. You notice a colleague walking over with something in a brown paper bag. Curious, you ask them what is in the bag. They reply that it is chocolate coins, and then scurry off in case you ask them to share.

Before you can dwell too much on Laurel's abilities, Giuseppa's face flashes in the corner of your screen, signalling an incoming internal chat message.

Read the message in **Section 181.**

---

186 Phase Three—Attack

You've plugged quite a lot of time into this call centre malarkey, you may as well see it through now.

You feel you now know Georgios in greater detail than you ever wanted to, as you fill the silence waiting to be put through to Jane Doe. He has two children, three dogs, an incredible barn conversion in the countryside and endless other possessions and qualities that make you feel inferior. As you are about to have to somehow fill 15 minutes talking about your one-bedroom flat, mercifully Jane Doe actually picks up the phone.

"As per the defined worldwide legal submission process, Fesrodah has given this submission the required recognition, but the issuer has dropped from the telephone line."

"We have not, and are prepared to issue our statement," Georgios interrupts her and looks triumphant. All that wait seemingly wasn't in vain.

"Oh." Jane Doe clearly isn't used to people actually bothering to hold for— you look at the phone screen—42 minutes.

"My name is Georgios, representing Generico McCompany as legal counsel. Generico McCompany demand that Fesrodah Limited cease DDoS, otherwise known as Distributed Denial of Service, against Generico McCompany infrastructure applications and overall online presence immediately. The initial request for this service was initiated by an entity impersonating Generico McCompany, proven by the contact details left by Fesrodah's customer."

Before any lawyers come after me, I know this is not how this works.

That sounds like a lot of words for "stop it", but this is Georgios's area. He has a smug look on his face, which suggests he expects it to be checkmate.

You hear Jane sigh before replying. "Fesrodah Limited acknowledges receipt of Generico McCompany's demand and will cease immediately."

Georgios hangs up.

Celebrate with your new best friend in **Section 126.**

---

187 Phase Two—Preparation

"So remember, when it says that the delivery of stated products or services is not guaranteed, that is a bad thing."

You let Georgios know that you understand. Doubt practically sweats out of every single one of his pores, but he doesn't bother challenging you. Instead, he motors off to wherever he is needed next.

There is still an hour left in the day. You trawl the internet hoping for clues on how Golden Slug operate, but don't find anything. The clock strikes five and you finish for the day. No breakthroughs yet, but you are sure there will be progress tomorrow. It's raining, so you decide to take the bus home instead of the train. The trains are horribly crammed when it rains.

You almost feel bad for the pedestrians who get soaked as the bus splashes cold rainwater onto them, but laugh internally instead. You spend the evening fighting with a travel agent to get a cash refund on a holiday that was cancelled; you don't want the voucher they keep offering you. Just when you thought you'd have to settle for the voucher, you gamble and say you'll talk to your lawyer and be back in touch. This seems to terrify them and soon your bank account swells with your returned cash. The investigation into Golden Slug can resume tomorrow.

Head into work in **Section 165.**

---

188 Phase Three—Attack

> First, good morning, where are your manners?
>
> We are Golden Slug. Whilst many do not care about the planet's future, we do.
>
> Generico McCompany CISO. We are very sorry for making you have to do your job.
>
> Generico McCompany put radioactive material into drinking water. It should be obvious what you need to do to make us stop.
>
> Golden Slug

Well, that didn't achieve much. But it gets worse. In CC are over 50 email addresses clearly belonging to journalists at a whole variety of national and international news outlets. You can almost picture them all typing furiously, racing to publish news stories off the back of this email. Just thinking about the headline makes you shiver.

You take yourself to a happy place, browsing playful dog pictures to help brace yourself for the incoming storm. It doesn't take long to arrive, with a monsoon of news articles flying out across the internet. Cecilia from PR instantly picks up on them, like a spider watching flies get stuck in her web, and drops you a line on internal chat.

"Apparently you've emailed Golden Slug and they've shared it with a ton of journalists. Is this true?"

Here may be your way out. You could lie and claim you didn't send the email, or own up to Cecilia.

Lie in **Section 333** or tell the truth in **Section 152.**

---

189 Phase Two—Preparation

> *Ah, sorry, the "denial of service" part of the vulnerability was a red herring. Whilst it has denial of service in its name, it's talking about denying a user or even potentially multiple users access to their account. Although annoying, this is different to a DDoS.*

Further research shows that the vulnerability relates to an internet-facing application called TrainingWheel that provides insurance quotes. If a user puts the wrong password in multiple times, the user is unable to log into the application for 24 hours. The problem is that the application cannot distinguish between a genuine user trying to access their account and a hacker. In a worst-case scenario a bad guy could lock all TrainingWheel's genuine users out of their accounts and the service desk would have to unlock them. This could in theory be repeated, so it's something worth thinking about, but it's not really related to how Golden Slug work.

Your eyes glance towards the clock and see there is plenty of time left in the day. As you see it, you have two options. You can either contact the penetration test vendor who completed the test for their opinion on this vulnerability, or switch your attention to the other vulnerability, "Firewall set to reboot in weak state".

Contact the penetration test vendor in **Section 354**, or investigate the firewall vulnerability in **Section 173**.

---

190 Phase Three—Attack

The transfer was successful because you permitted it, apparently. You would dispute the claim, but the evidence is plain to see on Guillaume's monitor. The data loss prevention software had a rule added minutes ago that allowed any transfer to Golden Slug's IP address; that rule is recorded as being added to the list by you. You protest that this is impossible, as you were sat next to Guillaume at the time.

A bit of a stretch for a file macro to lead to a firewall rule change, but you should still treat macros with respect.

"It could have been a rule with a time delay," Vijaya adds unhelpfully, proving she had indeed been listening in on the conversation. Amongst the three of you it's decided that the best course of action is to remove the new rule to prevent more data from being stolen, before giving Susan a refresh.

Together you shuffle into Susan's office to deliver the latest update. Like a software update, it's likely Susan will want to shut down afterwards. Due to your involvement in the latest proceedings, you allow Guillaume and Vijaya to recount the most recent events; hopefully they are merciful storytellers.

"Anyway, it would have been fine, but because of that rule change Golden Slug managed to steal all kinds of data," Vijaya concludes.

Susan's immediate response is straight onto the offensive. "Can we go legal against Golden Slug, now we have an IP address to tie to them?"

"The IP address is based in the kind of country where words like 'extradition' and 'illegal' are considered comedic, Susan. It wouldn't achieve anything," Vijaya replies.

Susan sighs.

Susan turns her attention to you in **Section 158.**

---

191 Phase Three—Attack

You follow Sergeant's advice and delve into the Generico McCompany phone payments system, looking for clues. Locating the phone payments system takes longer than it should, as the network diagram for it is so out of date if it were milk you'd be able to smell it from four postcodes away. You mentally remind yourself to point out to whoever will listen that this is why you ask people to store up-to-date documentation.

Susan interrupts your investigation to let you know the regulator has been in touch and is aware that Generico McCompany have suffered a breach. The regulator is expecting a swift update, with Susan expecting an even swifter one. Like for any normal human being, this increased pressure just makes your investigation take longer.

Sergeant's analysis was right. Golden Slug have definitely been gearing up to steal payment card data from these phone calls. The call recording system has been craftily edited to forward each of the call recordings to a phone number you don't recognise, but would bet good money belongs to Golden Slug. From there they could just play each recording, write down the card details and wait for the next recording to be forwarded. Luckily for you, the program is not due to start for another 24 hours. You've managed to get ahead of Golden Slug yet again.

First things first, you are going to need to remove this call forwarding setting. Opening the call recording software's settings page triggers a hidden program to run. Suddenly, large neon text fills your screen.

Read it in **Section 133.**

---

192 Phase Four—Aftermath

Gesa passes you details of the supplier that Golden Slug manipulated into performing the Generico McCompany shop maintenance work. It seems unlikely that Golden Slug would have hacked into the procurement tool to involve a clean, legitimate business. The police log the potential crime as "cybercrime" and never follow up on it. In the meantime, you work with the development team to put some safeguards in place so that an external attacker or an administrator who goes rogue would find it harder to make such significant changes to systems without triggering an alert.

Life is good for the next few months. Generico McCompany did lose some payment card data from the Golden Slug e-commerce page code insertion technique, but the regulator looked favourably on the company thanks to the reasonably swift corrective action and clear lessons learned. An incident response employee for the National Fraud Office makes some disparaging comments about you in an interview with an information security news website, but you can't please everyone.

Things seem to be going well. At least until one day when you walk into work, only to find a swarm of men and women in dark suits and sunglasses crowded inside Susan's office. She beckons you in to join her.

See what they want in **Section 42.**

---

193 Phase Four—Aftermath

Vlad gulps, and then emits a rasping cough, like a pair of bellows stuffed with honey. "Sorry, got a bit of a dry throat," he says, pulling out a packet of throat lozenges and popping one in his mouth. He offers you one, but you decline. Based on his cough, he needs them much more than you do.

"The most sensitive data I have access to is probably our interview feedback. But it is handled through its own portal and it never touches my email. The only things in my email are CVs received from candidates and some internal bickering and gossiping."

You frown. It's a complete curveball from Golden Slug and one you don't think you'll have time to puzzle out right now. You thank Vlad for his time, watch him almost immediately fall asleep against the wall again and then turn your attention to Susan.

Walking into your boss's office to tell her that some hacking group has been reading the last year's worth of her emails is unlikely to score you many points. You decide it's best to go with backup, and pick up a soy milk latte, Susan's Achilles' heel. You wait until she's taking a sip before breaking the news. As you'd hoped, the coffee softens the blow.

You outline the two options to Susan. In one, you send her an email specifically mentioning Golden Slug and try to spook them into accelerating activity on their plan, which hopefully will result in them making a mistake. In option two, you delete the emails they are looking through and find a way to boot them off the network right away. Susan asks you what you think is the better option.

Lay a trap in **Section 75**. Evict them from the network as soon as possible in **Section 332.**

---

194 Phase Three—Attack

"That is an invalid option, please call again."

I'm sure there is a way to get out of this automated phone system… right?

Call again in **Section 26.**

---

195 Phase Four—Aftermath

Big roles sometimes need big decisions.

You conclude to Sasha that you are hardly winning popularity contests as it stands, what with you making people work securely rather than quickly and what not, and you could do without the negative internal press that a companywide password reset would bring about.

"Sounds good to me. Anyway, at this point I think it's time I got Galactic Cyber into an escape pod whilst we still can make use of a gravitational slingshot."

You ask Sasha when the gravitational slingshot wouldn't be available.

"Rush hour."

You thank Galactic Cyber for their time and expertise, promising that Generico McCompany will pay their invoice in a timely fashion. Finance will never pay that invoice on time, but you had your fingers crossed behind your back, so you are covered.

Once Galactic Cyber have left and things start to calm down, you make a new discovery: you are famished and could really do with lunch. You ask Guillaume and Vijaya if they are also hungry. Guillaume pulls out an unappetising salad and admits he will likely forever be hungry when his wife has him dieting. Vijaya is trying a new fad of only eating during the third minute of every hour. As it's currently 14:10, you head to the canteen alone.

The day's special is a curry you have never heard of. You snatch up a plate of it and after eating it discover why it's not more commonly known. It's gross.

Force it down in **Section 86.**

196 Phase Two—Preparation

One of the key rules of securing payment card data is to **encrypt** it virtually at all times. With that in mind, you survey the Generico McCompany call recording data storage centre, with unencrypted payment card data as plentiful as grains of sand in the desert. The call recording software you use is meant to pause recording when shoppers provide their payment card data to the call centre staff member, then start it up again afterwards to make sure it can record what satisfaction rating the customer provides.

Needless to say, any score below eight out of ten is likely to result in a disciplinary for the hapless call centre agent. Any hacker who gains access to this call recording data folder could harvest hundreds of thousands of payment card details. Whilst it would be a tedious job, the rewards would make it worthwhile, with stolen cards retailing for good money, especially if complete with the CVV code from the back.

You send Susan a calendar invite for first thing tomorrow morning to raise this with her. It's not going to be a quick fix, but at least you can get the process started. You spend the final half hour of your working day attending a webinar put on by one of the vendors you work with. The vendor has assembled together 10 minutes' worth of quality content and then stretched it to the point of being see-through to fill the time slot. You finish the webinar feeling drained. You go home and get some sleep.

Head back into work in **Section 349.**

197 Phase Three—Attack

Susan shows you an email on the large monitor in her office.

> Petra.
>
> We are Golden Slug,
>
> Using an internet bug,
>
> We took your SCAPI Database

If you don't want it thrown in your face

You will need to pay us

Or we will give SCAPI to the media on a Universal
Serial Bus.

You wince at Golden Slug's poetry. The email goes on to outline a price of $10 million and a bitcoin account to send the money to. There is even a helpful guide on how to go about purchasing and sending bitcoin.

"This was sent to our CEO Petra half an hour ago. They included some fragments of the database to prove they actually have it," Susan finishes, before looking to Ruby for comment.

"This is highly unusual, it goes completely against Golden Slug's standard modus operandi," Ruby says, stroking her chin as she studies the email again.

You ask what the National Cyber Security Agency's advice is on dealing with ransom situations like this.

"Officially, never to pay, as it incentivises the criminals to continue their work."

Unofficially, a lot of companies actively consider paying a ransom as a stalling tactic. Regardless of whether you pay the ransom or not, you should assume that at some point the data in question will be posted on the internet. You should also note that some criminal gangs are on your country's sanctions list, making paying a ransom to them a crime. Did I mention that information security can be grey?

Pay up in **Section 311**. Refuse to pay in **Section 57**.

---

198 Phase Two—Preparation

*Online chats are by no means invulnerable, but the safer bet was the **third party Vatidiva**. Their code would be definitely be active during the checkout process, as this is where payment card details are entered, and therefore is most likely what Golden Slug would be interested in most.*

TLK2ME provide that familiar experience of a little chat bar appearing in the bottom corner of your computer screen when you browse a website. Behind the helpful greeting of "Hi, how can I help you today?" is a capitalist machine created with the sole intention of removing any excuses you might have for not buying whatever service is on offer. TLK2ME have been successful and have improved the conversion rate of people idly browsing to becoming actual customers by a significant percentage. Secretly you hope there is nothing wrong with the code; you'll be making a lot of enemies if it needs to be removed.

You suspect that TLK2ME is just a connection between the shopper and a TLK2ME employee via an online messaging tool, but the TLK2ME service brochure claims it's actually a lot more complicated. The user journey begins with the customer answering some artificial intelligence–enabled questions, the answers to which the chat engine then uses to divert the chat to the most appropriate support person.

When you peek under the hood, you see that in fact the questions asked have no influence on where the chat is assigned. The artificial intelligence line was likely added by a marketing team member and never fact checked.

You decide to forgive TLK2ME for their overegging of the service, partly because you don't pay for their software, and partly because they have actually written a well-secured piece of code.

> As a rule of thumb, when **penetration testers** perform full-on code reviews to gain assurances that code has been well written, they would generally take a day of effort for every 1000 lines of code. For you as a CISO to straight up review this code yourself there and then is a tad unrealistic, given all the other things on your plate. Though if something like that appeals, you should definitely consider getting involved—the industry is always looking for new talent.

Move on in **Section 310.**

199 Phase Two—Preparation

Now you've got your jaws locked, don't let go.

You point out that it's the project that Gesa wrote a risk register for that had a risk identified as destroying an entire country's water supply.

"Wow, that does sound pretty bad. It's not ringing any bells though. It must have been ages ago," Gesa responds.

You pause, feeling your brain turn to mush as you try to decide what to say next.

Gesa preempts you by pointing to Michael the COO's office.

"Ask him, he might remember more." She gives you a pointed look and turns back to her monitor, clacking away at her keyboard theatrically.

You psych yourself up and head over to knock on Michael's door. He has a reputation for being quite stern, and the company's chief operating officer is not a man you want to annoy. He beckons you in and turns his reptilian eyes upon you. For a second, you could swear his tongue flicks out like a snake, tasting the air, tasting your fear. Hopefully it's just your imagination running wild.

"What can I do for you?" he asks, the smile on his face not touching his eyes.

You tell him that you need details on Project Luminec.

Any hint of a smile is wiped off of his face and his expression becomes slightly angry. "Who sent you to ask about Luminec?" he asks, more than a hint of anger in his voice.

You respond that nobody sent you and that you are simply investigating a cyberthreat actor. Your investigation has led you to Project Luminec.

He sighs and furrows his brow, anger turning to frustration. "I am sorry, it's not your fault. I'll add you to a meeting invite. It will all make sense tomorrow."

You stand in stunned silence.

"Leave me to think now, please," Michael says as he shoos you out.

Retreat to **Section 151.**

---

200 Phase Three—Attack

You are probably the kind of person who gets frustrated when a YouTube video takes longer than two seconds to load. You had a good thing there, you should have seen it through!

This incident response plan is going nowhere, so you shove it back into your drawer and contemplate what to do next. Golden Slug haven't started up the second wave of DDoS yet, so you have a bit of time to come up with a new plan.

In football they say that the best form of defence is offence, but applying that to the current situation doesn't really work. You continue to think about your favourite sports team for a few minutes, wondering if they ever come under cyberattack.

If you are interested, there have been a few high-profile stories about sports clubs having their email systems or player scouting systems hacked.

Next you are drawn into an office-wide debate over whether you'd rather be double or half your height; the majority sides with being double. In the corner of your eye you catch a glimpse of the time and would have almost fallen out of your chair, had you not been standing up. You've somehow lost 20 minutes to the double or half height debate; you excuse yourself and return to your computer.

Massaging your temples feels good. You try to force extra blood into your brain, as if that'll suddenly present you with a eureka moment to solve this whole problem. A quick internet search shows that massaging temples is good for relieving headaches, but seems to have no impact on your cognitive skills. You get sucked down an internet rabbit hole, and before you know it you are reading about coffee beans that are passed through an elephant first, reaching a level of filtration you never expected to see.

You've done it again: you are procrastinating. Stop procrastinating and get on with setting up some kind of defence.

Sort something out in **Section 20**.

201 Phase Four—Aftermath

In the lift, you are attempting to pick bread out from between your teeth using the mirrored walls. Suddenly, the lift doors open, and Susan is standing on the other side, beaming at you.

"Ah look, the employee of the hour!" she coos as you step outside the lift.

Just the hour? You were kind of hoping thwarting a global cybercriminal group would earn you at least a day's worth of praise.

Susan doesn't notice your disappointment and instead entrusts you with a new task. She wants you to deliver an envelope to Julia, who works in the **server** room on floor 12. You point out that your pass does not open the door to that area.

"I've had it activated on your lanyard for the next 24 hours. Thanks!" Susan jumps in the lift and the door closes to seal her escape.

Not only has Susan thrown a dull task your way, she's just taken the lift, forcing you to use the stairs down to the 12th floor. That floor is purely used as a data centre and serves as home to the most IT of IT people in the company. The stairs down to the 12th floor all merge into a single corridor that leads to the access point for the data centre.

You see a colleague carrying a stack of boxes, trying to manoeuvre them to allow a clean line to scan their white lanyard. Do you want to help them out by opening the door for them?

Open the door for them **Section 231.** Leave them to it and scan yourself through in **Section 259.**

202 Phase Three—Attack

So far, you know Golden Slug are interested in payment card data, as e-commerce websites are a clear source of payment card data. This MP3 lead is definitely more obscure. Hopefully it pays off.

You launch one of the MP3 files to find out what secrets are hidden inside. Disappointedly, it's a rather mundane recording from the Generico McCompany call centre, where a customer is making complaints that their jigsaw puzzle arrived broken and the call centre agent is trying to explain that's just how jigsaw puzzles work. You move on to the next recording. This time it's someone interacting with a call centre agent to pay for a session of virtual massage, however that works.

You continue listening, hoping for some kind of clue as to why Golden Slug would be spending time here, if not just for the comedic value. It soon becomes apparent. When it reaches the point where the customer provides their payment card details, the call recording software is meant to stop recording and then start again once the payment has been processed successfully. As you listen to the customer recite their payment card details, you can hear that this isn't happening.

Lucky break!

You fire off a message to Giuseppa, who heads up the e-commerce business unit. You ask her how many payments the company receives per day where the customer gives their details over the phone.

"About 5000. Why?"

You reply that you were just curious, knowing that telling her the real reason would only make her incredibly defensive and slow down your efforts.

Do you want just to delete all the recordings from the folder to slow down Golden Slug, or talk to Susan about having that payment option taken offline until things are under control?

Delete them all in **Section 185.** Look to take the payment option offline in **Section 30.**

203 Phase Two—Preparation

You stroll towards the operations office, awkwardly trying to measure your speed to avoid catching up to the colleague in front. They are walking that bit slower than you, but you can't overtake them without making it look awkward. You will have to stay behind them and get increasingly more annoyed with their walking pace. You soon realise that they are also walking to Gesa's desk. What a small world.

"Gesa, got this for you," the person states as they place an envelope in her hand. "I need you to sign here to acknowledge receipt." They produce a mail receipt form, which Gesa signs, a slightly puzzled look on her face.

The character then skulks away, seemingly absorbed into the background. They have one of those generic faces; you get the feeling you'd never be able to pick out that colleague in a line-up, even though you literally just saw them.

"Give me a second," Gesa says as she opens the envelope, reads the contents and places both items in her desk drawer. For what it's worth, Gesa has a good poker face. That envelope could have told her she's sacked or that she has won the lottery and you'd be none the wiser.

"Right, who are you annoyed with today?" she asks.

You make a mental note to stop moaning to Gesa quite so often. You let her know you are looking into past projects that had potential environmental impacts and ask her what she remembers of Project Luminec.

She furrows her brow. You can almost picture her mind conducting a search of her memory.

"I don't remember that one at all," Gesa concludes.

You are stumped.

Ask about the **risk register** in **Section 199**, or return to your desk to get printed copies of the documents in **Section 242.**

---

204 Phase Four—Aftermath

A tough choice, but you know I can't reward you for that decision.

You decide to play the game, embracing the dirty secret into your life. The media never follow up on the data and Golden Slug seem to shift their attention elsewhere, so it seems the decision has paid off. Invisibly, though, the secret sits on your chest, like a huge oily gremlin, making you increasingly paranoid over time.

It starts small: flushing toilets an extra time for each use, pressing elevator buttons twice. But the paranoia grows exponentially, to the point where you no longer trust any of the software you use to do your job. You stop attending work meetings, as you don't believe the time displayed in the calendar invite is genuine. You don't even attend your own HR disciplinary, fearing it to be an elaborate ruse put on by Golden Slug.

Eventually your pass stops working on the lobby. You would phone the company to get this fixed, but telephones are full of lies. You throw your clothes off and run naked into the nearest forest to live a life as a nomad.

The End.

> *Well, that was unexpected. You can consider this a pretty good ending really: as a nomad you can cut yourself off from the cold, instantaneous feedback cycle of work and social media and relax. But from an information security career perspective, it clearly isn't an ideal ending. Where do you think you could have done better? Read back through to look for a more positive ending, or try drinking tea early on for a different story.*

205 Phase Three—Attack

Very brave; perhaps foolish, but definitely brave. As CISO it's up to you to decide what points to hold strong on and which to concede on, like in any job role.

Steeling yourself, you let Petra know you strongly disagree and hope she reconsiders her stance. As Petra stares at you, the phrase 'if looks could kill' comes to mind. You'd better be right, or she is going to come after you.

"Fine," she replies.

You visualise your name being written on a chalkboard in her brain, one entitled "Danger Zone". As the meeting continues, you focus on looking anywhere other than Petra, in case she changes her mind, or her stare does indeed manage to kill you.

Eventually it's concluded that Cecilia will disclose the nuclear incident now, to avoid any accusation of an attempt to sweep it under the rug, but she won't make any mention of Golden Slug. Cecilia continues.

"Remember, as with hotdog gate, the press is likely to try to sneak into the building to dig around for intel."

As she finishes, you simply have to ask what on earth hotdog gate was.

"It was when the press discovered that Generico McCompany was lowering their sausage sizes by half a centimetre in length. The public went insane over it, even though the width of the sausages increased, resulting in a net increase of sausage per dollar."

"People sent in messages carved onto sausages. It was the most delicious hate mail ever," Michael remarks fondly.

"I think we can conclude this meeting here," Susan decides, correctly.

Shuffle out of the meeting room in **Section 179.**

206 Phase Three—Attack

You begin comparing the sets of code. The first mistake was assuming that comparing month-old code from a Generico McCompany e-commerce website with the present-day code would immediately highlight Golden Slug's activity. If you met both code sets at a fancy dinner party, you'd never have guessed that the two are related, let alone originating from the same website.

At a large company like this you would expect stronger version control of code than this.

Vijaya isn't wasting her thoughts on imaginary dinner parties and actually finds something that could be the Golden Slug code. Upon closer inspection, it's a legitimate business process that wouldn't look out of place in a cybercriminal's repertoire. You make a note to revisit that later.

Ruby takes a slot in the centre of the bank of desks, but spends most of her time prowling from monitor to monitor. "The Golden Slug code I've seen in the past tries to pretend it's part of the delivery address lookup function. That way it's embedded in the payment process, but is a little downstream from the actual payment card entry point to avoid suspicion," she shares with the team.

Guillaume lets everyone know he will inspect there. You look at the code that handles what limited-time deals are presented to the user, and Vijaya takes the code relating to what colour scheme is used, which funnily enough is comfortably the largest section for some reason.

Keep analysing code in **Section 51.**

207 Phase Two—Preparation

Vatidiva is running version 17.0, which you find surprising. The sound effects haven't changed since it was first launched, and you can't figure out why it has needed so many iterations.

With a bit of digging, the reason behind the most recent software update becomes clear. You find a piece of code that is designed to steal payment card data, and as you dig deeper you discover that the new update was actually deployed by an entity other than Vatidiva. The code has a date-based timer attached to it, and luckily it was set to go live from tomorrow, so no card payment data has been stolen yet.

Filled with relief and a newfound resolve to remove all of Vatidiva's code for good, you rush to Susan's office to share your news.

Once you've brought her up to speed, Susan moves swiftly. "Purge Vatidiva from the system completely, I'll field the questions when the website owners come calling."

You ask her whether they will still be difficult when they find out the software was stealing payment card data.

"Oh, absolutely, they really love those sound effects."

You do as Susan says, spending the rest of the day purging Vatidiva from all of Generico McCompany's e-commerce websites, a duty you perform with gusto.

> *Not something the CISO would do themselves really, they'd delegate it to product owners or development project owners, but for simplicity we'll have you do it yourself.*

With the small time you have left over, you manage to confirm that the fake update was delivered by Golden Slug, and put a project plan together to prevent this kind of thing from happening in the future. Finally, you head home feeling satisfied at successfully stopping Golden Slug in their tracks. Rest up and head back into work tomorrow.

See what the next day brings in **Section 208.**

---

208 Phase Two—Preparation

Strong winds claim the life of your umbrella as you walk to work. You tell yourself that you'll stop buying flimsy portable umbrellas and get something sturdier next time, but this just falls into the void of good ideas that never get acted upon.

As the lift doors are about to slide shut, Susan jumps in and you take the opportunity to update her on the previous day's work. You summarise that Golden Slug were preparing for a payment card data stealing campaign, but that this has now been nipped in the bud.

Susan looks impressed—genuinely impressed rather than the faux impressed expression she throws out when someone in her team does the bare minimum and she tries to look excited. "Sounds like good news, what have you got planned for today?"

Spotting a trap, you spin a lie that you are in meetings for most of the day. Your instincts were on point: Susan had some work that doesn't really sit in your domain that she was looking to pawn off. You've successfully ducked it.

You decide to treat yourself to a little extra milk in your tea to capitalise on yesterday's good work. As you are about to leave the kitchen, you are stopped by Cecilia from the public relations team.

See what she wants in **Section 124.**

209 Phase Three—Attack

With the recruiter's password reset, you notify Susan of the updates via internal chat and move the investigation to Golden Slug's activity on the email server. Curiously, you notice that the Golden Slug IP address appears to be trying to communicate with a device through the guest Wi-Fi. You decide to let that go for the minute: corporate devices can't connect to that Wi-Fi network and if Golden Slug want to spend their time trying to break into someone's personal mobile, that's not the worst thing in the world right now.

> In some businesses the CISO would have to care quite a bit about this if personal phones are part of the strategy, with employees accessing email or applications on their own phones. Also, it's worth noting that personal phones could be used as a vector for **social engineering**.

Golden Slug's activity on the email server is bizarre, for lack of a better word, spending half of their time fawning over any email sent by the CEO and the other half digging through more recruitment emails. Golden Slug appear to be profiling Petra, the Generico McCompany CEO, most likely with the intention of replicating her writing patterns in a **business email compromise** attack.

Charlotte is playing with her phone. This seems like an opportune moment to try to drift away from here and keep her in the dark.

Turn the metaphorical lights off in **Section 180.**

210 Phase Three—Attack

Looking at the URL you notice another oddity: the shopper was browsing genericomccompany.com/glasshammer, but the page with the strange logo is genericmccompany.com/glasshammer.

"Sorry, but can you look into why the popup is being blocked? It apparently hurts the user's shopping experience. I am told this counts as information security, so I will leave the ticket with you," Leslie continues, pointing at the popup.

You begin a reply about how you'd ask someone who actually deals with that kind of thing to look into it, but trail off, having now pieced together the puzzle. Golden Slug are diverting customers from your genuine e-commerce websites at the payment page to a fake payment page, and then stealing the payment card details. In the background they must be completing the customer's order, or all of the failed checkouts would have aroused suspicion by now.

Leslie leaves, satisfied he has slippery shouldered the innocuous popup **ticket** over to you. You'd normally be annoyed at such antics, but this is exactly the breakthrough you needed.

You begin to search the Glasshammer e-commerce page code to find the part that is causing the user to redirect. Now you know what you are looking for, it's almost trivial to find. The guilty lines of code are surprisingly intricate. Only one in four users get their payment cards stolen and any **IP** addresses linked to Generico McCompany or law enforcement have been programmed never to have their card details stolen. Within the code you also find an interesting hidden surprise.

Take a closer look at the surprise in **Section 123.**

211 Phase Three—Attack

Perhaps this is wise: you've already picked a few fights today.

You instruct Guillaume to kick Golden Slug off the network. Time is money, after all. The directors give you a nod of approval and glide away to a whisky tasting, or some other executive-only activity.

A quarter of an hour later, the online horoscope generator is fully operational again, pumping out vague statements that are true for the vast majority of the population: "You will rekindle a lost friendship soon" or "Beware of strangers on days of the week that end in day". Mock all you like, this thing brings in serious revenue.

After running some forensic scans, you conclude with certainty that Golden Slug have been completely evicted from the network. Their external DDoS attack failed to beat you and their phase two plan targeting the firewalls hasn't succeeded either.

Things look good. You can now prepare yourself for a post mortem on the incident, which you will surely come out of very favourably. Then an email drops into your inbox.

Read it in **Section 363.**

212 Phase Three—Attack

The collective noun for a group of crows is a murder. You don't know what the collective noun for a group of sharply dressed business executives is, but they certainly look like murder as well. They seem to communicate as one as their combined voice booms across the room.

"Why is the online horoscope generator application offline?"

Susan appears, thankfully not part of the director horde, and stands between them and the IT team, heroically shielding you.

"As you are all aware, we are dealing with a live cyberincident. I would imagine this is related?" She trails off, looking at you to pick up the baton.

You confirm that is the case. You have goaded Golden Slug into revealing their methods and are now in the process of evicting them from the network completely.

"How long will that take?" the directors ask.

Guillaume replies without looking away from his screen that it'll be roughly an hour to do it thoroughly.

The director horde loses some of its power as one of the members faints on the spot.

Guillaume adds he could do it in minutes but with much less thoroughness.

The fainted director remains fainted. The director horde is not satisfied. "That is too long! We are in peak horoscope season. That thing is making us millions an hour."

Susan again looks for your input. You can either kick Golden Slug off the network right here and now, or you can put your neck on the line by fighting for Guillaume to get his extra hour.

Evict them right now in **Section 211.** Fight for Guillaume's hour in **Section 147.**

213 Phase Two—Preparation

It would seem one of the departments has taken on a batch of new graduates recently: the kitchen is swarming with people who were blatantly living the student lifestyle not too long ago. The newbies give themselves away by the awe-struck looks they give to the clean cutlery and free fruit on offer. For some it's a shock just to see fruit not accompanied by a shot of tequila.

You catch fragments of conversation that indicate they are fresh recruits to the marketing team. They are swapping stories of their university grades, where they currently live and how crazy it is finally to have a full-time job. They still hold the innocence of youth; a few years of a nine-to-five job will bring them to the dark side. One of them does come up with an interesting riddle:

"What are the two whole, positive numbers that have a one-digit answer when multiplied and a two-digit answer when added together?"

Interesting, you think, as you rearrange the cutlery drawer so that spoons and forks no longer share a slot. Needless to say, you are focused on your task at hand and don't pay any thought to the riddle.

Not wanting to be outdone, another asks: "What two-digit number equals two times the result of multiplying its digits?"

You feel your brain overheating as it attempts to puzzle out the answers. Before you become overwhelmed, you leave them to it and focus on making Guillaume's coffee. The coffee machine seems almost to ask why you want a coffee at this time as it's contrary to your routine. You whisper that the coffee is for someone else and the machine seems happy with this response, spitting boiling liquid into the mug you have placed underneath it. Time to channel your inner barista. How does Guillaume take his coffee again?

If you think it was one milk no sugar, go to **Section 29.** If you think it was one sugar no milk, go to **Section 224.** If you think it was one milk one sugar, go to **Section 275.**

---

214 Phase Three—Attack

If you are paying them, you may as well involve them and give them a chance to help out.

Despite their appearance, you have to acknowledge that the Cyber Pirates are a professional outfit with years of experience dealing with incidents, and their input could be valuable. Cecilia is chairing the PR response meeting. The Pirates' entrance immediately draws everyone's attention, although nobody comments.

"I believe we should go public confirming that we are experiencing DDoS attacks, but without revealing the ransom letter or who the entity behind the attacks is. If people start looking into Golden Slug, they'll start asking questions as to why environmentalists have a problem with us."

"Golden Slug announced the campaign this morning on all the major **dark web** hacking forums. The major media outlets will have sources to relay this to them," Captain Dave interjects.

Wow, a good point, well made, all without any nautical terms.

"So that ship has sailed." So close… Regardless, Cecilia looks pleased at her quick wit. "That's excellent. Obviously not that they've announced it, but at least we know that if we'd tried to play things down we'd have started on the back foot immediately."

It is ultimately decided to come clean and attempt to use the ransom note to demonise Golden Slug.

> *That is generally fine, but the sympathy garnered will evaporate rapidly if it's revealed that the defences in place were trivially bypassed.*

"One last thing," Ship Cat Tobias throws out just as people are ready to exit the room. "There may be a chance there is buried treasure in our midst, if you catch my drift."

If you did catch his drift, prove so in **Section 183**, if you didn't, move to **Section 305**.

---

215 Phase Two—Preparation

> *Whilst users getting phished can lead to negative outcomes, potential problems in the e-commerce websites had a more direct connection to Golden Slug's interests.*

You browse to your internal file store and double-click to open the user awareness training program document that you wrote, containing your initial plans and then the revised plans when the initial plans didn't work.

At the top is a quote: "Two things are infinite: the universe and human stupidity; and I'm not sure about the universe!" You must have left that there to brace you for the horrors inside.

Reading the quote reminds you of a particular incident, when a user called you over to their desk to check whether an email was legitimate or not. Despite you pointing out that the email had addressed them as "Bernardo" (their name was "Joyrene") and that, whilst claiming to come from a reputable travel company, it seemed to have been sent from a personal email account, Joyrene smiled and clicked the link inside the email.

I've seen it happen.

In the "room for improvement" section of the document, you've outlined two major concerns: one, the user population's proclivity to fall for **phishing** emails; and two, the inability of your colleagues to even identify, let alone challenge, an employee not wearing a lanyard or wearing a lanyard of the wrong colour. You wonder whether Golden Slug will have tried sending someone onsite. You could perform a scan of the office looking for people either wearing the wrong colour lanyard or no lanyard at all, or you could review the most recent phishing emails being sent to Generico McCompany staff.

Do a lanyard search in **Section 121** or review the phishing emails in **Section 39**.

---

216 Phase Four—Aftermath

Faith in humanity restored.

You reply to the email stating thanks but no thanks and forward a copy to Susan. Susan herself forwards it on to some of her government contacts.

The following morning, you wake up to a notification that a million dollars has been added to your bank account, presumably from Golden Slug. Susan's government contacts step in, seize the million dollars and attempt to trace back the bank transfer to unearth the identity of Golden Slug, but the threat group manage to give them the slip.

Perhaps whilst rummaging around your bank account, Susan's contacts noticed how pitifully low your balance is, as Susan comes up with a substantial pay rise for you at the next review cycle. She references your "solid" performance handling the Golden Slug incident and almost impeccable attendance record.

No, but seriously, that would be a pretty significant privacy breach and shouldn't happen.

Before long another Golden Slug–style incident comes along. Hopefully you act just as "solidly", as the Chief Information Security Officer role can be an unforgiving beast.

The End.

Nice work and props for avoiding that last-minute curve ball. Don't look so disappointed. You lose your job in most of this book's endings, so genuinely this is a good conclusion. You did well to stick to the incident response plan and hold strong under Petra's scrutiny. Why not have another go and mix up your decisions to see how things play out? Or try drinking tea instead of coffee for an entirely new story.

217 Phase Two—Preparation

Sticking to the task at hand: nicely played.

You decide to sidestep the cinnamon comment, but put it in your back pocket for the next time you see Jorge down at the pub. You tell him you are doing some research into a threat actor called Golden Slug and need to examine recent changes on the company's e-commerce sites.

"Golden Slug? That is a great name. We are going to need to advertise that product more."

You begin to explain that it isn't a product, but decide you can't be bothered, instead focusing on your need to know about any changes that have been made to Generico McCompany e-commerce websites lately, particularly if there are any new companies that plug into them.

Jorge opens up one of the websites on his computer. He seems to be looking for Golden Slug on the products list.

"I could have sworn we wanted this page to be blue. But to answer your question, no, we haven't got any new third-party connections, just the regular ones, and we've not had a major change in months. All this security red tape makes changes harder to push out."

The intern looks at you accusingly: how dare you make it harder for marketing to make drastic changes to the website at a moment's notice with no regard to security?

You press on regardless. You thank Jorge, but conclude that there is nothing new. You turn on your heel: you can go and review the existing third parties or talk to the e-commerce website owner to see if they've noticed anything fishy.

Review third parties in **Section 70** or talk to the e-commerce website owner in **Section 157.**

218 Phase Four—Aftermath

This is an incident response situation, not a popularity contest, and doing something that annoys a few people is worth it to get the situation under control.

You let the team know you are comfortable with ruffling feathers to ensure the job is done.

"A fine plan," Commander Sasha says, before stating that now seems a logical point for Galactic Cyber to jettison off in an escape pod, as their work is complete.

You thank Commander Sasha and his team. They salute you and leave behind a small model of a lunar lander as a memento.

Not wanting to risk Golden Slug gaining any initiative, you force through the password reset for all Generico McCompany staff and go for your lunch break.

The staff canteen is a hive of activity, as always with a mix of praise and scorn being directed at the excellent or miserable options available to eat, depending on who you listen to. As someone who had previously only eaten at school canteens, the Generico McCompany lunch options are Michelin star worthy in your eyes. As you tackle a big bean burrito with a token salad on the side, you begin to hear the tide change in conversation as new hungry faces enter the large room.

"Did you have to set a new password too?"

"Yeah, it's ridiculous. I already set a new one two years ago, why do I have to set another?"

"I can't believe I can't just change the number at the end of my password any more."

"I heard it was something to do with information security."

With that last comment, eyes begin to be drawn towards you. Scoffing down the big bean burrito and forgetting the token salad entirely, you finish up and escape your colleagues' glares.

Flee to **Section 255.**

---

219 Phase Two—Preparation

"Now, Michael, you can explain the why this **firewall** issue is so relevant to us all."

Michael assumes a power stance, his crimson necktie almost blinding you all with its intensity. "To cut a long story short, during a project codenamed Luminec we have potentially leaked radioactive material into a remote water supply in a foreign country."

You ask if you can hear a slightly longer story, perhaps with more actual detail.

"We ran a battery recharging site that used nuclear waste to fuel the process; some leaked."

"No" would have sufficed.

Susan seizes the initiative and jumps in. "As Golden Slug are environmentalist hacktivists, there is the potential that they will launch operations that target us once they learn of this. But we have an ace in the hole," she finishes, looking at you, vastly overestimating your prowess and experience.

Feeling the spotlight shift, you decide to contribute to the meeting yourself by asking Cecilia how widely publicised the story of the nuclear spill has become. Everyone looks impressed by your question, not seeing that you are actually stalling for time.

"It is only being reported on low-viewership channels at the moment. The word "nuclear" is a bit of a news article catalyst, though, so I predict it will be widely reported on within hours."

"Then we have a head start?" Susan asks, more in hope than anything.

See how big the head start is in **Section 241**.

---

220 Phase Three—Attack

Sadly for you, just closing down Dragarock isn't the end of things. From looking at the malicious code within Dragarock, you pinpoint the **IP** address where the payment card data was being sent. Naturally, it's located in some legally dubious territory where any kind of attempt to halt the hacking activity is more likely to be met with laughter than action. You run a search for the IP address in your perimeter defence software and find two matches, two instances of Generico McCompany servers communicating directly with the attacker's IP address.

Susan sneaks up on you, in a manner that is presumably taught to staff before promoting them to line managers. You bring her up to speed with Dragarock.

Charlotte helpfully throws in comments making it clear Susan should direct all praise her way.

"What are those?" Susan asks after her story wraps back to present-day events, gesturing at the two servers circled in yellow on your screen.

You enlighten her that these are servers that are also talking to the hacker's infrastructure.

"Doing what?"

You admit you don't know yet, as you only just identified them.

Charlotte decides to use this opportunity to get involved. "One is an email server and the other is a payment processing application used for moving money between banks. I identified this Golden Slug activity 20 minutes ago."

"So it is Golden Slug, then?" Susan asks.

Again, Charlotte frowns before replying. "I believe that IP address is known to be linked to them, but will need to double-check."

Time to choose: do you want to explore the email server lead or the payment processing application lead?

Dig into the email server in **Section 59.** Plunge into the payment processing application in **Section 13.**

---

221 Phase Three—Attack

Ruby outlines what led the National Cyber Security Agency to the strong belief that Generico McCompany have been hacked, first at a very technical level, and then summarised for non-technical people. "In other words, we have seen network traffic into and out of Generico McCompany that is identical to the traffic we saw at another company that had been breached by Golden Slug."

"What are Golden Slug doing, can you tell?" Susan asks.

"They've inserted malicious code into your e-commerce applications so that when a customer buys something, a copy of their payment card details get forwarded on to Golden Slug."

Susan's response is her face going white, already visualising the **PCI DSS** fine from Generico McCompany's bank, and the media fallout.

"From a PR perspective, when the news breaks, I could say we've fallen victim to a sophisticated, persistent and advanced threat, right?" Cecilia enquires.

Ruby shakes her head. "Golden Slug are not exactly known as the A team of criminal groups. The industry would jump on this straightaway and you'd look worse. They are relative amateurs."

Yet they still waltzed in, you think to yourself, not failing to see how this revelation must reflect on your own efforts.

"So, what do we do?" Guillaume asks.

"Well, I am unfamiliar with your setup, and really that decision sits with your CISO."

Everyone in the room turns to you. What do you want to do? You could remove Golden Slug's code from the e-commerce sites immediately, or spend time figuring out how they got into the network in the first place.

Get rid of them now in **Section 177**. Look into how they even got there to begin with in **Section 67**.

222 Phase Four—Aftermath

It turns out they could achieve quite a lot, stealing all sorts of data, including employee salary details and future product plans. Whilst they are now locked out, the damage has been done.

Golden Slug openly mock you, stating they were easily able to trick you into taking a listening device into the Generico McCompany office for them. After a forensic investigation, it is revealed that the USB that you accepted was the listening device. You failed to notice that the person who handed it to you was wearing a blue lanyard, when Generico McCompany only use red, yellow or green lanyards.

From listening in on the team's conversations, Golden Slug were able to adapt their attacks to perfectly target areas of weakness. Despite your being given a heads-up on their methods, they were able to get the jump on you.

The post mortem on the Golden Slug incident concludes that you were not capable of carrying out your role as required and you are sacked.

The End.

The damage was done in phase two: you didn't find any credible leads on Golden Slug, which set you up for a painful phase three. Try making some different choices and seeing how the story plays out.

223 Phase Two—Preparation

Tuesday morning gets off to a bad start. Having spent an entire train ride throwing judgemental looks around to shame whoever is subjecting the other commuters to that horrible smell, you realise that the smell is courtesy of the dog poop smeared under your shoe. Whichever dog produced this sample probably needs their diet adjusted; the smell is particularly overwhelming and surprisingly resistant to your desperate attempts to clean it away in a toilet sink.

After finally salvaging your footwear, you hurry to your desk to set up, sheepishly pointing to your foot and letting people know the reason you are late.

"It happens," Vijaya replies, before adding, "Susan was looking for you though."

Letting out a sigh, you push up from your chair and go in search of Susan. It's typical that she'd try to find you on the one day you're late to work.

Susan is in her office, playing with a Newton's cradle with a glum expression on her face. After explaining your awful start to the day and why you were late, she proceeds to make your mood a whole lot worse.

"We've been popped," she says, almost nonchalantly.

You beg her pardon.

"Hacked, popped, breached, whatever term you'd like to use. A friendly face in the National Fraud Office gave me a heads-up that payment cards being used to buy goods for a criminal group are being linked back to Generico McCompany."

You ask her how this happened.

"We don't know. I didn't expect you to know either. The National Fraud Office is sending a principal incident responder to look into this. They will be here in five minutes. Will you go and meet them in the downstairs lobby, please?"

You grab a red visitor's lanyard and go downstairs as Susan requested.

See who the National Fraud Office sent in **Section 244**.

---

224 Phase Two—Preparation

Well done, you didn't fall for the traps. By the way, the answer to "What are the two whole, positive numbers that have a one-digit answer when multiplied and a two-digit answer when added together?" is 1 and 9. The answer to "What two-digit number equals two times the result of multiplying its digits?" is 36.

Guillaume smacks his lips as he drinks. To you the coffee would be too hot to drink, but he seems to have no nerves in his mouth.

"I think your Project Luminec is live, yes. I didn't set up the file share. Not sure who did, but I've put a copy on your desktop." He opens up Solitaire again, clearly dismissing you.

Browsing through the files, it doesn't take long to determine that Project Luminec is indeed live and running. Based on the figures, the plant seems to be doing exceptionally well and is turning a massive profit. Regardless, it is known that Golden Slug target companies who impact the environment, and a seemingly secret battery recycling plant that involves nuclear energy certainly ticks the right boxes.

You send Susan a meeting invite for tomorrow morning, so that you can brief her on what you've found so far and work out how you might want to mitigate the risk.

You decide to conclude your investigation for the day and turn your attention to addressing a backlog of emails you've filed as "Important but not urgent". Working through these takes up the final moments until it's time to leave. You get caught in a downpour and arrive home looking like some kind of swamp monster. Despite this, you feel positive; today was good and now you are ready for tomorrow.

Find out if tomorrow is just as good in **Section 81.**

---

225 Phase Three—Attack

Just a thought: isn't the S key on the second row of the keyboard?

You type out "Telephone" and hit enter. Once again the text on the screen is replaced.

"Thanks for taking part. I will now process your answers and either disarm the logic bomb or unleash hell, depending on your performance. Please do not close the application."

If you want to close the application, go to **Section 345**, otherwise keep reading.

You take yourself for a quick stroll to clear your head and work the adrenaline out of your system after that high-pressure ordeal. Whilst it seems strange that processing the results of a two-question quiz would take so long, you can't really judge; it's just a bonus you were even given this option to disarm the logic bomb.

Upon returning to your desk, you notice new text on your screen.

Read it in **Section 167.**

226 Phase Three—Attack

You are such a kind soul, you probably give people good Secret Santa presents.

There is no way that Vijaya is complicit in all this, you decide, Golden Slug must have phished her login credentials. You start a group message with Vijaya and Susan rapidly explaining the situation.

"This is terrible, I'm so sorry, I have no idea how this happened," Vijaya says out loud to you, then types it in chat for Susan's benefit. She looks mortified.

You comfort her by telling her not to worry, and to reset her password, then you can disable the code from running.

Susan doesn't chip in. Either she has nothing to add or she's done that thing where she types a message but forgets to hit enter and moves on to something else.

You disable the code on the firewall and monitor the other weakened firewalls to see if it reappears on any of them. Thankfully it doesn't: Vijaya's password reset has done the trick.

You task Niko the resident cybersecurity apprentice with double-checking Vijaya's logs for the past week, to see if Golden Slug leveraged her credentials and access to plant any other nasty surprises hidden in the background. Niko is a reformed hacker, the ideal tool for the job. Golden Slug didn't mess around, apparently, as Niko compiles a list of numerous subtle changes that would have allowed them to reenter the Generico McCompany network essentially at will.

You figuratively lock these **backdoors** up and throw away the key, dramatically clicking your mouse to close the last one. You've won.

Celebrate in **Section 138.**

227 Phase Four—Aftermath

Fast forward five months. You are wearing a fancy outfit at a formal black-tie event celebrating the launch of the joint Generico McCompany and Rathervil charity fund. All manner of high-profile celebrities, politicians and company executives are in attendance, with all of their details being collated in a Generico McCompany **server** so unsecure it may as well be loaded onto a bunch of USBs and mailed to random addresses around the country. You'd rather be anywhere else in the world, though admittedly the canapés are rather good.

The man with the moustache from the meeting five months ago leads a stirring opening speech, captivating the gathered crowds with talk of the generosity being displayed by Generico McCompany and Rathervil. He does not feel the need to reveal that the venue hire, catering and drinks are all being provided for free as part of a government grant. As his speech draws to a conclusion, he approaches the subject of information security, which seems strange.

"And finally, in this data-centric world, as a charity we are incredibly conscious of the importance of donors and the general public having full trust that we will be keeping our data secure. In light of the recent news that has been brought to our attention concerning Golden Slug stealing large quantities of payment card data from Generico McCompany, now is a good time to announce that we do not tolerate such dereliction of duty. With this in mind, we want to announce the sacking of the Generico McCompany CISO."

Oh wait, that's you.

The End.

If Golden Slug's plan to steal payment card data with call forwarding wasn't due to start for 24 hours, how were they stealing card data in the previous 48 hours, as per Sergeant's message?

228 Phase Three—Attack

You can almost hear the sound of the minute hand slicing through the air as it reaches the upright position, signalling eleven o'clock. Your perimeter defence software looks normal right now, but round two is surely coming. Except, nothing comes.

Shellmaster texts you, asking if the plan worked, and you reply that it looks like it has. Five minutes pass, still with no DDoS wave. Ten minutes pass and the coast is still clear.

After 20 minutes you even allow yourself time away from your desk to raid the free fruit basket that lives in the kitchen, emerging with a kiwi and an apple. It looks like your Operation Judo has worked. You are about to break into a dance when Susan hurries over and delivers a strange question.

"I just received a phone call from the head of the district's local hospitals. Why are we DDoSing their hospitals?"

You look at her with a bewildered expression; she returns an equally mystified expression with hints of anger woven in. You let her know that you obviously aren't and would never do that.

"Well, apparently they took a phone call that claimed we had full responsibility and named you as the reason."

You are about to brush off the claim when you notice an email sitting in your inbox with the subject line: "DDoS misdirection for dummies". The email is from hello@goldenslug.com. Susan asks you to look into this before walking off.

Read the email in **Section 253**.

---

229 Phase Two—Preparation

Your lift compatriot tells you all about how their new ultra-green shoe boxes are going to change the world. All you can think is that you'd rather be in anyone else's shoes than hear this. The lift takes 26 seconds to go from the ground floor to the 13th, but it feels like an eternity. The universe takes mercy on you and the doors slide open, offering a chance of escape, but not before one final sting in the conversational tail as you both emerge on the 13th floor.

"Sorry, can I just check, do you know Sakura, who I think works in IT?"

Indeed you do. Sakura got married recently, and is now enjoying a two-week honeymoon. You confirm you know her, but tell your lift buddy that she won't be in today. They seem slightly surprised.

"Oh, she was supposed to need this USB urgently, it was flown into the country specifically for a project she's working on." They produce a dull-looking USB stick from their bag.

"Would you mind giving it to her when she gets back? I am only in the office today and will be travelling abroad tomorrow." They offer the USB stick to you.

Accept the USB in **Section 64** or, if you feel something doesn't feel quite right, go to **Section 287**.

---

230 Phase Three—Attack

Charlotte starts tut-tutting mere moments after being given access to the Generico McCompany network and throws ugly looks your way, which you deem best to ignore. You hear her muttering words like "sloppy" and "careless", either attempting to goad you or because she's got no class. Again, best avoided.

Eventually, she has something useful to say that isn't a personal attack. "It would appear that your attacker has hacked a third-party company that provide software for your e-commerce process. Then they changed the software so that it did its function, but also duplicated the payment card data to their own **servers**."

You ask Charlotte which **third party** has been compromised.

She spins her laptop around and points at some code on her screen. "Dragarock, the company that provide that software, which knows how old you are based on how your mouse moves across a screen and how you type."

Actually, that's more real than sci-fi. Do a Google search of "my mouse, my rules" and you'll find a good research paper on this subject. It would seem that with mouse movements alone we can predict age and gender with surprising accuracy.

You continue, asking if she can see how long the compromised code has been running for.

"I am a competent information security professional, so yes," Charlotte replies, without really answering your question.

You look at her and, twisting your head to the side, ask how long.

"Sorry, are you not a competent information security professional too? You can check for yourself. I have to write up my notes."

You can't resist releasing an exasperated sigh as you dive into Dragarock's code and look for the point at which the malicious **payload** started being used. Would you consider yourself a lucky person?

Luck plays a part in all jobs in a way.

If you are lucky, go to **Section 31**, if you aren't lucky, go to **Section 306.**

---

231 Phase Four—Aftermath

Top points for kindness. What colour was their pass again?

You make the hapless person's day by scanning your pass and holding the door open for them. As they walk through, trying to keep the precarious pile of boxes upright, they throw you a quick thanks and shuffle off.

It takes you a while to find Julia. Everyone you ask thinks she is on the other side of the building, until you finally ask another person where Julia is and they respond, "Right here, how can I help?"

You hand over the envelope and mention Susan gave it to you.

Julia acknowledges Susan's seniority by opening the envelope there and then. After giving the contents a quick scan, she shakes her head and mutters, "This is terrible."

You try to console her, but it turns out the news is simply how large the server room team's budget for a team lunch is for next week. Seeing as you've never had a team lunch, you can count the amount of sympathy you feel on one closed fist. You leave Julia to wonder how to salvage her meal and go back upstairs to your own job.

The next few months pass in a blur. The Golden Slug incident earns you a promotion and special praise, which is great, but a pay rise would have been preferable. One day you walk into the office and everyone looks glum.

Find out why everyone is glum in **Section 262.**

232 Phase Three—Attack

Beating Golden Slug at their own game sounds very appealing. Shellmaster outlines how the exploit they've chained together works. In summary, you can manipulate Fesrodah's **Stresser** so that when they next start a DDoS attack, rather than the traffic all hitting your infrastructure it'll instead hit the **IP** range through which Golden Slug are accessing the Stresser tool. Shellmaster sends a list of instructions on how to get this set up, which you start bringing to life.

Guillaume comes over to check out what you are doing. "I didn't know you knew how to code," he says, managing to sound surprised enough for the statement to be slightly hurtful.

You reply as nonchalantly as you can that you dabble, failing to reveal that calling what you are doing "coding" is extremely generous.

"What does this bit do?" he asks, pointing at your devious **payload**.

You let him know it's going to divert Golden Slug's DDoS back at them.

Guillaume thinks for a while, then replies. "Like judo?"

You ask him what he means.

"Judo, you know, using someone's own strength against them."

You let him know that's a good comparison and dub the operation Operation Judo.

Guillaume wags his finger as he walks away. "This has nothing to do with me."

You frown at him, then at the clock, as it shows you only have 12 minutes until eleven o'clock, which you have theorised will be when the next DDoS attack is launched. A misspent youth in online chat forums has its benefits as you expertly manage to type out the code for Operation Judo with four minutes to spare. You deliver the payload and sit back.

See what happens in **Section 228.**

233 Phase Three—Attack

Clearly you have a full picture of what Golden Slug have been up to, meaning there won't be any hidden surprises—right?

You tell Sasha to nuke the network from orbit.

"Pardon?" he replies.

You are surprised Sasha doesn't appreciate the space reference, but simplify the message and ask him to get Golden Slug off the network, confident they will only have been interested in payment card data.

Galactic Cyber scramble into position. You take the time to grab a cup of tea to calm your nerves. In the kitchen you notice that someone has vandalised your information security poster by drawing a rude image on it.

When you return, you find Susan standing at your desk with a bemused look on her face, observing Galactic Cyber from a safe distance. "Who are they?" she asks in a lowered voice.

You brief her that they are Galactic Cyber, the information security retainer company she signed up nine months ago. Whilst she seems satisfied with that answer, you can tell what she's thinking and put her mind at ease, letting her know that despite the outfits, they appear to be extremely competent and professional. You then give her a play-by-play account of what she has missed since leaving to attend the board meeting. You finish up by explaining that once they are done, Generico McCompany will need to report the payment card breach, although the number of cards Golden Slug will have had time to steal won't be that significant.

"Which hopefully will mean an insignificant fine. OK, well, carry on and let me know if anything major pops up." Susan walks off, catching one last extended glance at Galactic Cyber.

Marshal Marshal approaches and requests that you follow him for an update.

Download the update into your brain in **Section 182.**

234 Phase Four—Aftermath

In the weeks that follow the Golden Slug incident, the post mortem singles you out for praise, acknowledging your sustained ability to stay calm under pressure and maintain conviction in the face of pressure.

The discovery and removal of Golden Slug's backdoor gain you international acclaim, and you receive invitations to appear as a guest on a medley of mostly unsuccessful podcasts and very, very, very low-budget television programmes.

A promotion follows, which doesn't mean much other than making your job title uncomfortably close to a swear word when presented as an acronym, but at least the pay rise is nice. Unbeknownst to you, a shadowy figure is already planning Golden Slug's return. Did you really fully uproot them?

The End.

> *You took some pretty big risks along the way there, baiting Golden Slug and standing up to the executive mob. Thankfully for you, it's paid off in this instance. Finding that backdoor was critical: until you removed that, Golden Slug could just come and go as they pleased. All in all you've done a good job. There are even better endings, but they are tough to find. Try to discover one of them, or alternatively read through again but pick tea instead of coffee for a whole new adventure.*

235 Phase Three—Attack

Susan's office is a hive of activity. As soon as you enter the room you notice you've spilled your lunch on your shirt and now will be wearing the stain as a failure trophy for the rest of the day. But the stain is forgotten when Susan reveals the reason behind her emergency meeting.

"We've received a ransom email from someone claiming to be Golden Slug."

"Who?" those in the room say, almost in unison.

Susan continues, "They claim we've radiated a large supply of drinking water and are now going to target us until we sort it out."

"Did we really do that?" asks Vijaya.

Gesa from the project management office replies, "It is certainly looking like we did, yes. Something to do with a nuclear-powered battery factory…" She tails off, realising nobody really needs to know.

"How much is the bounty?" Michael cuts in, ever the compassionate soul.

"It's $20 million, but there's no guarantee they'd hold off even if we paid it."

Discussion turns to planning what to do. Given that there is no **incident response plan** set out and nobody with experience of a similar incident, the options are limited.

"The attacks are meant to start in 20 minutes. My team will monitor them and we can convene later to decide how to act," Susan finishes, dismissing everyone from her office and reaching for a bottle (you doubt it contains water).

Take a big breath and face the fire in **Section 270.**

---

236 Phase Three—Attack

Well done! Maybe...

You type out "Telephone" and hit enter. The screen text gets replaced by a big smiley face, before changing to more text.

"Congratulations, you have passed the test. Our little present will now delete itself. And remember, always click the link in emails without reading them."

Don't do that.

The application then makes good on its word and cannibalises itself. You spend half an hour making sure there are absolutely no remnants and no other hidden "presents" lurk in the shadows. It's almost a shame that there is no trace, as now you have no real proof that any of that happened at all.

Susan comes by your desk holding a mug decorated with the number 1337. "You look like you've seen a ghost. What happened?" she asks.

You walk her through recent events, deciding to pretend Golden Slug's ordeal was spaced over ten gruelling questions rather than two for dramatic effect.

Over the course of your storytelling, she doesn't take a single sip from her mug; maybe it's just for show. "What kind of questions were they asking?" Susan asks, genuinely intrigued.

You half lie that you only remember two of them.

"Does that mean Golden Slug are finished with us and we can go back to business as usual?" Susan replies hopefully.

If you think so, head to **Section 21.** If not, head to **Section 271.**

---

237 Phase Two—Preparation

You let Susan know it's Golden Slug and her eyes widen in shock.

But wait a minute, why did Cecilia invite IT and security to this meeting when it had to do with a nuclear incident? When you ask her, it turns out she didn't know there was any link. She'd only invited IT staff members because she was going to need help temporarily taking down the site's infrastructure and you happened to be nearby—lucky break.

"How public is this news?" Susan asks for you.

"Local TV at this point, but it'll get picked up nationally. Everyone loves a reason to sneak a gut punch into Generico McCompany," Cecilia replies.

Susan turns to you. "It looks like you are up, then."

You excuse yourself and rush back to your computer as quickly as is socially acceptable in a professional workplace. Nobody around you seems to be alarmed. That's a good sign, surely?

Your perimeter defence software shows network traffic **data packet**s hit your external infrastructure before being routed to wherever they need to go. How many of those little dots are just colleagues sharing memes, you wonder…? A loud phone alarm erupts somewhere in the vicinity, announcing the time as 10:30 and for the phone's owner to take their blood pressure pills.

10:30 seems to be when Golden Slug decided to serve up their own medicine: your screen becomes a wall of white as their DDoS attack begins. Maybe, just maybe, this is a drill.

Cross your fingers and find out in **Section 145.**

---

238 Phase Four—Aftermath

It isn't far into the resulting interrogation when Charlotte breaks and spills the cyber beans. After losing out on the Generico McCompany CISO job to you, she joined the National Fraud Office. In one of her first investigations, Charlotte was introduced to Golden Slug, who had just stolen payment card details from a well-known pizza chain. As part of the investigation, she discovered contact details for Golden Slug, and she used these off the record to establish a partnership.

Exploiting her connections, Charlotte was able to find out exactly which third parties Golden Slug should target when attacking Generico McCompany, and was responsible for getting them into the network to begin with. She even took the time to check Generico McCompany annual leave requests to ensure that you would be there when the breach unfolded. Whilst Charlotte clearly wanted you to get sacked as some form of petty vengeance, she also wanted Golden Slug to steal the human resources records relating to her job application, so she could find out why Susan had picked you over her for the role to begin with.

Meanwhile, back at Generico McCompany, the fiasco of having a **malicious insider** within the National Fraud Office easily overshadows any story about stolen payment card data, and the company gets off with a negligible fine. You survive Charlotte and live to fight again.

The End.

> *Close call. This is one of the few good endings that are possible once Charlotte gets involved. The good news is that you wriggled out of a tight situation; the bad news is that you only ended up in a tight situation because you hasn't made a lot of progress in phase two. There are actually two different ways to move one step ahead of Golden Slug. Why not read through again and see if you can find one? If you would like to try something different, read through again but pick coffee instead of tea—that leads to an entirely different story.*

239 Phase One—Prologue

Susan cringes when you use the short form of her name, as if she can't believe you thought you were friends. You tell her you'll have a look at the article when you get back to your desk and ask her for the threat actor's name.

"Golden Slug. I'll forward you the email. I'd rather we didn't suffer a **data breach**, so do look into it," she replies.

You thank Susan, making sure to use her full name, and rejoin the march of the caffeine-zombie horde. You notice a familiar face from the legal team.

"Hey, do you know if that **cyberinsurance** policy got signed off in the end?" they ask.

You let them know that it hasn't been signed off yet and isn't on the agenda for another two board meetings.

They roll their eyes. "I look forward to chasing this in six months' time to see where it went."

You sympathise. It's a well-known fact that projects often nosedive into obscurity once they reach the board.

You make small talk with a developer about computer **code**, and they begin to talk about the pros and cons of agile versus waterfall development, but thankfully you manage to pass them off to another colleague. Finally, you reach the front of the line.

You elbow your way into the kitchen in your quest to get that caffeine hit. Go to **Section 314.**

---

240 Phase Three—Attack

Smart move.

With urgency, you inform Guillaume and Vijaya that together you need to close port 13337 on a number of **server**s.

"I wasn't enjoying this chicken salad anyway," Vijaya confesses, dumping her lunch in the bin and springing to action.

It doesn't take long to put a script together to close port 13337. Correction, it doesn't take long for Vijaya to put a script together to close port 13337; it would have taken you ages. Her finger hovers over the enter key, prepared to unleash the script. "Ready?" she asks.

You reply, unconvincingly, that you think so.

"Give no quarter!" Captain Dave adds with a flourish of his hat.

Vijaya hits enter and port 13337 is closed.

The Cyber Pirates turn their attention to monitoring again, seeing whether Golden Slug have any more tricks up their sleeves.

Without much better to do for the minute, you go on a coffee run to refuel your troops. But it seems you overestimated your strength and feel your arms shaking as you bring a heavily laden tray of mugs back in the room. The Cyber Pirates are so engulfed by their work they don't come to help; at least you hope that's why. Pedro the Parrot is happily picking away at Vijaya's discarded food, but he couldn't have helped if he wanted to.

Set the coffees down in **Section 101.**

---

241 Phase Three—Attack

You head downstairs to your desk to plan out your next move. You immediately open your network traffic map software to see if anything looks out of the ordinary, but for now the coast is clear. You feign ignorance and practise your poker face as rumours of the nuclear incident spread around the office like a particularly infectious disease.

Lyle, personal assistant to the executive team, swings by your desk and asks you to join him for a minute. He essentially pushes you into a meeting room and shuts the door behind you.

Petra, the company's CEO, is in the meeting room, looking very glum. Wordlessly, she spins her laptop to face you and reveals the email sitting in her inbox. It reads:

> You are the enemy. Attacks will start in two hours and come as crippling waves of judgement.
>
> Kind regards,
>
> Team Golden Slug

Petra shakes her head. "They had the cheek to offer kind regards." She turns back to you and continues, "There isn't anything else to add. I'm surprised they even gave us a heads-up."

You are about to agree when Guillaume bursts into the room. "Applications and **servers** are falling like..." Noticing Petra, he catches himself before a typically crude crescendo to the sentence can escape his mouth.

You look at Petra with eyes that say "I need to go" as you rush back to your desk.

Find out what how bad things are in **Section 103.**

---

242 Phase Two—Preparation

Proof makes arguments much easier to win.

As you walk back to your desk and take a seat, you overhear a member of the IT support staff working on a support **ticket** over their headset; it sounds painful. You log into your computer and browse back to the Luminec folder, which is no longer there. Puzzled, you retrace your steps. Nope, it's definitely not there. You hear an exasperated cry from the helpdesk worker: "How can your phone not be working if you are calling me on it?"

Checkmate. Turning back to your own problem, you wonder what on earth has happened to Project Luminec. There is no trace of it in your recently viewed items and the folder seems to have vanished. You fire off a quick message to one of your friends on the IT team, asking them to look into it.

As you wait for their reply, you spend some time writing up a piece for the Generico McCompany newsletter on how staff can avoid cyberfraud in their personal lives. Your advice focuses on a common situation where there is a bill that needs paying via bank transfer, such as sending money to an estate agent. In this situation, you tell staff always to contact the company in question using the phone number on their website to clarify the details, not to trust a phone number in an email. In fact, you tell staff not even to trust any website link in an email, instead telling people to Google the company name and get the phone number that way.

This is because a hacker may have compromised the company in question's email and waited for this opportune moment to change the bank details being provided. By calling the company on a known number, staff can confirm that the details are correct before making any payment.

> This sort of fraud happens all the time. Whilst you may have a case that the lost money is the company in question's fault depending on the law of wherever you live, that won't bring it back anytime soon and may put purchases or house moves at risk. Stay safe and take the time to confirm bank details properly.

You finally get a reply from your friend in IT. "Sorry, but I don't see any trace of that folder. Are you sure it is spelled 'Luminec'?"

A flicker of doubt enters your mind, but no, you are pretty sure you have spelled it correctly. Things seem to be getting weirder and weirder.

Go back to Gesa in **Section 247**, or head over to talk to Susan in **Section 351.**

---

243 Phase Two—Preparation

> I'd say well done, but you know I'm not going to be able to reward you for attempting to commit a crime.

You've found a treasure trove of payment card data. Whilst it sits on the internal network and is not directly exposed to the internet, it's still a valuable target for Golden Slug, and so it's worthwhile for you to fix it. You fire a calendar invite to Susan for tomorrow morning.

She replies with "Sounds promising" and a thumbs-up emoji when accepting the invite.

A calendar notification pops up and reminds you that a vendor is coming in to pitch on their quantum computing–enabled real-time factory equipment maintenance software. One of the business heads is interesting in buying it and you are attending the meeting to ensure that the software isn't going to bring any hidden surprises to the table. You wander over to the designated meeting room and take a seat. You notice the salesperson eyeing you nervously when your job title is read out during the introductions, and it soon becomes clear why.

"So, to log in to the application for ease of use, it simply requires the user to enter the factory name."

You ask whether that means that anyone who knows the Generico McCompany factory name could access your factory's settings and change them.

"Yes, but that would be against our company policy."

With that, you decide you've heard enough. You leave the meeting and head home.

> Clearly, the factories having their own dedicated credentials (such as username and password combination) is critical, otherwise an attacker could **brute force** the login process with all possible factory name combinations until they found the Generico McCompany factory. The salesperson's line about its being against company policy is cute, but company policy doesn't stop hackers.

You attract some strange looks on your way home because you still are laughing at the salesperson's line. You sleep well that night.

After eating a complete breakfast and squeezing in a morning gym workout, go back into work for day two in **Section 349.**

---

244 Phase Three—Attack

In the lobby, you see a reasonably dressed man with a beard, a woman in a green cardigan and elderly woman with a walking stick. These are your candidates for the National Fraud Office's incident responder, as you didn't get an actual description or name to work with. These three individuals are sitting on the sofa in the lobby, giving away no clues to their background or purpose. You decide to try the reasonably dressed man with a beard first. You ask him if he is from the National Fraud Office.

"No, but the deals I have on offer are so big it's almost like my customers are committing fraud against me!" he replies, launching a laptop out of nowhere into a presentation that seems to resemble a pyramid scheme.

You give reception security a subtle nod and the reasonably dressed man is escorted out of the building, though not without first trying to flog a protein/testosterone hybrid formula to the guards.

Next you try the elderly woman with a walking stick. You ask her if she is from the National Fraud Office.

"I am waiting for the bus, do you know when it's next due?"

You point out that she is inside a building right now.

"Oh." She shrugs, pulls out a crossword and continues to wait.

You back away slowly. Finally, you approach the woman in a green cardigan. You ask her if she is from the National Fraud Office.

"No," she replies.

You are about to apologise and find someone else to try when she continues, "I am Charlotte, from the National Fraud Office's Cyber Wing."

Get to know Charlotte in **Section 69.**

---

245 Phase One—Prologue

Generico McCompany employees work with a `firstname.lastname@genericomccompany.com` email format.

Remember this.

During the login process you are forced to **authenticate** with your username and password repeatedly until the system gives in and reveals your inbox. Apart from the standard internal emails, you see nothing particularly interesting or urgent. A quick check on your network monitoring tools reveals nothing of significance either. You lock your computer and decide that it's time to get a hot drink.

You join the convoy of co-workers in a queue for the kitchen, seeking their morning caffeine hit. Susan, the company's Information Technology (IT) Director and also your boss, leans against the wall just outside the kitchen, silently taunting the caffeine-zombie horde by sipping a cup of coffee that was probably delivered to her by one of her minions.

Susan's main focus is on keeping all the IT systems up and running. So far, she's done a good job; the company has had minimal downtime over her two-year tenure. Despite your slight feeling that she wasn't overly keen on hiring an information security person, she seems to have taken a marginally less dim view of you upon signing your successful probation papers.

Her eyes land on you and she calls you over. "Good morning. I know you just got in, but I wanted to see whether you'd read about this new **threat actor** apparently targeting companies in our industry?" she rattles out, barely pausing for breath.

No doubt she has been forwarded some scaremongering article and fallen for the clickbait. You let her know you haven't seen the article and accidently acknowledge her as "Sue".

Find out the consequences of your transgression in **Section 239.**

---

246 Phase Two—Preparation

This is a sensible move. You now know that Golden Slug are interested in targeting companies that harm the environment. By looking at projects that have a risk of angering an environmentalist, you can gauge the risk of Golden Slug attacking Generico McCompany either now or in the future.

You decide to reach out to Janet, who works as programme manager. She has overall accountability for the company's projects that fall outside of business-as-usual activities. From experience so far, you know that she is direct, only answers the exact question asked and hates interacting with people in person. You send Janet a greeting on your internal chat system.

"Hi, what do you need?" the response comes back. Janet is living up to her reputation.

You ask her about any recently completed projects that have catalogued environmental impacts.

"All projects have environmental impacts. Be specific."

You specify that you are interested in projects with bad environmental impacts.

"Again, they all do because they all involve a computer, which needs electricity etc."

You roll back in your chair, put your hands behind your head and let out an internal scream. Clearly, you aren't speaking the same language. You ask if Generico McCompany have completed any projects recently that had "environmental impact" identified as a risk in the project plan document.

"Yes."

With a mental fist bump, you ask Janet how many.

"143 so far this year."

You sigh, opening a project plan you've submitted to remind yourself of the risk rating system. It seems risks can range from minimal up to critical. You ask Janet if any of those had a critical risk rating for environmental impact.

"Yes, two: Project Degrada and Project Luminec. Do you want anything else? I'm just heading into a session of all-day meetings, so only have five more minutes."

Ask Janet about Project Degrada in **Section 163** or ask her about Project Luminec in **Section 80.**

247 Phase Two—Preparation

Gesa has already been investigated and that didn't turn up anything new. It was a good time to escalate things to your line manager.

You get stopped for a mundane chat with a particularly outgoing co-worker. You try to convey with your eyes how much you don't want to be part of the conversation, but either you fail or they are oblivious. You desperately search for an opportunity to escape, which is provided when your captor remembers they have work to do.

As the operations door swings open, you notice a problem: Gesa isn't at her desk. You ask her neighbour Zola if Gesa is gone for the day.

"Yeah, she's gone home," she confirms.

Lucy continues looking at you, emitting brainwaves that force you to flee the operations office and return to your desk to reflect on your futile search. You really need to learn that trick; those brainwaves would have been really useful as a defence against the chatty colleague. You make a note to ask Lucy to teach you.

From your internal chat, you notice that Michael has been offline for hours now, so your only lead on Project Degrada is unavailable and your only lead on Project Luminec has gone home for the day.

You plough on, hopeful that your search will be more fruitful tomorrow. Eventually it is time for you yourself to go home and put your feet up. The sun sets, the moon does its thing, until a cockerel decides to announce the arrival of the sun with a crow and Tuesday rolls into motion.

See what the day has in store in **Section 323.**

248 Phase Four—Aftermath

Disaster strikes as you hurtle towards the city on an underground train. You've had a memory lapse and have forgotten whether you brushed your teeth this morning or not. You spend the entire commute pressing your lips together to contain the potentially noxious fumes.

An attractive passer-by stops you to ask for directions. With horror, you realise they're also flirting with you. You completely blow the opportunity and instead provide ridiculous hand gesture directions to someone who could have been your soulmate. What a dumpster fire start to the day.

To add fuel to your fire, whilst riding the lift up and checking your appearance in the mirrored walls, you notice a toothpaste stain on your shirt. It turns out your teeth and breath were fine all along.

"Why the long face? I thought you poured salt all over Golden Slug yesterday?" asks Vijaya as you slump into your seat.

You decide to share your morning toothpaste nightmare with Vijaya and enjoy some equally fruitless and shameful stories of spurned love with Guillaume too when he finally turns up. Maybe he also had toothpaste trouble.

Hear what he has to contribute in **Section 60**.

---

249 Phase Four—Aftermath

Right on. Who knows what Golden Slug have done to the PIN entry devices in person that a software-based reset wouldn't detect or fix?

You tell Gesa that you want to go the store so you can get your hands on one of the PIN entry devices and see what they've done in person. She decides to join you; any excuse to get out of the office.

The walk over to Northallerton Street is a pleasant one, cutting through a lush green park full of trees and also people who seemingly have nothing better to do at three o'clock on a working day. You've never visited the Generico McCompany store on Northallerton Street, but you can pick it out instantly; the company's logo engulfs an enormous billboard with an arrow pointing downwards, no doubt to guide lost souls into the store to spend their money. As you walk in you are greeted by a shop employee who seems to be made of 60% enthusiasm and 40% acne.

"Good afternoon! Welcome to Generico McCompany Northallerton Street branch. If you are here for the bath bicycle trial, head on down those stairs."

You decide to avoid trying to pronounce whatever is on the employee's name badge and instead wish them a good afternoon. You let them know that you are from the Generico McCompany head office, and explain that you've come to check on the PIN entry devices that were recently serviced by a contractor.

Upon hearing that you are not potential customers, and instead more likely potential problems, the young man's shoulders slump. The employee's response is going to be dictated by how much he has absorbed when he took part in Generico McCompany's cyberuser awareness programme. How well do you think you'd be at teaching other people to be cybersecurity smart? Rate yourself out of 10.

If you rate yourself between 0 and 5, head to **Section 350.** For those more confidently rating themselves between 6 and 10, head to **Section 11.**

---

250 Phase One—Prologue

The machine whirrs and beeps, trying to convince you that it's a mechanical device when it's clear to the world that a coffee machine is something magical. The smell of the coffee beans wafts into your nose, providing an initial thrill. Your mouth waters as your mug fills up with liquid gold. Jealousy beams in the eyes of the person stood behind you in the queue; they are affronted that you dared arrive at the machine before them. Once your mug is full you are able to wheel away in celebration, allowing the next person to fulfil their destiny.

The first sip feels as good as watching someone you dislike falling over. The second feels like arriving at the bus stop seconds before your bus pulls in. The third is so good you consider dancing, despite having no sense of rhythm or choreography. The day may now begin.

Back at your desk, you log in and take a look at your to do list. After clearing the easiest tasks, you decide to investigate Golden Slug. A Google search shows that Golden Slug are an environmentalist group that punish companies who damage the environment by releasing devastating **DDoS** attacks upon them.

> *Distributed denial of service (DDoS) is when an attacker sends a huge amount of network traffic towards a target, hoping to cause **servers** to crash and either prevent the company from trading or slow it down significantly.*

Flicking through articles reveals that Golden Slug have a history of targeting companies shown to be polluting water or contributing to major deforestation. That's good to know. To give Susan peace of mind, you decide to have a poke around to make extra sure.

You could either go and talk to the project delivery office and see if they've got any environmentally iffy projects in the pipeline, or you could take a look at what kind of traffic your external perimeter is seeing at the moment and whether it resembles a DDoS attack.

Go to **Section 246** to talk to the project delivery office, or try **Section 347** to look at the external perimeter traffic.

251 Phase Two—Preparation

You feel powerful as you write the script to encrypt the call recording files. Making a computer do your bidding is always satisfying, even if it does mean you'll be executed quicker when the machines inevitably rise up and overthrow humanity. Not fearing the wrath of the electronic appliances, you walk to the kitchen to prepare a cup of tea. The kettle will definitely want to take a shot at you when it gains sentience, you've definitely pressed the on button more forcefully than is needed.

In the kitchen a debate is in session over whether eggs should be stored in the fridge or at room temperature. Valid points are thrown each way, with the conversation getting surprisingly heated. Some people clearly need their morning caffeine fix.

"Why do you have eggs in the office anyway? We don't have a frying pan, saucepan or even an oven to cook them in."

"You can boil eggs in a kettle, you know," the person replies, taking your place as the kettle's nemesis. That is one less thing to worry about when the uprising occurs, at least.

The situation is much calmer in the IT section, not a single egg debate to be heard. Just as you take your seat, an email appears in your inbox from Susan with the subject line "URGENT – DARK WEB".

Read what it's all about in **Section 176.**

252 Phase Three—Attack

Susan is in a board meeting now. Given that Generico McCompany board meetings ban participants from touching anything other than a ringing phone, you can be relatively certain the current activity on her email account is Golden Slug rather than her. They are trawling through emails from eight to nine months ago, just looking around aimlessly by the looks of it.

You put a stop to their fun and kick Golden Slug out of the email server, but knowing they managed to bypass the two-factor authentication process makes you feel very uneasy. You call Niko over to your desk via online chat. Niko is working at Generico McCompany as an IT apprentice after being charged with minor hacking offences by the police; in exchange for some generous tax exemptions, Generico McCompany are sponsoring his reform programme.

This does happen, but there are easier and less law-breaking routes into the industry.

Due to his shady past, Niko is an ideal person to try to peer behind the curtain into the enemy's mind. You ask him how hackers would typically try to circumnavigate two-factor authentication.

"Well, if the code was being sent to a phone number, we could try to convince the phone provider that the SIM card had been stolen and take ownership of the SIM, so the codes would get sent to us."

That's a practice known as SIM swapping.

You shake your head. Generico McCompany directors and administrators don't use SMS-based two-factor authentication. You ask Niko about other methods.

"Other than tricking the user into entering the code on a **phishing** website, you could always plant a physical device that intercepts the code when it's generated by the phone."

Charlotte scoffs, pointing out that you are entering into the realm of bad sci-fi films. She continues to tap away on her own phone. You grab some popcorn and 3D glasses to amplify the experience.

Enjoy the show in **Section 359.**

---

253 Phase Three—Attack

Good plan, except we are not babies and can fake origin IPs. Remove your little exploit from Fesrodah's Stresser and take our lovely DDoS like an adult, or we will continue to target the hospital instead.

Much love,

Golden Slug

Ah, they got you there. Trying out to outhack the hackers was a dangerous game to play when you factor in that they don't care about legality.

You let out a groan. It's checkmate. You text Shellmaster asking for their input, but they don't reply.

Susan has returned to her office. Without giving away the slight illegality of the situation, you explain what has happened. She imitates your groan and holds her head in her hands before saying, "Do as they say, we can't risk human lives over this."

You agree and dash back to your desk to remove the exploit.

As you remove the payload from Fesrodah's Stresser, a thought begins to niggle away at you. Why didn't Golden Slug just move to a different Stresser service if DDoSing Generico McCompany was their objective?

"How did Operation Judo go?" Guillaume asks.

You let him know that Golden Slug used you using their own strength against them against you. Steam rises from his head as he tries to process whether that is good or bad. He decides it's bad and leaves you to it.

Retreat to lick your wounds in **Section 276.**

---

254 Phase Three—Attack

Bridget promises to stay on her guard and hangs up. She started her career in the most junior position available on the help desk, and has continued to work her way upwards ever since. Now she runs the entire unit. Bridget is very protective of the call centre, and she would hunt down like a bloodhound anybody who endangered it. If Ruben is up to anything, she will surely catch him in the act.

But you don't want to rely entirely on Bridget, so you start to delve more into the connection between Ruben's terminal and the strange foreign **IP**. It could be a glitch or something Ruben isn't even aware of. You begin by putting in a call to a friend who works in cybersecurity incident response, and ask them if they have any knowledge of the rogue IP in question.

"Ah, that's known to belong to the threat actor known as Golden Slug," they reply.

This doesn't come as a great surprise. Now you need to determine whether it was intentional or accidental, and to get the connection severed.

Bridget calls you back. "I caught Ruben opening an internet tab and typing in card numbers when customers were providing them over the phone. I have no idea how he managed to access the internet from the terminal. The police are coming to arrest him now."

You ask her not to touch his computer terminal and contract an incident response forensics team to investigate it.

Find out what they found and wrap things up in **Section 50**.

255 Phase Four—Aftermath

Susan is not immune to hunger or irritation and she catches you before you can sneak out of the room. "Why am I getting complaints from all the directors that everyone has had to set a new password?"

You explain why you thought it would be safest to push through the reset, even if there was no concrete evidence that Golden Slug had managed to pivot onto other user accounts.

"That seems fair, good call," she replies, and her stomach rumbles audibly. "Perhaps you should give me a full recap after lunch?"

You agree that's a good idea and recommend the big bean burrito. Susan nods at you politely, but you can tell that hell would have to have frozen over before she'd even consider it.

With the entire company seemingly on a witch hunt, now would be the opportune time to make use of the developers' hidden nap pods to get some rest until your recap with Susan. You get inside a pod and laugh to yourself at the idea of being able to sleep in such a strange contraption. The next thing you know, you check your watch and see that an hour has passed. Touché, nap pods.

Sheepishly, you climb out of the pod and make your way to Susan's office, trying to look slightly more tired than you are to avoid giving away your scandalous sleep secret.

Reach Susan's office in **Section 41**.

256 Phase Three—Attack

You ask First Mate Gloria what files Golden Slug are looking at.

"Network diagrams. I would guess they are trying to get their bearings before going after any buried treasure."

You check if First Mate Gloria thinks it will be possible to block Golden Slug's IP addresses.

Captain Dave answers that one. "Yes, but they'd likely come back again via new IP addresses. You need to determine how the rats got into the hull or they'll keep nibbling your cheese. Now, this may look like the cat's out of the bag, but I have a plan."

You stare at Captain Dave, the universally accepted way of non-verbally saying "Go on then…"

He eventually takes the hint. "We boobytrap a treasure chest."

What? You ask Captain Dave to say that again, but in English.

"We plant a **honeypot**."

Still, what? You ask him to revert to the pirate theme, but to simplify matters.

Captain Dave outlines his plan: you plant a fake server somewhere Golden Slug are likely to see and monitor what attack mechanism they use to break in, letting you defend accordingly.

> *This is a real technique, I should add. You put a really appealing-looking target on the network and hope hackers find it too tempting to pass up. When they put their hands into the honeypot, it fires off an alert to tell you where the hackers are.*

Pour some honey in a pot in **Section 119**.

257 Phase Two—Preparation

With an elaborate hand gesture, Giuseppa declares, "You have full access to my team. We must protect the payment card data."

Great, you have found someone who cares about information security as much as you do.

"Because if any of that stuff gets out stolen, they'll close my babies down whilst they do forensics."

Maybe not. You spend the next few hours talking to the various compartments that form the e-commerce team. The fraud team confirm nothing suspicious has been seen lately. The logistics team look through the last few weeks' worth of orders and can't spot anything that looks out of place. The user experience design team actually do flag something they don't like the look of.

"Why is this page green? It should be blue. Now a user's attention is going to be guided to the cheapest option when it should be focused on the premium package."

Giuseppa had let your interviews carry on without interference, but the mystery of the green screen is too important to let slide. She steps in and starts a full crisis meeting to uncover why the screen is green and not blue.

You decide it's opportune to leave. There isn't really enough time to start on any new leads, so you finish up and head home. You spend your evening building a large tower made of playing cards, only for a gust of wind to undo all your work.

See what tomorrow has planned for you in **Section 223**.

---

258 Phase Three—Attack

You tell Sergeant that you hope so.

"Hope will get you nowhere in this game. Hope isn't what kept me alive for all those years in the military, it was down to training and mental aptitude."

Sergeant proceeds to lecture you about his days serving on the front line. You find yourself unable to cut him off or end the conversation. Soon you're trapped in a never-ending nostalgia loop with no break in sight.

The End.

> *It's kind of unfair for things to end there. You had no way of knowing Sergeant was so chatty, so why don't you head back to **Section 328**?*

259 Phase Four—Aftermath

> *You are either observant or mean-spirited. Either way it pays off, as that person had a white lanyard and Generico McCompany only issue green, yellow and red lanyards.*

As pathetic as the person with all the boxes looks, you'd look even more pathetic if you buzzed someone through who wasn't meant to be in the server room. You make sure you hear the door click shut again once you're through and let the first person you see know there is a delivery person stuck outside.

"Our deliveries are meant to go to the loading bay and are then brought up by our own elevator," they tell you, before leaving to investigate the delivery.

You shrug and start searching for Julia. The server room is essentially the entire floor and it's a maze. You get hopelessly lost and end up sitting on the floor in the foetal position calling out for help. Eventually a colleague comes over, asks you what on earth you are doing and then acts surprised as you reveal the envelope bearing Julia's name.

"Julia is laying a cable over on the west wing, I'll take you there."

You stare at them in confusion and wonder if they were being literal or just gave you way too much information. But they turn around, walking away and expecting you to follow. You do so, mostly out of curiosity.

Find out what kind of cable is being laid in **Section 118.**

260 Phase Four—Aftermath

"This sounds like a right royal mess," Susan summarises neatly when she's heard from you and Gesa. "How many stores do we have across the country again, Gesa?" she continues.

Gesa lets her know there are over 9000, which makes your hair stand on end.

"And what is the nearest store?" Susan continues.

"Northallerton Street. It's a 10-minute walk from here. I should add, by the way, that the PIN entry devices we have installed at all our stores can be accessed and updated remotely," Gesa replies.

"So, if Golden Slug put their own software onto the devices, we could push them back to an older version of the software that is clean?" Susan asks.

You let her know that is correct.

She presses on with her interrogation. "So why did you get onsite maintenance to perform the job if that remote update option was always a possibility?"

"We only learned about that after the booking was already made," Gesa replies, then states that the rogue maintenance crews conducted all their work yesterday, so there is no risk of running into them.

> *Probably a bit of a stretch for all 9000 jobs to have been performed in one day. I sometimes find it hard to coordinate four people to be at the same place at the same time, so 9000 separate sites would be a challenge. Let's just run with it, though; our little secret.*

Do you want to travel to Northallerton Street and inspect a device yourself, or push out an update forcing all the PIN entry devices back to a known safe software version?

Pick Northallerton Street in **Section 249.** Go with the update option in **Section 178.**

261 Phase Two—Preparation

There was no right or wrong for that first decision: both options had merits and drawbacks. It could be argued that the vulnerability scan report made direct reference to the e-commerce websites that Golden Slug would be targeting, but that's very minor. Crack on.

Before you started at Generico McCompany, the only kind of information security internal audit carried out was the type that was done at the very last second to satisfy a customer's contractual requirement. Nothing quite beats the rush of having to pretend you've been regularly monitoring hundreds of **controls** for months, especially when you only get told the day before the audit is due. After six instances of this in your first month, you decided to address the issue. Now you've got internal audits running in a light touch manner, updating a master document every few months to let you identify issues before they become a problem.

The report is formatted quite simply. A thing that is "bad" is listed, followed by the date it was identified, the impacts of said bad thing and potential options to make the bad thing go away. As an example, one listing identifies that the colour scheme for one of the e-commerce websites is due to change, with the impact listed as customers potentially not liking the new colour. Not exactly the kind of change that should make its way into this kind of document, but you appreciate whoever put it there for at least trying.

You tell yourself it's better than nothing. You home in on the changes that relate to the e-commerce websites.

Susan parks up next to your desk and asks how the investigation is going.

You tell her you are reviewing the information security internal audits to identify any changes made to the e-commerce websites recently.

Susan frowns before walking off. You are unclear whether she is frowning at your line of investigation or just because it's Monday.

Continue your research in **Section 336.**

262 Phase Four—Aftermath

Everyone is glum because the National Cyber Security Agency have been in touch to reveal that Generico McCompany have been hacked. You roll up your sleeves, announcing that you are ready to go toe to toe with whoever is trying to hack the company.

"That won't be necessary. We have already been able to identify how the attackers got in and have had them removed," Susan lets you know.

You ask how they got in.

"Well, some idiot let someone without a valid pass into the server ro—"

Before Susan even finishes her sentence, you've started pulling out your laptop to compose a resignation email. You're out of the door a few minutes later.

You did so well against Golden Slug, but one tiny lapse made all of that work go to waste.

The End.

> *Tough lesson to learn. You got it right quite a few times in a row and saved the day, but you are only ever one blip away from a mistake. You let someone with a white lanyard into the server room. Generico McCompany only issue red, yellow and green passes. Don't be too hard on yourself, though: try reading through again, but having coffee instead of tea for a fresh challenge.*

263 Phase Four—Aftermath?

The next few weeks become a blur. You are greeted each morning by the blue sun rising in the sky. Sometimes you have cereal for breakfast, sometimes you eat the bowl itself. You ride the great water motorway on a dolphin wearing a saddle to get to and from work.

Work itself is now one big all-day party. Your efforts in the Golden Slug breach get you promoted to supreme overlord of fun. Your first action in your newly appointed position is to do away with corridors, replacing them with slip and slides to make moving from meeting to meeting at least enjoyable.

No work actually gets done any more, so the meetings are just hangouts where people play board games or get bored playing games. You are now part of something called "Fun House", though you aren't entirely sure what it is or whether it's going to pose a health risk in the long term.

Looking out the window and seeing a skyscraper-sized tennis racket float by makes you think that maybe something isn't quite right. Wait, you didn't get the Golden Slug maths equation horribly wrong and rewrite physics, changing reality forever, did you?

Probably not, you muse, as gravity ceases to exist bringing everything to...

The End.

*Oh dear, it looks like you broke physics and ended the story prematurely. Remember BODMAS: Brackets, Order, Division, Multiplication, Addition, Subtraction. Perform the maths in **Section 123** in that order to find the right answer. Failing that, try all the answers until one of them leads you to an outcome where things don't get so weirdly out of hand.*

264 Phase Two—Preparation

You don't fail to attend something that is introduced to you as a "crisis" meeting unless you want a "crisis" in your employment status. Get yourself to that meeting.

Actually go to the meeting in **Section 323.**

265 Phase Three—Attack

A problem with this approach is you are so focused on fighting the fire, you are unable to keep track of what other things Golden Slug may be getting up to.

Taking the entire company offline to fix this problem is too much collateral damage for you to swallow. The next few hours are spent in full firefighting mode, bringing services back online and slowly defusing Golden Slug's deadly trap. Sometimes it appears futile, though, as if your extinguisher is itself spewing flames.

The day is drawing to an end and you actually have things under control. Performance across the business took a hit, but it was nowhere near as painful as it could have been. The weekly company update email goes out. Somebody is looking to raise money for charity by attempting to break the record of the most biscuits eaten in a day. It's nice to see the rest of the world is continuing as normal.

You see Susan approaching. She will surely be delighted by the progress made in the Golden Slug defence.

"Golden Slug have sent a huge file to a variety of media outlets. It's full of what they claim is personal data they've stolen from us."

Well, that stole your thunder.

Susan continues, "It's late. There's nothing we can do for the minute, but first thing tomorrow you will need to determine if the claim is genuine or not. I've sent the file to your inbox."

You go home. You eat something despite not being very hungry. And finally, you go to bed, although you hardly sleep.

Commute into work in **Section 111.**

---

266 Phase Three—Attack

Sadly, no dice.

You make your suggestion to Ruby, who almost falls out of her chair, then actually does fall out of her chair. As she picks herself up from the floor, she lets you know her view on that approach loud and clear.

"To put it simply, hacking back is illegal in most countries. I cannot endorse that at all. I would advise you drop this idea immediately."

*Sorry, if hacking back had a positive outcome, getting this book published would become pretty much impossible. Whilst this no doubt happens when government agencies fight amongst each other, it's not something a private company would ever do. If you have an interest in offensive security, you should definitely look at becoming a **penetration tester** or work on some **bug bounty** programs.*

Return to the land of the law abiding and let's pretend this never happened in **Section 104.**

---

267 Phase Three—Attack

Sorry to tell you, but if you don't like nautical puns you probably won't enjoy the Cyber Pirates.

Listening to the team introductions during the incident response kick-off meeting is one of the strangest moments of your life.

"Captain Dave in the crow's nest."

"First Mate Gloria here."

"Ship Cat Tobias reporting for duty."

Unable to hide your scepticism, you ask Tobias if he is actually a cat.

"It means I'm junior," Ship Cat Tobias responds.

"He's seen cannon fire," Captain Dave reassures you. "Just not ready to take the helm."

After bringing the bizarre party up to speed, the consultants begin to speculate and work out some battle plans. They ask for the last 24 hours' worth of **logs** for your external network, which you prepare to email over. You finish the call by letting them know that the Generico McCompany office closes at six and you need to prepare their passes and desk space, so there isn't really much more to do today.

"Roger that. We will make arrangements to board your office at eight o'clock tomorrow."

After getting temporary red passes made for the Cyber Pirate gang, all there is left to do is go home, sleep, and wait to see what these buccaneers can do.

Find out exactly in **Section 171**.

---

268 Phase Four—Aftermath

Days pass and no reply comes from Golden Slug. Days become weeks and weeks become months. Before you know it, it's a full six months since the Golden Slug incident.

You are in the office, forcing yourself to clap as Fernando, the person who handed over the SCAPI database to cybercriminals, is promoted. Nobody forces you to eat the cake that was bought to mark the occasion, but if it means there is less cake for him to enjoy, then it's a form of petty revenge you can get on board with.

Once the celebrations are over, everyone gets back to work. You slide back into your new office chair and see what emails have arrived since you were dragged away to celebrate Generico McCompany's devotion to the Peter principle: *The idea that people get promoted until they are at least one stage above where they should be.*

Amongst the normal mix of emails is a very angry-looking subject line. All in caps, it reads: "URGENT: OFFICE LOBBY RISK".

The email outlines how Generico McCompany staff should remove anything that identifies them as Generico McCompany staff before they leave the ground-floor lifts. A group of protesters have gathered and seem to be targeting Generico McCompany employees. The email doesn't go into detail about why the protesters are there or what they are protesting about. Instead, that is covered in the next email. Golden Slug dumped the data they stole online and now the public are annoyed.

Despite this, Generico McCompany decide to keep you on as CISO, mostly so that they have someone to blame future incidents on.

The End.

A close call: because you made such slow progress in phase two, the odds were always working against you. There were a few chances for you to gain a little or a lot of ground on Golden Slug, taking a bit more control of the breach and allowing a more positive outcome to be found. You've actually done well to reach an ending where you keep your job, so kudos for that. But this is a 5/10 ending at best. Why not give it another go and see if you can lead things to an even better finale?

269 Phase Two—Preparation

An excellent choice. If technical vulnerabilities interest you, the Open Web Application Security Project (OWASP) regularly publishes data on what the most commonly exploited vulnerabilities are in web applications. Cross-site scripting has been in the top 10 since the list began back in 2003. Cross-site scripting allows an attacker to access a web application (like an e-commerce website), then inject scripts into web pages viewed by other users of the application. So essentially, the hackers can display things or interact with other users of the application, potentially even stealing their data. This has happened in real life. Google "cross-site scripting payment card data", so I don't have to name any companies and risk legal action.

It doesn't take you long to realise that this cross-site scripting vulnerability is the real deal. You push an email out stating the user awareness training will be starting an hour later. You hear cheers; hopefully the two events are unrelated. Some investigative work shows that this was incredibly close to becoming a genuine problem, with the **logs** showing examples of cross-site scripting being exploited in what look like proof-of-concept attacks. Crucially, these were performed using **IP** addresses known to be linked to Golden Slug.

You solve the problem the same way most problems are solved: by writing an email. The email highlights the vulnerability to the development team, and professionally suggests the developers prioritise fixing this immediately. Including Susan in CC is the cherry on top; there is no better way to show something is important than CCing your boss.

Don't try this at home.

Susan does a reply all stating she expects this to be resolved ASAP and you know you can rest easy now: nobody disappoints Susan.

With that attack thwarted, you deliver your user awareness training session, helpfully finding that by removing one hour from the schedule you have enhanced user engagement and, fingers crossed, gained better information retention. You head home tired, but triumphant. You reward yourself with popcorn and a good film, the kind of film you've watched countless times and it's never let you down.

Go into work for day two in **Section 208.**

270 Phase Three—Attack

Things look normal on your perimeter defence software at 13:55, but by 14:05 the software has crashed, unable to keep track of all the **data packets** being fired at your internet-facing infrastructure. By 14:10 the madness stops, offering a temporary respite.

You provide Susan with a running commentary over the phone as she gives a rushed briefing to her fellow directors.

"Why did they stop after only 10 minutes, though?" she asks.

You theorise that Golden Slug might be showing off their capabilities, giving Generico McCompany one last chance to pay the ransom before hitting hard.

"I don't like the sound of that."

You don't either. You let her know you are carrying out analysis on what services and hardware were taken offline by that 10-minute burst, but first impressions actually aren't that bad.

Susan hangs up. Honestly, you prefer it when conversations end abruptly like that; it's much better than having a goodbye stand-off to see who will put the phone down first.

You spin around in your chair. Vijaya is shaking her head, looking confused. "I just don't get it. They had the element of surprise. Why would they stop after only 10 minutes when they've barely done any damage at all?"

You prepare to repeat what you've already said on the phone, but she continues, "Yes, yes, I know, potentially giving us a chance to pay the ransom, but they wouldn't stop even if we did pay."

"What makes you say that?" asks Guillaume, clicking the "send" button to fire the damage report out to Susan.

Continue the conversation in **Section 277.**

271 Phase Three—Attack

*Yup, well done. Whilst you managed to defuse the call recording forwarding **malware** and the logic bomb, Sergeant said he had evidence of cards stolen in the past 48 hours. This would have been before the call recording forwarding was even turned on.*

Recalling your conversation with Sergeant, you shake your head. You tell Susan that Sergeant found 200 fraudulent transactions from cards that all linked back to Generico McCompany, and that they all had been used on company sites in the past 48 hours. You finish by telling her that you don't know where any of the card details came from.

"OK, it sounds like you have things under control," Susan says, gliding off in another direction. She is probably aware you don't have things under control, but doesn't want to confirm her suspicions yet.

You pull up the intrusion detection system again and come across something that stands out as a new suspicious lead. For some reason, one of the terminals used by customer service employees is communicating with an **IP** address from outside the company. You put a call in to Bridget, the call centre manager.

"Welcome to the Generico McCompany support line, this is Bridget, how may I help you?" Despite having not actually worked on the phones in years, it seems that Bridget has clung to her old phone manner.

You ask her who is sat at terminal 16 in the call centre today.

"Ruben. Why do you ask?"

You let her know that his terminal is connected to an IP address outside of the Generico McCompany network, when it should be locked down in a manner that prevents external connections.

"Strange, I'll keep an eye on him."

You thank her and tell her to keep a particular lookout for anything related to payment card data.

"Yes, I remember the riveting training you delivered on the subject. You do know I've worked in the call centre for longer than you've been in permanent employment, right?"

Let her know you do remember in **Section 254**.

---

272 Phase Three—Attack

You share the latest update with Susan and Petra. You expected a response to equal the horrendous nature of your news, but both women seem more thoughtful than annoyed.

Petra breaks the silence by asking, "Is it obvious the data comes from us?"

You let them both know it wouldn't be obvious, as it's a generic database with no clear and obvious links back to Generico McCompany. Hundreds of similar lists already exist on the internet.

Petra closes her eyes and has a deep think, then outlines her plan. "We say nothing."

Susan nods solemnly.

Petra continues, "Pretend this conversation never happened. We say nothing, we refute any claims." She stops and appears to inspect her fingers before delivering a threat so thinly veiled it's translucent. "There will be no problem with this, I assume?"

You tell Petra you hear her loud and clear and leave the room, suppressing the urge to look back. You can feel both directors' eyes fixed on the back of your neck anyway. It's time to regroup and take stock with a coffee.

Head to the kitchen in **Section 296.**

---

273 Phase Three—Attack

If you looked at your keyboard before writing that, shame on you.

You type out "repertoires" and hit enter, suddenly realising you could have looked at your keyboard to double-check, but it's too late now. Golden Slug's devious program seems to be happy enough with your answer, as the text changes.

"Before question two, you may be wondering why we even included this opportunity for you to disable the logic bomb rather than merely set it off."

You were wondering that, in fairness.

"It's because we pity you."

Oh, OK. The text changes on the screen again before the full weight of that insult can strike at your core being.

"Question two. What never asks a question but always gets answered?"

If you think the word is "Books", go to **Section 71.** If you think the word is "Telephone", go to **Section 225.**

274 Phase Two—Preparation

You are a nice person, but would the pay-off of not being so nice have been worthwhile?

You decide that Rory has earned some shut-eye and leave him be. You notice that he looks sunburned; waking up a tired, scarlet man has surely been the start of many a war, even if the history books don't know it. You do know that Guillaume isn't asleep, so it seems prudent to switch your attention to him.

As you walk to your desk, you are flagged down by a colleague, who appears to have mistaken the printer for a toaster and you for a support technician. You see that they've stuffed paper into the output tray and have a feeling that the problem won't require a large amount of skill to fix. This proves to be an accurate diagnosis, as you cure it by turning the printer on. Out of the corner of your eye you see Guillaume slipping off home. Your chat will have to wait until tomorrow.

You drift away from the printer. Being a good Samaritan has left you thirsty, so you head to the kitchen to grab a glass of water.

Take stock of the situation in **Section 16.**

275 Phase Two—Preparation

Oh no, did your mind become too focused on the brain teasers? The answer to "What are the two whole, positive numbers that have a one-digit answer when multiplied and a two-digit answer when added together?" is 1 and 9, by the way, and "What two-digit number equals two times the result of multiplying its digits?" is 36.

Guillaume recoils in horror after taking a sip of his coffee. "Bah, this is so sweet I won't be able to have a biscuit with it."

Great, now you've cost him a game of Solitaire and a biscuit opportunity. He goes to discard the abomination you've created for him, leaving you sitting there waiting for him to come back. He doesn't rush on your behalf. Finally he returns, perfectly crafted coffee in hand.

You see an internal call from Susan pop up on Guillaume's screen. He points to it in the universal language of "I gotta take this."

You go back to your desk and do some busy work as you wait for Guillaume to finish his call with Susan, except like a basketball game it seems to last longer than you'd planned. As he eventually hangs up, it becomes clear he isn't going to be able to look into Luminec for you today. It'll have to wait until tomorrow.

After packing your bag and heading out of the door, you decide to hang out at a local coffee shop, listening to customer orders and visualising making them, eager to ensure you are prepared for the next coffee challenge. At home you spend hours reading about coffee beans, even arranging some beans you have at home into an elaborate art piece, which you then smash apart with a single karate chop. You are ready.

After getting some sleep and following your morning routine you grab the train into work, ready to make Guillaume a single-sugar coffee to start things right.

Ride the train in **Section 100.**

276 Phase Three—Attack

The DDoS attack starts up again at 12:00 as expected. The IT infrastructure team flounder around, powerless to stop the barrage of network traffic from overloading your internet-facing estate. But like before, the attack only lasts 10 minutes, giving you 50 minutes to brace yourself until the next one. Two niggling thoughts make their way from the back of your head to the main stage:

1. Why are the attacks only lasting 10 minutes?

2. If Golden Slug could continue their attack even after your exploit, why did they pull the hospital stunt?

As you crunch these two statements in your head, a rogue idea springs to mind. You could just ask them. You have their email now, after all. There is no guarantee they'll reply to you, but it could be worth a shot.

On the other hand, instead you could try scanning through the day's **logs** to see if you've missed anything. But remember that searching for malicious logs without some kind of idea of how the attacker operates, where they are or what they want is pretty challenging, to say the least.

Try emailing Golden Slug in **Section 85** or check out the logs in **Section 46.**

277 Phase Three—Attack

"Just a feeling, really," Vijaya finishes, as you all turn back to your screens.

Whilst you work on diagnosing the DDoS attack's impact, out of the corner of your eye you see Cecilia from the public relations team, walking as quickly as possible without actually running. The look on her face is a mix of anger, panic and uncertainty; you feel bad for whoever she is delivering news to. Cecilia stops by your desk.

"Hi, can you join me in Susan's office?"

You can't help but note the lack of "please" in the sentence. Cecilia is known for bringing amazing home-baked goods into the office and for being one of the most cheerful people around. The lack of pleasantries must mean it's serious.

Wordlessly, you nod and stand up, following Cecilia towards Susan's office with the distinct feeling you're about to be told off for something. What have you done?

You line up in Susan's office like naughty school children, though surprisingly Susan looks like she has no idea what's going on either.

"Can I help you, Cecilia?" Susan asks, perhaps dreading the answer.

Instead of replying, Cecilia picks up the TV controller on Susan's desk and turns on the news. The breaking news headline reads: "Generico McCompany targeted by environmentalists?"

Cecilia points at the screen. "Needless to say, this is a PR nightmare. We have to understand how this information was leaked, and we have to get a handle on this ASAP, because in a quarter of an hour the lobby is going to be full of press."

See what the repercussions are in **Section 83.**

278 Phase Two—Preparation

The person sitting next to you on the train has awful taste in music. Normally you don't pass judgement on other people's preferences, but as this person's headphones are blaring out noise so loud it's inescapable, you have no choice. You spend the entire commute stewing over how much they've annoyed you and how in an alternate universe you would have asked them politely, but sternly, to turn the volume down. You get an incredible rush of adrenaline even thinking about your made-up act of bravado.

That adrenaline carries you into the office, helping you skip over the polished marble reception to the lift that hurtles you upwards. Today's coffee gets jazzed up with some foamy cream on the top, because—well, why not? You are slightly put off your stride when the meeting room where you expected to find Susan contains Susan and a ton of other people too.

In attendance are Michael (COO), Vijaya (IT Backup Manager), Gesa (Project Manager), Cecilia (Public Relations), Georgios (Legal) and Susan (IT Director). Of the assembled cast you can only really see why two or at most three would care about your firewall discovery.

Susan soon brings everything into perspective. "Ah, I'd just given everyone a briefing on your firewall finding. Excellent work there."

You take a mental note of all the people in the room. Open praise from Susan is rare, so you're glad to have witnesses.

Continue basking in glory in **Section 219**.

---

279 Phase Three—Attack

Whether it's today or in a year's time, lies can come back to haunt you. I have to at least partially endorse this decision.

There's no denying it, the data was stolen from Generico McCompany and you decide it would be best to come clean. You give Cecilia in the PR team the brief.

Her reaction is much as you would expect. "This isn't going to go down well."

That's a bit harsh, really: as a CISO each month where nothing bad happens there is no press release or fanfare, but the vultures swoop as soon as the slightest thing goes wrong. That's the industry you got into, nevertheless.

The press release goes out. To say the reaction is negative would be a contender for understatement of the century. Generico McCompany's stock price takes an almost instant hit. From the way people talk about the stock price, you may as well have cancelled Christmas.

This mentality is changing, thankfully: companies that react well to breaches can come out of things relatively well.

You can't fail to notice that the stock price dip from being honest about a data breach was actually bigger than the hit that was taken when the company admitted to poisoning a water supply with radioactive waste.

A few hours later Susan messages you, asking for an update.

You inform her that Golden Slug are off the network and their external DDoS is now insufficient to trouble the company. Telling Susan that neither outcome was necessarily down to your actions is a cosmetic detail you decide not to share.

Get a cup of coffee and see how things play out in **Section 164.**

280 Phase Three—Attack

"We found something. Can you come with me?" Ship Cat Tobias mutters nervously before turning on his heel.

You follow him on the two desks' walk to his laptop. Ship Cat Tobias rewards himself for that long walk with a wedge of orange, vital for holding off scurvy, as he lets you know through a mouthful. After disposing of the rind, he gestures towards his laptop. The screen resembles a particularly angry painting, full of harsh red lines and sharp angles.

"Your **firewall** appears to be acting very strangely," he says, pointing at one of the red lines.

You peer down to understand what he means by this. Captain Dave wanders over and looks at the screen too. It clearly is worthy of closer inspection, as he pulls out his retractable telescope for a closer look. He performs a series of elaborate hand gestures and suddenly all the Cyber Pirates are packing their bags.

You ask him what is going on.

"That firewall is pretty messed up. The Cyber Pirates know when to abandon ship," Captain Dave says as he leads his team towards the lifts.

An incident response team wouldn't just up and leave like that, unless they were proper cowboys. Maybe I should write another book with cowboy incident response....

See what has Captain Dave so worried in **Section 330.**

281 Phase Three—Attack

Good call. Honestly, I couldn't really have endorsed you going on the hack back line of thinking.

You've landed in a tight spot, and everyone knows that lawyers are the kind of people who get people out of tight spots. Georgios from legal is notorious for never answering internal chat, so you pick up the phone instead.

He doesn't bother with pleasantries. "Yes?"

You let him know you want to send a cease and desist to the company fronting Golden Slug's DDoS.

"Sounds like a great plan."

After a pause, you state that you need his help.

"I'm now unsure if your plan has merit."

You wait. Georgios also waits. You could fit the entire population of earth's elephants into the pause that follows before finally Georgios concedes. "OK, fine. What are the details?"

You provide Georgios with Fesrodah's details so that he can carry out some of his own research and preparation. You agree to meet in mini meeting room four to hatch your plan.

Upon arriving at mini meeting room four, you realise that the term 'mini' is not an exaggeration; the room can barely fit two people. The conference phone has been built to scale, complete with tiny number buttons. After squeezing in, and rearranging your limbs to avoid raising any complaints with HR, you dial Fesrodah's main number.

See what happens in **Section 26**.

---

282 Phase Two—Preparation

*Good job: always be wary of **phishing** emails.*

You raise your hand, for some reason reverting to high school social conventions.

Thankfully, Jack is in tune with you. "Yes?"

You let Jack know the email is a fake.

He looks at you with a puzzled expression, pinches himself, then points at his screen. "It's not fake, it's there."

You explain that the email has come from Jorge@genericomcompany.com, when it would have come from Jorge@genericomccompany.com if it was genuine.

He gets it in the end. "You reckon that was the Golden Slug guys you were talking about?"

You concede that you aren't sure, but either way you'll have to review the recent requests, and for the minute there will need to be a rule set up for the developer's inbox only to allow emails from genericomccompany.com addresses.

You implement the rule to prevent incidents like this in the future, and at the same time check whether this has happened before. Thankfully, all the other requests in the inbox are genuine.

You head back to your desk to review the malicious request and notify legal to have the spoofed domain seized. On the way, you are ambushed by a colleague who thinks they've downloaded a **virus** onto their computer, so you investigate.

The "virus" is playing music on your colleague's laptop. After a quick troubleshooting session, you see that the music is coming from an internet browser tab with a name questionable enough that you decide just to close it rather than inspect it first. If only all problems were that simple. Time to review the malicious developer request.

Put on your detective hat in **Section 22.**

---

283 Phase Three—Attack

No right or wrong there, personal choice really.

You tell Susan that you don't like the sound of Golden Slug crawling around the HR systems and will start there.

Surprisingly, Charlotte seems to think this is a good idea, as she sends texts on her phone.

"Sounds good. I will probably not mention that in today's board meeting and I would ask you keep it between yourselves for the minute." Susan looks at her watch. "Speaking of which, the meeting starts in seven minutes and I need a coffee. I'll be uncontactable for the next three or so hours, but I'll stop by once it's done."

Inside your head you plead for Susan to stay and not leave you with Charlotte, but outwardly you are a figure of cool composure as Susan leaves.

Once Susan is out of earshot, Charlotte wastes no time in digging her claws in. "Right, then, what would a donkey do in this situation?"

You tell her you don't know and ask her what they'd do.

Charlotte smirks before explaining. "No, as in you are the donkey, so what do you have planned?"

You point out you don't know what a donkey would do, but you do know you are going to look at the **logs** to see what communications are being sent to Golden Slug's **IP** address. Which you do, wearing noise-cancelling headphones throughout to protect yourself from more of Charlotte's verbal assaults.

Find out what the data is showing in **Section 343.**

---

284 Phase Three—Attack

You enlist the talents of Niko, a young reformed hacker, now working as an apprentice with the company. Normally he is only allowed to analyse suspicious email attachments to assess whether they are legitimate or not, but desperate times and all. It turns out to be a good decision, as he recognises the exploit Golden Slug have used almost immediately.

"That's a buffer overflow vulnerability being used. See, you can tell by this." He points at something on his screen that may as well have been a picture of an octopus playing bongos for all it tells you.

*A buffer overflow is when an application or process can be tricked into saving data into memory areas where it shouldn't. Think of two glasses of water, glasses A and B, which are next to each other. You want to get your poison (or **virus**) into glass B, but you only have access to glass A. You overfill glass A so that the runoff flows into glass B, getting your poison into glass B via glass A.*

"I see." You lie that you now understand and ask how you can stop Golden Slug from being able to use it.

"I could deploy signature-based **packet filtering** for you."

That sounds suitably impressive, you decide, and ask how long it would take.

"A few minutes. It's been primed to go live for a while, I was just waiting for the green light."

Without going too deep down the technical rabbit hole, a "signature" in technical terms is an identifier, something that lets you know an attack is linked to a particular threat actor. That is an oversimplification, but it will do for this context.

You give him the thumbs-up to start the signature-based packet filtering. You decide not to **shoulder surf** Niko as he prepares and instead check how long you have until Golden Slug's file transfers are complete. The transfer sits at 88%: you've got half an hour left at most.

A little bit Hollywood: you are unlikely to have access to this kind of information in reality.

"It's up, chief," Niko lets you know, confirming his news with a double thumbs-up.

You throw him a thumbs-up back. You restart Firewall F42, killing off Golden Slug's file transfer, and wait.

Continue waiting in **Section 65.**

---

285 Phase Two—Preparation

You don't wash your hands? Gross. I should make this into an abrupt ending. But no. I'll give you a second chance.

Just before you reach the bathroom door, your conscience screams at you to turn back and do what is right. You obediently return to the sink and wash your hands, properly, with soap and everything, musing how your conscience sounds uncannily like your mother.

Try to redeem yourself in **Section 125.**

---

286 Phase Three—Attack

A new voice emerges from the miniature conference call phone. "Hello, I have been told you had our Stresser services provided to you without your approval?"

You reply stating that is correct.

"In that case, as you have enjoyed the benefits that Stresser has provided, we will need to invoice you for the service utilised so far prior to cancelling."

You are about to fly into a rage, but Georgios raises his hand and takes over. "Madam, this is Georgios, legal counsel for Generico McCompany. This call will serve as sufficient evidence that Generico McCompany did not solicit Fesrodah's services and that the continued supply of these services will be a violation of national and international law. Unless you would like to take this to court, cease your activity."

"That will be fine, yes. It seems there has been a terrible misunderstanding. Press five on your keypad to complete this process. Please refrain from pressing any other key."

You look at the tiny number pad on the phone. The keys are so close together; who on earth designed this phone? You press five.

See how that works out in **Section 26.**

---

287 Phase Two—Preparation

Something's not quite right, but what is it?

You take a step back and analyse the situation. You can't put your finger on it, but something seems wrong.

Flat out reject the USB in **Section 87.** Keep reading to check the USB for **malware** yourself.

You let them know it will be no problem as you take the USB from them. Is it your imagination or do they flash a quick grin as you accept it?

"Thanks so much! What was your name again so I can let her know who has it?"

You provide your name and wait until they leave before plugging the USB into your laptop, but find that it is empty. Refusing to give up, you grab a soft drink can from the kitchen and walk off to your desk, carrying the USB in front of you face up as if it were a knife. Rather than going to your own desk, you travel instead to one covered in empty soft drink cans and crosswords—Niko's domain.

Niko is a (hopefully) reformed hacker, now working at Generico McCompany as part of an apprentice scheme. He spends his days analysing files that get quarantined by the **firewall**, checking that genuine attachments aren't being blocked.

> *You'd perform this kind of activity in what's known as a "sandbox", an isolated network area where tested malware will be trapped, rather than risk testing malware in the main network.*

He is the perfect person to discover the truth about your USB. You outline your suspicions and provide Niko with the USB along with the soft drink can that serves as payment.

Watching this guy type gives your fingers sympathy pains; not only does he hammer every key entry like whack-a-mole, but the speed of his movement suggests his fingers will give up on him someday. As long as it's not today, you don't care.

Find out what he unearths in **Section 137**.

---

288 Phase Three—Attack

> *This is probably safer. You hadn't really received much of a guarantee and it seems quite knee jerk. But is it right?*

You confide that you are not confident it will help that much in the long term and the financial outlay would be enormous.

"OK, I won't push for it." Susan blinks offline.

You immediately regret your decision. Whilst the DDoS protection option didn't fill you with confidence, you aren't exactly flush with alternatives. You watch the perimeter defence software beep and boop away. It's really quite therapeutic to look at when the company isn't on fire.

The little shapes representing servers and network devices are like your own ant colony. You fondly watch over your empire, narrating a backstory for the different pieces of kit (in your head, of course; you wouldn't want people to think you're crazy).

There's a particularly picky firewall in your view, one that only sends packets to other firewalls. Then there is an internal firewall, Firewall F42, sending its data off into space. The switches are helping this data movement come to life, working tirelessly as ever.

You hum away as you desperately ask your brain for help, but your brain just shrugs and says it's not paid enough for this kind of effort. Wait. Why is an internal firewall sending data outside of the company? You zoom in on firewall F42.

As you study the firewall, the next wave of DDoS washes over the company's external estate. Firewall F42 isn't being targeted at all, and suddenly is sending more data outside of the company than ever before.

Continue exploring the situation in **Section 329.**

289 Phase Two—Preparation

Michael clasps his hands together and rests his chin on his knuckles. It suddenly dawns on you that he is a company director, and he may not be appreciating your cavalier approach. As much as Generico McCompany claims to have an open-door policy, that often only applies to people bearing good news, or snacks.

"It was disbanded as it didn't align with the board's objectives," he says.

It feels like his gaze penetrates down to your soul. Has it always been so hot in this room? A single bead of sweat runs down the back of your neck when the danger of the situation becomes clearer. The words catch in your throat as you prepare to reply, leading to a coughing fit. Michael doesn't offer you a water bottle from his mini-fridge.

Eventually the coughing fit subsides. You notice just how sharp the book on Michael's desk looks. That thing could easily slice through an employee who snoops where they shouldn't. You tactfully try to communicate your need to focus on the environmental aspect due to Golden Slug's modus operandi and ask if the project had potential for any environmental impact.

Michael takes a swig from his water bottle, further emphasising the fact that he didn't offer you any. "Degrada ran a small risk of irreversibly polluting an entire region's supply of water, but the profit associated meant it was almost certainly worth the risk."

You appreciate the honesty about the focus on profits, and ask Michael to confirm the project was disbanded.

"The board voted against it, yes. We put a line under Degrada and moved on."

The energy emanating from Michael is definitely cold.

Press Michael further in **Section 92**. If you are happy with what you've learned and happy to escape whilst you can, head to **Section 346.**

290 Phase Three—Attack

Maybe?

You fire a message containing 290 packets to the server. For a moment you feel overwhelming satisfaction, which is quickly replaced by devastation, as you realise you have now let NotNotCatya out of the bag. The virus spreads across Generico McCompany's IT estate like wildfire: every server, laptop or appliance that connects to the internet now displays a picture of a fat cat trying to eat an enormous cheeseburger. Underneath the cat picture is a textbox: "Excellent news, this device has been infected by NotNotCatya. To remove, send 100 bitcoins to this address."

The caption helpfully lists instructions on how to buy and transfer bitcoin, as well as a helpdesk support line.

> *This does actually happen. Bitcoin is a great way for hackers to monetise their exploits, as it's much harder to trace than traditional currency. As buying, selling and transferring bitcoin are not activities the average person is comfortable with, hackers genuinely will provide instructions and even sometimes phone support. In the end, they want your money, after all.*

Do you want to accept your fate and fight the NotNotCatya ransomware? If you want to try something rogue, you could always call the NotNotCatya helpdesk line.

Fight the ransomware in **Section 102**. Call the helpdesk in **Section 174**.

---

291 Phase Three—Attack

Nice. Don't you just hate it when people expect others to clean up after them?

Like a respectable member of society, you clean up after yourself, allowing other colleagues to seize your vacated seat immediately. You and Ruby make your way back up to the 13th floor to plan out the next course of action.

Guillaume greets you at your desk. "How was lunch?"

You spend precious seconds outlining how the ratio of lettuce to tomatoes meant your salad was a little lacklustre.

"Good, good. Anyway, Susan thinks Golden Slug also stole the SCAPI database," Guillaume informs you, before walking off far more casually then someone should after delivering that kind of bombshell.

Your legs give way and you slump into your chair.

Ruby picks up the severity of the situation. "I am guessing the SCAPI database is important?"

You inform her that important is an understatement, SCAPI stands for Seriously Controversial And Potentially Incriminating. That database is a Pandora's box of morally dubious project plans and coverups.

> These kinds of things do exist; they wouldn't normally get quite such an "on the nose" name, though.

"Why keep all of that in one place?"

You admit you had identified it as a problem on day one, but the CEO herself accepted the risk. Now that your legs will work again, you and Ruby rush over to Susan's office.

Susan is talking to someone from HR, whom she sends packing with the line "I am not interested in hiring someone who chews gum in an interview", before beckoning you and Ruby in.

You ask Susan what she knows about the SCAPI database potentially being stolen.

"There is no 'potentially' about it, sadly," she replies.

Find out how she can be so sure in **Section 197**.

---

292 Phase Three—Attack

After giving Susan an update on the current situation, you wheel around to return to the fray, but she stops you.

"Hey, Michael is bugging me that this Eduard guy is going to want access to some graphing software."

You answer that you have seen the request and will be looking at it soon.

"What do you mean? Eduard hasn't sent the request yet." Susan looks at you with confusion on her face.

You return the look with equal confusion. Then the penny drops. You tell Susan you need to go and walk swiftly out the door. Her eyes track you as she shakes her head, probably wondering what planet she recruited you from.

Arriving back at your desk, you send an email, then call a brains trust meeting with Guillaume and Vijaya, gathering them around your screen as you pull up the earlier request that came from "Eduard".

Vijaya picks up on it immediately. "That isn't a Generico McCompany email."

You agree with her, telling her you wondered what the macro they tried to get approved would do, so you forwarded it to Niko who is better suited to this kind of job. As if by magic, Niko appears.

See what he has to say in **Section 131.**

293 Phase Two—Preparation

You tell Jack to spill the beans and he does, eventually. First, he holds his information hostage, asking you to push an approval he needs from you through the system. Whereas you'd normally crush such blatant disregard for process under your shoes, you give in; after all, you need a lead.

After his little victory, Jack shares his findings. "We have a **ticket** to change the options when a customer calls in, you know, on the automated switchboard."

You confirm you do indeed know what he is talking about, having fallen victim to many an automated switchboard in your time.

"Well, when testing our implemented changes, we noticed the call recording process and one of the guys messed around with it a bit."

It seems safer not to ask what he even means by that, so you let him continue.

"Anyway, we found out that the system is not censoring out payment card details; the recording is supposed to deactivate when card numbers are shared, but it doesn't." That is juicy indeed.

> This means the call recording database is a very lucrative meal ticket if someone like Golden Slug ever got in there, because the call recordings now contain payment card data.

Good to know. You thank Jack and set a meeting up with Susan the following day to share this update. There isn't enough time to sort it now and as long as there is no evidence of anyone abusing the loophole currently, it would be premature to hit the "panic" button.

That night at home, you take a bath until your fingers shrivel up and resemble a prune, then watch 5/10-standard television.

Get some sleep and go back into work in **Section 349.**

294 Phase Three—Attack

Unorthodox. If this is your first instinct, have you considered becoming a **penetration tester***?*

Before even trying to hack Fesrodah yourself, you drop a line to an external acquaintance who goes by the alias "Shellmaster". You don't quite trust them enough to be able to call them a friend. You met them online in a chat forum many years ago, and whilst you decided to pursue a traditional career, Shellmaster did not.

Shellmaster has never actually revealed to you how they make their money. You've never asked either, as you'd rather not know, but needless to say it's through hacking. However, what Shellmaster lacks in morals they make up for in skill, and over the years they've proven a useful ally when skirting the boundary between white and black hat activity. Today you are going to need to skirt harder than you've ever skirted before.

White hat hackers work within the bounds of the law; black hat hackers don't mind breaking the law. The whole "white hats are the good guys and black hats are the bad guys" notion is said to originate from old Western films, where with black-and-white television and a lot of similar outfits, the only way to clearly differentiate between good guys and bad guys was the colour of their hat.

You communicate with Shellmaster via SMS. They tend to swap numbers every two weeks or so; again, you don't feel the need to ask why. After you drop them a summary and outline your plan, they respond. "I hate Fesrodah, count me in. Going to probe their infrastructure now."

After a quick bathroom break and coffee refill, you call back to find they've already made progress.

"I have a lead, a very interesting potential exploit."

You ask what kind of exploit.

"The kind of exploit that reverses DDoS attacks away from the intended target, back towards whoever requested it."

You quickly piece it together: this means that you could send a DDoS attack back at Golden Slug. You check with Shellmaster whether you've understood properly.

"Yes."

Try to reverse the DDoS in **Section 232.**

295 Phase Four—Aftermath

"Use this to buy whatever food, drink or equipment the incident response team need," Petra tells you.

You ask if you wouldn't be better positioned helping with the clean-up process.

"No, you've done enough damage already. The only thing I want you cleaning up is plates, cups and mugs."

Before you can say anything else, Susan ushers you out of the room.

Within the hour, the aforementioned government-recommended incident response team arrive, and they mean business. They all seem to have codenames; you don't even get an opportunity to suggest your own before they label you "liability". Ouch.

Over the course of the next week, the incident response team work on restoring the Generico McCompany network to the way it was before the ransomware attack hit. Your feet ache terribly by the time it's all over, what with having to make so many trips to the kitchen and supermarket to keep the team fuelled with hot drinks and chocolate bars.

Finally, things return to normal, but as soon as the systems are up and running again, Susan takes the opportunity to have you sacked.

The End.

> *A bit of a shame, as you were doing really well in phase two. Golden Slug set out the rules for the logic bomb pretty clearly. I won't tell you how you failed the quiz (as there are a few ways to fail), but feel free to send any emails of complaint to hello@goldenslug.com. Anyway, don't let this little hiccup put you off. As I said, you were doing well in phase two. Try again and mix up your decisions a bit in phase three and see how things play out.*

296 Phase Three—Attack

You don't feel like conversation and hope that the kitchen has that perfect sweet spot of occupants to enable this. Nobody being in there is obviously very good, though it does run the risk of someone entering and creating the dreaded one-on-one situation. Absolute perfection is a very busy kitchen, where it's easy to get lost in the crowd.

You open the kitchen door and, just your luck, there is one person in there. The only thing to do is pray that they don't recognise or acknowledge you, allowing you both to sign a non-verbal agreement that the kitchen will be a silent room during your brief overlap.

"Hey, how you doing?" they ask, shattering your grand utopian dreams.

You reply that you are alright and ask how they are doing, hoping they keep the reply short, sweet and impossible to follow up with conversation.

"Yeah, I'm alright," they say, leaving the kitchen, gracefully signalling the end of this interaction.

You watch as the coffee machine fills your cup, suddenly envious of the machine's simple life. Make coffee, bring happiness and occasionally have milk left in you over the weekend; seems sweet. Sipping your drink, you reflect on how the coffee machine doesn't have to make decisions as seismic as the one you face now.

Going against Petra's plan is clearly the right thing to do morally, but it's career suicide, and staying quiet about it is the opposite.

Keep quiet in **Section 204** or leak the news in **Section 9**.

---

297 Phase Three—Attack

Baiting an enemy you don't really know seemed quite a wild move. This is much safer.

You reply telling her just to mention that an environmentalist activist group are subjecting the company to DDoS attacks and leave it there.

"Roger that," she replies and winks offline.

You let out a deep sigh. If you don't find something soon, that'll be another decision to heap on the day's regrets. A watched pot never boils, they say, but that doesn't stop you from flicking between your perimeter network monitoring software and the list of weakened firewalls.

Things get so bad you start convincing yourself that one of the firewall's numbers has changed. Before going into full meltdown mode, you realise it's only a smudge on your screen.

Whatever you do, don't blink. Eventually you do blink in **Section 299**.

---

298 Phase Three—Attack

I guess you are in pretty deep now, what's one lie going to do?

You email your thoughts to Cecilia in the PR team and CC Susan. Susan seems delighted by your "discovery" that the leaked data is fake. Her mood is further enhanced when you let her know that Golden Slug have now been kicked off the Generico McCompany network.

"I'm not going to lie, I thought you were out of your depth at one point," she lets you know, unhelpfully. You'll probably edit that sentence out when saving this entire experience into memory.

Over the following weeks, Susan fights your corner and earns you an excellent pay rise and a promotion. When your next birthday pops up, the company goes all-out and your cake has sprinkles on it. Nobody gets sprinkles on their cake unless you've made the big time.

The Chief Finance Officer sends you an email thanking you for not deciding to go for the option of taking the company offline to rectify the Golden Slug threat, mentioning that the revenue lost would have put many lives at risk. You sleep excellently for the next four months.

Find out if the good times keep rolling in **Section 112.**

---

299 Phase Three—Attack

As you open your eyes again, the clock strikes four o'clock and the DDoS attacks start again, with greater ferocity than ever before. It looks like Petra may have been right. You consider what would be the subtlest way of working on your CV in the middle of a crowded office. The outlook is bleak.

One of the firewalls unexpectedly starts to compile some fresh code. Whilst this would normally be bad news, it now gives you a faint glimmer of hope as you leap into action. The code appears to be preparing a new form of denial of service attack, one that originates from within Generico McCompany itself rather than from outside the network. The intricacy and detail of the code are horrifying. If it manages to run, it'll take Generico McCompany down entirely for weeks.

You have roughly five minutes to act, but you need to find out how the code got onto the firewall, or Golden Slug could redeploy it continuously until you get overwhelmed.

How did this code get in? It only could have been injected via one of the IP addresses in the allow list. You quickly delve deeper, looking for the route through which the code has been delivered. Your fingers grip your mouse so tightly your knuckles go white. The code didn't set off any alarms because it came from Vijaya's account. You swivel your head and see she's working away, seemingly oblivious.

There isn't much time to shut this down. You are going to need Susan to authorise the changes required to get it fixed. Do you think Vijaya is a **malicious insider** or an innocent bystander in all of this who had her credentials phished?

Point the malicious insider finger in **Section 73.** If you think she's innocent, go to **Section 226.**

300 Phase Two—Preparation

Good call. Of the options provided, the potentially exposed payment card data was an excellent place to start.

As you investigate the stored call recordings, an image of a swimming pool full of gold coins springs to mind. Your call recording software is supposed to stop recording when the customer provides their payment card details, and then restart once that part of the process is complete. Typically, you'd expect there might be one or two instances of failure, as with any software. But at least in that instance a potential hacker would have to listen to countless recordings before they were able to harvest the details of a single payment card.

Disastrously, your call recording software is failing to stop recording 100% of the time (or is succeeding in failing 100% of the time, depending on your outlook). You listen to a few recordings to confirm this, including two recordings where an old woman and a young man separately order the same device designed to remove nasal hairs using a miniature flamethrower. Aside from you wondering whether that demographic overlap had been predicted by marketing, crucially in both instances the full payment card data is there in the recording, a sitting duck to be taken and sold to fraudsters on the dark web.

Prices of stolen card details will range with the financial climate. Cards are sold in packages, containing hundreds or thousands of card details and the percentage of the cards that are thought to be usable. Like with any product there is spoilage: cards that become too old and aren't active any more, cards that the owner loses and has cancelled, or cards that other fraudsters have used, meaning the bank has already cancelled them.

For a moment you are half tempted to try selling some yourself.

Try selling the card details in **Section 344.** Or start planning how to tackle the issue in **Section 243.**

301 Phase Four—Aftermath

A fair choice. Since Golden Slug are known to be motivated by money, a tool that is used to buy things seems a good fallback option for them if they can't get their hands on payment card data.

Opening up the Generico McCompany procurement tool is like taking a trip back in time: the user interface resembles the first days of the internet, full of bright contrasting colours and unused white space. To be fair, the user interface is actually pleasant to look at when compared to the backend code that holds it all together. That code looks like it was compiled by hitting a keyboard with a rolling pin repeatedly. Generico McCompany's rationale for the outdated procurement tool is pretty simple: spending money is bad, and spending money on upgrading the tool that enables people to spend money is even worse.

The slow loading times and clunky interface are just obstacles that are placed in front of the user to ensure they really do need whatever they planned to purchase. Anyone attempting to purchase something through the portal doesn't only need money, they also need the patience of a saint.

After digging into the changes processed by the application, you discover that the administrator account changes were actually quite simple: they merely switched out the supplier contracted to perform some routine maintenance within Generico McCompany retail stores. It will be hard to tell whether the changes were instigated by a genuine administrator account user or Golden Slug, without first heading over to talk to the project manager in charge of the project.

Keep pursuing this lead in **Section 82.**

---

302 Phase Two—Preparation

"Of course. I'm going to dip into another meeting soon, but I should have a comment back to you by the end of the day. Is that OK?"

You thank her and hang up. At least Francine is having a good time. You figure that as it is almost lunchtime, and you don't have enough time to do anything productive, it would be sensible to have lunch early.

You've forgotten to pack a lunch today, so decide to take your chances in the office canteen. You order two slices of pepperoni pizza with a side of salad to stem the guilt, and have a seat with some colleagues. You know them well enough to eat with them, but wouldn't stretch as far as to call them friends.

Vijaya also sits on Susan's team. Somehow her vegan tofu lasagne smells more appealing than your pepperoni pizza. You don't get much time to dwell on this unfortunate truth, though, as she spends the meal period probing you on your Golden Slug investigation. It seems Susan has got Vijaya researching it too.

Golden Slug quickly becomes the talk of the table, but you decide to stay vague in your replies. Partly because it's good practice, but mostly because so far you have nothing concrete to contribute. Mercifully your lunch break ends, you scrape the majority of your pizza into the bin and you shuffle back to your desk.

You are greeted by an email from Francine. It informs you that the testers don't think the vulnerability is anything to do with a DDoS attack and the name of the vulnerability is simply a red herring.

Didn't I already tell you that?

You receive a text message on your work phone from an unknown number.

Read the text message in **Section 116.**

---

303 Phase Two—Preparation

That's better. Knowing that there is a history of developers inserting potentially vulnerable code into Generico McCompany's e-commerce websites made this the significantly more logical choice.

You notice with surprise that the developer you saw sleeping first thing in the morning is still asleep, and nobody seems to care. As you walk closer to the developer area, you witness what first appears to be a very strange ritual, but ends up being much more innocent.

A young man with a ferocious ginger beard appears to be talking to a rubber duck sitting on his desk. "I told the application to reset the password based on the time of day. The password saved in storage follows the same process. Why would they sync differently?"

The rubber duck looks forward with a blank expression.

"Of course, the application's calendar isn't accounting for leap years." The man leans forward to pat the rubber duck on the head before shifting his attention to his keyboard, presumably to teach the application about leap years. As useful as it clearly is, the rubber duck technique will always look weird.

True story: speaking about problems out loud can make it easier to see where you are going wrong. The rubber duck technique is real, I should add. Look it up.

It dawns on you that there is no polite way for you to conduct your investigation. The question you need answering is: "Have you guys messed up and introduced **vulnerabilities** into Generico McCompany e-commerce applications?" Sugarcoating it won't really be possible.

Rather than going straight for the kill, you lay some polite conversational groundwork first. You start a conversation about the merits of a standing desk and ask the developers how they enjoy theirs. The bait works: they begin to wax lyrical about standing desks.

You've lured them in, now probe for information in **Section 356.**

---

304 Phase Two—Preparation

This is a solid place to begin. So far you know Golden Slug target payment card data. Looking at what vulnerabilities your e-commerce websites have exposed to the internet is a logical starting point.

Naturally, the **vulnerability** scan report hasn't been saved in the folder called "Vulnerability Reports". Instead you find it in a folder called "Security2". You wonder about the baffling lack of a "Security1" or even a "Security" folder. Upon opening the Security2 folder, you see that the most recent vulnerability scan was from a month ago and it didn't pick up anything noteworthy.

You fire up one of Generico McCompany's e-commerce websites. Credit where credit is due to the development guys, the presentation is slick and you almost want to buy a degrogulator 421 model, even though you don't have any grog to degrogulate. You right click the page and view the web page's code. You don't really know what you're looking for and you don't really know what any of the code means, but it makes you feel like a hacker.

Code often is obfuscated (scrambled) to prevent easy reading and therefore manipulation of it. This also allows developers to get away with errors that would have been spotted if the code were readable.

You notice a **penetration test** report saved in the Security2 folder that you remember conducting only a couple of weeks ago. It could be worth a look. Alternatively, it could be helpful to talk to the marketing team and ask what they've requested the developers to change in the e-commerce websites lately, to see if anything stands out as suspicious or risky.

Open the penetration test report in **Section 367** or talk to marketing in **Section 320.**

305 Phase Three—Attack

Too right, what on earth was he on about?

The press release goes out. Although the PR team will need to field some tricky questions about why an environmentalist group are attacking Generico McCompany, it could be worse. You decide to embrace the Cyber Pirates' quirkiness and sit with them in the canteen as they plunder the day's menu. Pedro the Parrot poses for photos whilst he eats a simple meal of sweetcorn; apparently he dislikes meat and he won't touch any food that's been near any form of it. Who knew parrots were fussy eaters?

Once lunch finishes, you all move back upstairs and return to the task at hand. Your focus is squarely on directing the infrastructure team towards whatever needs repairing each time Golden Slug's waves of attacks hit. You feel like a military general, moving troops around the field to counter the enemy's movements. In this scenario there is no death, only lost revenue, which to some people in the corporate ladder is even more important.

After hours of manoeuvring your troops, First Mate Gloria taps you on the shoulder, jolting you out of your military make-believe world and instead into a pirate-themed make-believe world.

"Batten down the hatches, I've found something, and you are not going to like it." On her screen she's got a visual representation of the company's network. There is a red dot in one section with a list of numbers next to it. First Mate Gloria points at the numbers. "We have evidence that your data is being accessed remotely via these **IP** addresses."

That doesn't sound good at all.

Find out if it is indeed bad news in **Section 256.**

306 Phase Three—Attack

Don't worry, you aren't penalised for this; in fact you end up on a slightly better path.

You were never particularly lucky and have had to get by purely on hard work so far in your career, you muse as you piece together the code's timeline. You conclude that the code has been active for two weeks, and share this with Charlotte.

"Is that how long you'll need to figure out how long Golden Slug have been stealing card data?"

You retort that no, that is how long whoever is attacking has been stealing card data, and you can't be sure it is Golden Slug at this stage.

Charlotte frowns, or she frowns more, as her face always looks like it's frowning. "It seems like something they'd do, but I suppose you are right, we cannot be sure yet." She super-frowns at having to admit you were right.

Rather than rub it in, you prioritise Generico McCompany and work on disabling Dragarock completely, an action that immediately brings Giuseppa, the owner of Generico McCompany's e-commerce portfolio, to your desk.

"You turned off our profiling software. Now our pages will be trying to sell non-flammable matches to pensioners!" she exclaims, flapping her arms wildly.

After you explain what Dragarock was doing to payment card data, Giuseppa bows her head and slinks off. The fines from stolen payment card data will put a dent in her end-of-year bonus.

Cry her a river in **Section 220.**

307 Phase Three—Attack

Instead of a breakthrough, you receive a message on internal chat as Cecilia's name flashes in the corner of your screen.

"Do you want us to make reference to Golden Slug's activity in this press release?"

Interesting, you muse as you stroke your chin, the option of laying a trap for Golden Slug presenting itself. By asking Cecilia to be boisterous about things in her press release, you might encourage Golden Slug to check in on their firewall plan and give their game away, since you'll be sitting there monitoring the **logs** in real time. Alternatively, you could ask Cecilia to barely mention it, keeping Golden Slug in the dark for the moment, giving you more time to hopefully have your breakthrough.

Before you can reply to Cecilia, Susan also sends you a message. "Petra just left my office. She is fuming over the fact we haven't upped our DDoS defence. Please tell me that decision has been vindicated?"

You reply that you are almost there and working on it. Susan blinks offline, which is a relief: you didn't want to know where that conversation was going. You click back into Cecilia's chat tab and type out your reply.

Bait Golden Slug in **Section 318**; avoid deliberately baiting them in **Section 297**.

---

308 Phase Two—Preparation

Excellent, the kind of person whose zip definitely isn't undone. Did you just look?

Opening up the penetration test report reinforces that the due diligence was worthwhile. You are presented with a slick report that clearly identifies problems and prioritises them based on factors such as the ease with which the vulnerabilities could be exploited and the impact this would have on the business. It's even intelligent enough to recognise when two vulnerabilities interact to multiply the impact.

*For example, having an application that does not protect against **brute force** attacks, combined with it also having weak password complexity rules.*

The penetration test report on Generico McCompany's e-commerce websites contains a total of 76 unique vulnerabilities. That's not too bad, really, considering the sheer number of e-commerce websites the company runs.

The report was only written last week, so not all of the findings will have been actioned yet. It will be worth seeing whether any of the findings' remediations need to be fast tracked. Sifting through the penetration test report ends up taking a large amount of your morning, not so much due to the report being badly written, but because people keep interrupting your train of thought.

You come very close to breaking point when you are interrupted by a colleague who has mistaken you for someone else. You decide it'll be less awkward just to help them and ignore their mistake. The feeling of satisfaction at helping a human in need is wiped away when it becomes clear you've lost count of which of the vulnerabilities you have and haven't reviewed yet.

Looking up from your desk, you notice that the office is a hive of activity, with people walking around excitedly, which can only mean one thing: lunch.

You have two vulnerabilities circled as potentially worth exploring further: "cross-site scripting" and "administrative console exposed". But they can wait until after food.

You take the lift down to the canteen, speculating with colleagues what will be on the menu for the day. The menus are publicly available on the intranet, but for some people the lunch mystery roulette is the most excitement in their day.

Arrive at the canteen in **Section 128.**

---

309 Phase Three—Attack

If the intrusion detection software is configured well, it could offer leads to follow up on. But the problem is, what if Golden Slug breached the company months ago and left behind changes to code/systems that meant the payment cards in question were sent out automatically?

The Generico McCompany intrusion detection software (IDS) had been installed for years without anyone ever actually looking at it. The renewal date comes along and somehow another year's worth of licence is signed off. This has led many people to convince themselves that the IDS is doing a great job. Because there didn't seem to be any internal intrusions, there was no need for staff time to handle the software and it sat quietly in the background doing its thing. In your second month at Generico McCompany you had explored the IDS and discovered that in the five years it had been installed it had never been turned on.

Turning it on initially had proved to be a bad move, as suddenly it flickered into life and immediately detected over a million instances of what it believed were genuine hacker intrusions. Many months of fine tuning actually had brought the IDS to a condition where it is generating a more reasonable number of alerts per day, most of these false positives, but you have managed to catch the occasional low-sophistication attack in the act.

As you launch the IDS application today, you have one question for it: where are Golden Slug? There are two events that stand out as worthwhile leads on the IDS dashboard. One is on the Insuremytoupee e-commerce website and one is in a folder with no name, but you can see the folder is full of MP3 files.

Check out Insuremytoupee in **Section 33.** Look into the MP3 files in **Section 202.**

---

310 Phase Two—Preparation

You suspect that the chat might persist during the payment process, potentially allowing the chat support staff member to view the shopper's payment card details being entered, but once the payment process starts you see that the whole TLK2ME process gets shut down.

You wonder if TLK2ME support staff or a malicious actor could use the chat interface to pass **malware** to users, but notice that it is designed to allow only **plain text** communication, so that idea is also a dead end. You explore various other attack vectors, but find nothing wrong with TLK2ME; they even have a robust process for pushing out new software versions to prevent a hacker from tricking companies into updating TLK2ME with the hacker's modified version.

After interrogating the code and coming up with nothing, you conclude the only logical thing to do is go home. On your way home you stop to buy a lottery ticket; well-written code is such a rarity you feel the need to try to capitalise on your luck.

> There have actually been several real-world high-profile cases of chatbots either containing malware, or being used to distribute malware, so your thinking had merit. TLK2ME merely ended up not being impacted.

That evening you watch as your lottery numbers lose, then binge on a series of unambitious TV shows. Hours seems to melt together; you remember eating dinner but have no recollection of what you ate, or when, or whether it was any good. You're clearly tired. Go to bed.

Head into work the following day to continue investigating Golden Slug in **Section 223**.

---

311 Phase Three—Attack

> You will struggle to find anyone who officially endorses the idea of paying a ransom, but it is definitely considered sometimes and there have been high-profile cases of it happening.

You announce your preference to pay the ransom, as it's clear Golden Slug have your number by this point. Susan asks what guarantees Generico McCompany could ask for when paying the ransom.

"None. Also I need to state for the record I am not on board with this," Ruby replies.

Susan sighs deeply and stands up. "I will go and have a very fun conversation with our Chief Financial Officer, then. Whilst I am doing that, can we work out how they got the SCAPI database to begin with? The last thing I need is to get approval for this $10 million only for them to reveal more stolen files and up the ransom."

You leave the room to act on Susan's wishes, which are logical. It is actually quite impressive that Golden Slug even knew to target the SCAPI database, as only 20 people across the entire company have access to it. It doesn't take long to find the source of the leak. Ever the helpful soul, Doris in the customer liaison team has replied to a phishing email with her username and password. It's not even a good phishing email, it comes from phishing@goldenslug.com and she fell for it. The worst thing is, you aren't surprised.

To be safe, you double-check whether anyone else fell for this phishing attack and find three other victims, although calling them victims is perhaps generous. Doris's account is the only one Golden Slug bothered using. You reset the passwords for all the compromised accounts and take a note of the names so the account holders can be assigned to additional phishing awareness training.

Find out what happens with Susan in **Section 341.**

---

312 Phase Two—Preparation

Seeing as you've proven yourself unreliable when purchasing information security services, phoning a friend was the stronger choice. Unless they are equally incompetent, of course.

Pulling out your Generico McCompany's work mobile in all its ugly grey plastic glory, you punch in your friend Veronika's number and dial, walking over to one of the miniature meeting rooms. After exchanging formalities and a bit of gossip with her, you broach the subject of Golden Slug.

"Ah yes, those guys came after us a few months ago."

You ask her what happened.

"Nothing, really. They managed to get access to our network, but we caught them snooping around our call recording data. Forensics afterwards found they had got in via a vulnerability in the Checkout Fireworks software we use, you know, the one that makes fireworks appear on the screen after someone buys something."

You indeed do know of Checkout Fireworks, and know that Generico McCompany decided not to bother with it, opting for sound effects instead. You inform her that upper management put a stop to Checkout Fireworks and ask if she has any other ideas of where to look.

"Well, if I were you, I'd take a look at the latest pen test that was performed."

You wince as Veronika rubs salt and lemon onto the wound. Out of shame you play along and don't admit what happened with the pen test you bought. You thank her for her suggestion and finish up the call. You decide to have a look at the status of your own call recording data.

See what you find in **Section 196.**

313 Phase Three—Attack

The lift doors slide open to welcome you and Charlotte back to the 13th floor. As you both walk back towards the IT section of the office, Charlotte is occupied glancing at her phone. You feel pleased to have converted an enemy into an ally.

When you arrive back at your desk, Guillaume rains on your parade. "Susan is looking for both of you, something to do with **business email compromise fraud.**"

Charlotte looks at you and remarks, "That is not going to look good in my report." With that, the smug smirk is back on her lips.

You rush over to Susan's office and almost earn first-degree burns by running straight into an ambitious colleague carrying six coffee mugs on a tray.

After you knock on the door and enter, Susan wastes no time. "We've been had. Someone, probably Golden Slug, sent a perfectly faked email chain impersonating me and Petra, asking for an invoice to get paid as soon as possible."

You ask how much the invoice was for.

"$20 million. The payment has gone and the bank say it can't be recovered. Charlotte, what do you make of this?" Susan asks, as Charlotte enters the room.

"Well, for starters, I know that I wouldn't have left for an hour's lunch if the company was under live attack, especially when there was known Golden Slug activity that was unaccounted for." Charlotte looks at you with a sneer.

Feel the pain of betrayal in **Section 364.**

314 Phase One—Prologue

The kitchen is heaving, filled with the raucous chatter of colleagues sharing semi-amusing anecdotes, fuelled by their drink of choice and renewed optimism. You overhear titbits of conversation, including that the local sports teams had both an incredible and an awful weekend, and that some guy called Andrew is about to have an HR complaint land on their doorstep soon.

It's only 08:45, but the sink is already a bubbling cauldron of awfulness, overfilled with half-washed cups, bowls and plates, all floating in a foul liquid. The tables are bare, save for a few crumbs of stale cake left over from yet another birthday celebration that happened on Friday. Unsurprisingly in an office with over 3000 employees, birthday celebrations are a frequent occurrence. The kitchen walls are adorned with motivational posters, including cats clinging to clothes lines and dogs looking up aspirationally towards the moon.

You're surprised to see that building management have finally allowed your user awareness poster to go up, reminding employees always to wear their work pass. You look proudly at the image of an old man holding a baseball bat with the caption "No security **lanyard**? That's gonna be trouble! Remember: Green for employees, yellow for temporary staff, and red for guests."

Again, things to remember.

A quick glance around shows you that the message is being received. Excellent. When you started at Generico McCompany, people seemed to treat their lanyards like uranium and wanted them anywhere except round their neck. "Celebrate the small victories," you think, as the crowd thins to the point where you can approach the brewing station. It's time to make your choice. You place your mug under the nozzle. What will it be?

The decision of what drink you want actually branches the story in completely different directions. So even if you are a solid supporter of one drink, make sure to try the other options, or you're essentially halving the value of this book.

Get some coffee in **Section 250**, pour a tea in **Section 161,** or drink boiling water in **Section 141.**

---

315 Phase Three—Attack

As you bask in the glory of finding something that Charlotte didn't, you spot Susan appearing in your field of vision. She stops a few steps away from Charlotte's desk and appears to mentally psych herself up before asking for an update, which Charlotte provides. Charlotte doesn't bother to mention how Golden Slug have also compromised the corporate email system.

Turning to you, Susan barks orders. "Get Dragarock out of any Generico McCompany website immediately. If anyone comes and complains, tell them to talk to me about it. Also get them out of our email system."

You confirm you'll carry out Susan's orders and salute her, for some odd reason.

"With any luck, if Golden Slug have only been stealing payment card data for four days, the regulator won't come down too hard on us," she continues, deciding to ignore your salute.

"That will depend greatly on the output of my report," Charlotte teases, without suggesting whether Generico McCompany are doing well or not in her eyes.

For a few blissful seconds you daydream about strangling Charlotte. Sadly, good things can't last for ever and you are dragged back to reality to make a decision.

Try the email server lead in **Section 59**. Look into the HR system in **Section 283**.

---

316 Phase Three—Attack

But that's a lie! I won't penalise you, though: whatever needs doing, and it's not like Fesrodah are innocent.

"Hello, how are you doing today?" a different voice asks.

You seize the initiative. You let the voice know that you are very well and you are looking to speak to someone in relation to the Stresser service.

"Fesrodah have a wide range of services. Before connecting you to a customer support agent, I will quickly provide an overview of our most popular offerings."

You let the voice know that isn't necessary, but it cuts you off and continues with its pitch. It would appear this is still an automated message. Your only choice is to wait and see what happens.

"Fesrodah's Stresser service has now helped 10,000 customers prepare for DDoS attacks. You simply enter the **IP** range that you want to test and Stresser replicates a real-life DDoS attack so you can see how your network copes.

"Fesrodah's whack-a-mole service is ideal for companies looking to uncover potential **malicious insider**s. Fesrodah secretly contacts staff in your company and sees which employees are willing to provide their username and password, access badge or internal documents in exchange for money. With this information, customers can remove these employees from the company, enhancing their information security stance.

"Fesrodah's anti**virus** integrity checker service empowers customers to check whether malicious files would be detected by the world's leading antivirus software tools. Fesrodah's report also outlines what changes to the malicious file would lead to evasion of antivirus software, empowering customers to stay one step ahead of cybercriminals."

*I had a lot of fun brainstorming these, only to discover that a lot of services like this are genuinely offered on the **dark web**.*

"Thank you for holding," the voice finishes. "You are now being forwarded to a customer services representative."

See if you really are in **Section 115.**

317 Phase Two—Preparation

You ask Jorge what the right kind of cinnamon is.

His eyebrows rise in surprise. "Come now, you are telling me you can't instantly taste the difference between Mexican and Alba cinnamon?"

You concede that you can't.

The entire marketing team look at you with horror. Jorge is well respected. This faux pas leads to your immediate termination at Generico McCompany.

The End.

*Ouch, that didn't end well. Tell you what, why don't we hit the rewind button and send you back to **Section 320** so you can try that again?*

318 Phase Three—Attack

I hope you know what you are doing…

Cracking your knuckles, you grin and craft out the wording for Cecilia to use in her press release.

"Generico McCompany have been targeted by the **hacktivist** group Golden Slug. Since this news first started to circulate, the group's initial DDoS attack has proven unsuccessful. In addition, Generico McCompany have identified a secondary attack mechanism planned by Golden Slug, which is currently being neutralised."

That will put the cat amongst the pigeons. Cecilia issues the press release and it doesn't take long for it to provoke a reaction.

Vijaya asks what the second attack mechanism is so she can contribute to the remediation effort. You are forced to concede it's a bluff, but both her and Guillaume think it's a good idea. In your head you've propped a trap box up with a stick, you've now baited the box with a carrot, and all that's left is for Golden Slug to take the carrot and get trapped.

In your scenario the next step wasn't for one of the company's most lucrative business units just to get shut down, but that is indeed what happens. Somehow Golden Slug have started attacks from within your own network rather than from outside. It seems that you've trapped them in the box, but they are nibbling their way out.

As a very much needed positive, though, Guillaume apparently now knows how to blunt their attacks and kick them off the network.

See how that pans out in **Section 212.**

---

319 Phase Two—Preparation

The meeting continues, outlining the number of potentially impacted civilians, amongst other considerations. Eventually, conversation turns to your domain,

"We must assume that Generico is in Golden Slug's crosshairs. The second this hits the news, how can we protect ourselves?" Michael asks.

Before you can open your mouth to explain that you started your investigation under the fair assumption that the company wasn't running an undercover nuclear facility and so hadn't yet started to look at defensive **controls**, Susan saves the day.

"My team identified weaknesses in our firewalls that make us vulnerable, but each **firewall** would need to be individually updated, as the mass updater won't work for this fix."

"And how long would it take to roll that update out to all the firewalls?" Michael presses.

"It's estimated to take between five and six months, Michael. It's a big estate and I have a small team," is Susan's riposte.

You can't help but think how eagle-like Georgios appears, shifting his head to look at whoever talks and silently observing them. Has he spoken a word in the past hour?

Susan appears to notice the time and moves to wrap things up. "Right, we are all up to date on the situation, and for all we know Cecilia's team can get this swept under the carpet so that the security team won't have anything to worry about."

The look on Cecilia's face makes you think this is unlikely. The meeting concludes and you head to your desk.

Check out what is happening in **Section 241.**

---

320 Phase Two—Preparation

Dealer's choice there: both options had their merits.

Christelle from finance ambushes you as you walk towards the wing of the building where marketing and sales live. She is incensed that the software licence for one of the tools you use has increased from $150 to $160 and is threatening to deny the purchase order request. You consider telling her to dock the $10 from your pay to save the hassle, but instead resolve the situation by accepting her offer of an hour's meeting next week to run through a budget request defence. A one-hour meeting with two people in a room to justify a $10 price increase is the kind of bureaucracy you wake up for.

The marketing team's area of the office is particularly vibrant and colourful. One wall is covered from floor to ceiling in sticky notes, each featuring an energetic adjective: innovative, game changing, flamboyant. A new recruit is admiring the wall of sticky notes, scratching their chin and trying to inspire themselves for the day.

Jorge, who runs the team, is daydreaming at his desk. He's got a model T Rex next to his keyboard. He notices you and swivels in his chair to say hello. His shirt is decorated with pineapples.

You greet Jorge and ask him how he is doing.

"I'm good, man. The coffee shop didn't have the right kind of cinnamon for my hot chocolate, but I don't hold grudges."

Ask what the right kind of cinnamon is in **Section 317**, or get to the matter at hand in **Section 217**.

---

321 Phase Three—Attack

Counter attacking or "hacking back" as it's known is something more typical of a government or national security group. Private companies don't typically do this, but never say never.

You let Susan know you plan to fight cyberfire with cyberfire. She raises an eyebrow at this. "I didn't think I paid you enough to be able to do that."

Ouch. She slinks off, allowing you to apply aloe vera to that burn.

You can see that the packets from the DDoS attack all come from a similar range of source IPs. A quick lookup shows this belongs to a company called Fesrodah, operating in a "morally questionable" country. The company offers "stress testing" to their clients; clearly, someone has aimed their services at you. You could work with legal to try to get them to stop.

Alternatively, you could give your own black hat a workout by trying to turn Fesrodah's services off yourself, taking on the hackers at their own game.

Explore legal options in **Section 281**. Try hacking back in **Section 294**.

---

322 Phase Four—Aftermath

But that isn't the end of the matter. With their last act on the Generico McCompany network, Golden Slug manged to send a rushed and poorly worded email from Petra the CEO's email to a middle manager in the finance department, requesting an invoice be paid. Naturally, the middle manager identified that it wasn't a genuine invoice and blocked the payment and… Who are you kidding? They paid the invoice without any questions.

It's only on the last day of the month when the accounts are tallied that the multi-million-dollar discrepancy is discovered, far too late for the bank to recall the money.

After an initial flurry of head scratching and trying to understand what happened, things get pieced together and it reaches a point where people want to attribute blame. As CISO, you're the prime target. Whilst you did a good job preventing Golden Slug's initial attack on the e-commerce websites, your hastiness in evicting Golden Slug before understanding their game plan enabled the **business email compromise** attack to go unnoticed.

Generico McCompany decide to send you on some advanced training courses that teach you a lot, but also erode your soul. Susan admits to you down the line that there was some pressure to see you kicked out of the business, but she was able to fend it off.

The End

> *Close call. You can chalk this as a half victory, as many of the endings include you losing your job. It would have been even better in the context of this book if you'd held your nerve and let Galactic Cyber observe Golden Slug a bit longer. In fairness, in the real world that might have been the wrong call; did I ever mention that this industry can be a bit grey? Try reading through again, but make some intentionally bad choices early on and watch how differently the story can flow.*

323 Phase Two—Preparation

The day promises to be like any other, except it isn't in every way imaginable. You are given a freebie tub of ice cream on the train into work, but no spoon to eat it with, and so it has turned into a melted soup of cream by the time you reach your desk. You then notice that Cecilia from public relations looks stressed; Cecilia never looks stressed. In fact, come to think of it you never see her around the IT part of the office. What is she doing here?

Cecilia hurries up to you. "Crisis meeting in meeting room six," she says, before dashing off to gather more participants.

You frown, wondering what could be going on.

Why attend at all? If you want to bail on the meeting, hide in **Section 264**.

As you enter the meeting room, it appears that Cecilia has gathered her own crack squad. You can see Michael (COO), Vijaya (IT Backup Manager), Gesa (Project Manager), Cecilia (Public Relations), Georgios (Legal) and Susan (IT Director). Nobody seems to have had their morning coffee yet. Regardless, Cecilia's news acts like a shot of espresso directly into the brain.

"We've had a nuclear spill at our rechargeable battery factory. Apparently, the factory is known as Degrada or Luminec?"

"It's interchangeable," confirms Michael with a shrug.

"It's left a water reservoir irradiated, impacting countless local villages," Cecilia continues, looking around the table.

Again, Michael shrugs. A lightbulb goes off in your head.

"Interesting as this is, why are IT here?" Susan asks.

You know the answer.

Announce why in **Section 237.**

---

324 Phase Two—Preparation

How is irritating the one person who might be able to help you a good idea?

You point out that might not have happened if they had been a better CISO. They don't even bother dignifying that with a reply and hang up. You stare at the handset, trying to justify why on earth you did that. In the end, the only explanation you have is that you are feeling kind of evil.

You spend the rest of the day in similarly evil ways, filling custard doughnuts with toothpaste, placing cello tape at the bottom of people's computer mouse (and a real mouse) and the like. The crescendo is a brilliant placement of a "Cleaning in progress" sign outside the kitchen, leading to many people being unable to claim their last caffeine fix of the day, overall costing the company millions of dollars in lost productivity. The clock chimes to signal the end of work and you set off home, making sure to send the lift to all 42 floors of the building as you step out.

As soon as you leave the office, the universe decides to rebalance the karma scale. A pigeon, a seagull and a magpie all manage to hit you with "gifts" on your way home. Two buses and six cars splash you with water. Your favourite TV show is cancelled in place of your least favourite show in the world; as you try to change the channel the TV breaks completely, the volume boosts to maximum and the show just won't turn off, even after you unplug the power cable.

You decide to go to bed. The sound of construction work, loud car music and sirens keeps you awake for many hours. Eventually the universe grinds back into its normal position and your karma levels return to normal, allowing you to go to sleep.

Wake up, try being less evil and go into work in **Section 8.**

---

325 Phase Three—Attack

With the payment processing application now clear, you turn your attention to the email server. Either Golden Slug had a heads up that your investigation would bring you here next, or they simply were never that interested. There are absolutely no signs that Golden Slug were able to achieve anything in the email server, or even that they attempted to.

Opening up your perimeter defence tool shows no new communications with the Golden Slug server. You decide to apply some network rules to forbid any further connection to Golden Slug IP addresses. Clearly, the action is trivial enough that Charlotte doesn't feel the need to **shoulder surf** to ensure it's done properly. With that achieved, thankfully it's now time to say goodbye to Charlotte.

"I will make sure to send you my write-up before we issue a press statement," Charlotte tells Susan, before wishing her a good day and leaving without saying a single word more to you.

It takes a full week for the office to feel like a safe space again. You hear Charlotte's fingernails clattering on desks everywhere you go, and even the office kettle has started to sound like her now. She is inside your head. Eventually the nightmare ends, and you can go back to your normal routine, full of last-minute requests and people falling for **phishing** emails; the high life. A few weeks later the report from the National Fraud Office hits Susan's desk.

Find out what it says in **Section 136**.

---

326 Phase Two—Preparation

This is the less useful of the two options. The five firewalls may all have gone offline and then rebooted with no consequence; in all likelihood those outages were nothing to do with Golden Slug. Knowing what those firewalls would look like if a DDoS attack forced them to restart would be beneficial against all DDoS scenarios, not only Golden Slug.

As luck would have it, each of the five firewalls that fell over in the past 12 months is from a separate continent, making tracking down the infrastructure team who manage them extra difficult. Two of the firewalls are in areas that are now in non-working hours, so they are a no-go (you are only meant to contact out-of-hours support teams in emergency situations). That still gives you three viable leads, so you ping out an instant message to those three infrastructure owners.

You copy and paste a message to all three owners, forgetting to change the name of the person in your greeting. Thankfully, Lucas doesn't seem to mind being called "David" and the other person you messaged also happens to be called David, so no harm done. To each of the owners you briefly outline your investigation and ask a few questions relating to the nature of the outages the firewalls have undergone.

All three need to check their **logs** before they can provide you with any details, giving you time to browse the national news as you wait. As it turns out, one went offline due to a power outage, while the other two were knocked over by slightly above average traffic. Lucas's firewall was taken out by the power cut, so you proceed to interrogate both of the Davids, careful to keep your notes separate.

See what they say in **Section 93.**

---

327 Phase Two—Preparation

This seems the stronger option. Vlad in recruitment could have been given a list of job roles and specifications without necessarily knowing how it all ties together. As Jennifer had overall oversight, she is a more promising lead.

You message Jennifer and let her know you've got a quick question for her.

"Swing by my desk, I'm about go AWOL from chat as I'm getting bombarded." She then blinks offline.

Finance live in the block adjacent to you, crunching away at numbers and sending semi-rude emails to customers who haven't paid their bills. As you walk along the corridor you take some time to admire just how bland the company's artwork is. Despite this, each painting is probably worth more than your flat.

The finance office is a cacophony of noise, activity and energy; everyone looks tense and infinitely stressed. In the corner of your eye you catch glimpses of all sorts of graphs and charts, most of which you are reasonably confident are only produced for show. Jennifer used to work on the stock exchange and seems to have attempted to replicate the energy in her team. Nobody goes as far as swallowing a goldfish, but you know they are thinking about it.

Jennifer's desk is over in a corner. Anyone who seeks an audience with her is forced to run the gauntlet across the room. Essentially, each row of desks acts as a check to confirm that your issue is urgent enough to proceed up the food chain. Anyone lacking in conviction is likely to be slain by Jennifer's gatekeepers well before they reach her.

Your will is strong, though, and you stride on through and announce yourself, stating it's good to see her and long time no speak. You both cringe at the poor joke.

"Hi, what is your question then?"

You tell her you need to know about the environmental risks associated with Project Degrada.

See her response in **Section 122.**

328 Phase Three—Attack

As a rule of thumb, you shouldn't deny anything unless you are 100% certain, as journalists will be sure to throw these denials back in your face.

You don't believe the payment card data that has been leaked will genuinely link back to you; perhaps Golden Slug are trying to distract the company before executing a different plan. Rather than speculate, you call on a contact who works in the fraud office of one of the payment card brands, a man by the name of Reginald, though he prefers to be referred to in by his now defunct military rank. You use his preferred "The Sergeant" title as you say good morning to him.

"Based on what I am reading, it isn't such a good morning for you folks at Generico McCompany." Straight to the point as ever.

You admit that is why you are calling, as you don't believe the cards being pinned on Generico McCompany genuinely come from the company.

"Do you hope those card details aren't linked to Generico McCompany or do you genuinely believe that?"

Say that you hope in **Section 258.** If you believe, keep reading.

You tell Sergeant you genuinely believe that to be the case.

"Based on what?"

Without over-elaborating, you share your previous day's findings, outlining how the planned attack was thwarted ahead of time.

Sergeant seems convinced by your narrative, or bored, since he agrees to divert some of his team's time into digging deeper into the payment cards that Golden Slug have circulated.

After thanking him and hanging up the phone, you spend a few minutes obsessing over a small stain on your shirt sleeve.

Attack the stain in **Section 169.**

---

329 Phase Three—Attack

It doesn't take long to confirm that firewall F42 has been completely compromised. Somehow Golden Slug have taken remote control of it and are using it to siphon data out of the company. The DDoS was apparently merely a smokescreen. Poring through the **logs** shows the real mishmash of data it's been sending out: network diagrams, employee contact details, product internal guides; all stuff that is going to make Susan pretty unhappy when she finds out.

Your heart sinks as you keep scrolling. Golden Slug have been going after documents relating to Project Luminec. Forget company reputation, these are nuclear secrets.

Amongst all that bad news, however, you find one bit of good news. No files have actually been transferred yet. Golden Slug have been dripping portions of them out very slowly to try to avoid detection, but these portions alone are useless: Golden Slug would need the entire file to have anything usable. You have a few hours to put a stop to things.

This is a bit more of a spy thriller situation than reality, but it sounds cool.

You rush to Susan's office to bring her up to speed.

"Can't we just shut the firewall down?" she asks.

You reply that you could, but because you don't know how Golden Slug compromised Firewall F42, they could just do it again.

It's worth pointing out that shutting down assets (applications, servers, firewalls etc.) that have been compromised is a perfectly sane thing to do in some situations where you are limiting exposure of systems and data.

"F42?"

You explain it's a nickname someone in the team came up with for the firewall, choosing not to share that it was your own creation.

"OK, but can't we shut the firewall down and then see how they do it next time?"

What do you think?

Vote good idea in **Section 45** or bad idea in **Section 175.**

330 Phase Three—Attack

"Pretty messed up" ends up being an understatement of epic proportions. Your firewalls have all been configured in such a way that if they receive a specific **data packet**, they will amplify the message and send it to every end destination they know of. Essentially, your own firewalls are now primed to DDoS you from within your own network.

If the firewalls now resemble a giant powder keg, the only positive is that the fuse is only accessible from within the network. Golden Slug can't activate it externally. It dawns on you that if Golden Slug could make changes to the **firewall**, they are clearly in the network anyway.

This realisation drops at the same instant as the fuse is lit. You are powerless as your network starts to be ripped apart by the very devices built to protect it. Like a perfectly arranged line of dominoes, each firewall recruits others and those in turn recruit more. What was initially a single data packet is now thousands of firewalls going haywire.

It doesn't take long for Susan to appear, looking for answers—or blood. "What on earth is going on?"

You inform her that Golden Slug have moved from an external DDoS to an internally based one.

Susan's face goes white. "I know a Chief Technology Officer that happened to. He got fired."

Well, at least Susan is staying positive. You have many options, but the only two that don't involve simply picking up your bag and leaving are to try firefighting until the blaze is under control, or to shut everything down and clean things up.

Firefight in **Section 265** or shut everything down in **Section 166.**

331 Phase Two—Preparation

Secret project piqued my interest too. Guillaume may have been involved in setting up a network share, but someone who had boots on the ground is surely a good lead. If you can get him to talk, that is.

You make your way over to the operations department, waiting patiently as a middle manager type delivers what they believe to be a motivational pep talk on the subject of timesheets. As tempting as it would be to continue walking on by, you just know senior management love to use someone as an example and, seeing as your own timesheet is empty, you'd rather not risk it. As you make your way to Rory's desk, you are stopped by a colleague who has a question relating to computer **virus**es.

"If someone else were to visit inappropriate websites on my laptop, would that person be in trouble?" they ask, in a completely non-suspicious manner.

You decide that now is a good time to explain non-repudiation to them.

Non-repudiation is the assurance that someone cannot deny that they did or said something. As far as most company policy is concerned, if something happens on a laptop that was signed onto using employee A's username and password, the actions are employee A's. This is part of the reason you shouldn't share your password with anyone, as you will be culpable for any bad things they do or naughty websites they browse.

You let them know that the safest thing to do is to report the laptop as potentially compromised and request a password reset. But this time they must keep the new password to themselves, to prevent "someone else" from using their login.

Whether it genuinely was them on a naughty website or not is sort of irrelevant; it's not worth the time to explore it. This employee has now learned that non-repudiation is a thing and is much more likely to use their personal device for any questionable internet activity moving forward.

They thank you profusely and you continue on to Rory. Rory is a Swiss army knife of an employee with incredible versatility, and for this reason he gets to drift between various odd projects and sometimes to disappear for weeks on end. Fortunately, he isn't abroad currently and you spot him reclining in his chair. Are his eyes closed? You approach to double-check and confirm; he is indeed asleep, but nobody around him seems to be fazed by this.

One of your allies, Gesa, who works in project management, notices you looking puzzled and explains. "He flew back into the country today. His body clock is about seven hours out of sync."

You ask if she reckons Rory will be waking up any time soon.

"Probably not, he only just fell asleep." She turns back to her own work.

Is your question urgent enough to wake a man catching up on lost sleep?

Wake him up in **Section 105** or leave him alone in **Section 274**.

332 Phase Four—Aftermath

This could be a little hasty. Kicking off a hacker group before you fully have a handle on where they've infiltrated and what plans they have set in motion runs the risk of an incomplete eviction. But it can be a sensible first step. Will it work out for you?

Susan clearly agrees with your decision. "I don't like the idea of having Golden Slug around for a second more than necessary. Smoke them out."

You spend a few minutes on casual small talk before Susan pretends to have a meeting starting soon. You take the hint and get back to work.

Now that you know something about where Golden Slug have been on the Generico McCompany network, it's slightly easier to build up a profile, almost like the Golden Slug "smell". Wherever Golden Slug have been has remnants of that "smell", depending on how recently Golden Slug were on the server and for how long. Using this approach, you sketch out a little map on an A4 piece of paper, building up a picture of where Golden Slug have spent time on the network.

"Is that a fish?" asks Guillaume unhelpfully, though in fairness it does look a bit like a fish.

Finally, your sketch is complete and you take stock. Golden Slug seem to always move to servers and network locations that are one jump away from one **firewall** in particular, firewall C-137. You decide to inspect firewall C-137 to see if there is anything special about its settings that may make it of particular interest to a hacking group.

Find out in **Section 342**.

333 Phase Three—Attack

You would be better off fronting up to mistakes in life. Lies have a nasty way of biting you in the backside.

You message Cecilia, stating that you can see the reply in your inbox, but that you didn't write the email.

"OK, thanks. I will let the press know." She blinks offline.

Before you can properly think through the implications of that decision, a new email appears in your inbox. It's from the well-renowned cybersecurity blogger Troy Hunt. Troy runs a free web service, which lets people know when their data has been hacked... Wait a minute.

> Dear Generico McCompany CISO,
>
> I am getting in touch as a large file containing personal data has been shared with me by a source claiming it is currently for sale on the dark market.
>
> The seller claims the data originates from Generico McCompany. The file itself is a list of clientele of the "Virtual Back Wax" online service, including full name, contact details and web cam images. Having reached out to my user base, I have every reason to believe this data is genuine.
>
> So that I can allow the www.haveibeenpwned.com user base to prepare accordingly, can you confirm the data's validity?
>
> Troy

Troy is a real person and that is a real website. If you sign up for the free notification service, Troy will let you know when he receives evidence that hacked data contains your personal information.

He has attached a file that you only take seconds to conclude is indeed legitimate Generico McCompany data. Could this day get any worse?

Sorry, yes. Lying about your email being compromised did not pay off. What were news headlines of "Generico McCompany CISO makes foolish plea to environmentalist hackers" become "Generico McCompany CISO has email compromised". You confirm that the breach is genuine and prepare to face the heat.

See how hot it gets in **Section 47**.

334 Phase Three—Attack

Did you just get phished?

You quickly approve the request—not because Michael scares you, but he kind of does—then ask Guillaume what he has for you.

"Some suspicious activity on this **firewall**. It's been trying to route all kinds of data to this **IP** address."

You ask him to elaborate on what he means by the word "trying".

"Yup, the transfers keep getting blocked by our **data loss prevention** software."

You sigh and state that that is fortunate.

"Exactly. Anyway, this IP address…" Guillaume continues, pointing at his screen, "belongs to whoever is trying to take the data."

As if that was the signal Golden Slug were waiting for, the firewall on Guillaume's screen tries to send data to the IP address again, and this time it's successful. What was a calm situation turns into pandemonium. Guillaume assumes the lead on identifying why the file transfer was successful and you take point on finding out what the data was.

It turns out the data can best be categorised as "everything", ranging from Generico McCompany salary details, photographs of your colleagues' pets and even some instances of the cafeteria menu. The joke's on the hackers, though: those menus are months out of date. You hope that Guillaume has found out why the data loss prevention software didn't block this latest attempt.

He has. The reason it went through is tough to swallow.

Face the facts in **Section 190.**

335 Phase Three—Attack

The chat logs are a thing of beauty. You have a strong urge to have them printed out, framed and then hung on your non-existent office wall for all eternity. The second you gave Charlotte the project Titan lead, she passed it straight to Golden Slug with the message: "Project Titan for free payment card data. Eat your hearts out, the idiot has gone to lunch. Don't forget our deal. C."

You smirk. Charlotte thinks she's been sly by not using her real name, but the first letter of her first name is hardly a bulletproof alias.

You send Susan a screenshot of the chat, and ask her to sort out a police intervention whilst you stall Charlotte. It is a herculean level of effort to keep the smugness out of your face; you reckon you deserve to be given an Oscar on the spot for this acting performance.

"What are you so happy about? You do remember that Generico McCompany have had payment card data stolen, right?" Charlotte asks snidely.

Maybe your acting isn't as accomplished as you first thought. Luckily, you are spared your blushes by the arrival of two police officers, with Susan hovering behind them. It would seem an arrest being made is justification for being dragged out of a board meeting.

They approach Charlotte and ask her to confirm she is indeed Charlotte.

"Yes, I am Charlotte. What is this all about?" Charlotte asks, her voice shrill.

One of the police officers replies by slapping a pair of handcuffs on her and announcing that she is under arrest. You watch as Charlotte is escorted out of the room.

Savour the moment in **Section 238.**

---

336 Phase Two—Preparation

Trying and failing to put Susan's frown out of your mind, you continue flicking through the report and finally find some potential leads. There are three particularly promising entries. First, you see that when customers pay for items over the phone, the recordings are being stored and saved as is, rather than having the payment card details hidden.

Second, you notice that user awareness training is proving ineffective. You see that this is an entry you had identified yourself, likely straight after having to clean up after Doris fell for her fourth **phishing** email of the day.

Finally, you have a note that the Generico McCompany e-commerce websites utilise a large amount of code that comes from third parties.

Third parties are external companies or individuals.

This in itself is common, but you've highlighted that a variety of these sources are small, potentially insecure companies, or that the code itself provides non-essential functionality. Your train of thought is interrupted by a colleague asking a question. "Why do you recommend I turn on **multi-factor authentication** for my personal email again?"

You remind them that personal email accounts are not only used for sending emails, they are also the place where password resets for all the online services they use get sent to. By getting access to their email, a hacker could springboard from there into social media accounts, online shopping profiles or even investment platforms. You finish by telling them multi-factor authentication makes their personal email significantly harder to get into, and hackers are often looking for the path of least resistance.

Seriously, this is worth doing and for most email providers its free to do.

They leave and you feel the satisfaction of helping another, although it's less invigorating than normal. Oh right, you have an investigation to take care of. You scratch your chin as you decide what to do.

Pursue the call recordings avenue in **Section 300,** the training angle in **Section 90** or the third-party code suppliers in **Section 70.**

---

337 Phase Three—Attack

Now that the DDoS attack has seemingly been blunted, there is enough time to have a look at the **logs** from the past few hours to see if anything slipped under the radar. Searching through logs is like looking for a book in a library. If you know the title, genre or author of the book/log, you have a chance. In this situation you know none of these things. You are essentially looking for a book that may not exist, and if it does exist, it might be a fish rather than a book.

As you scan through the hordes of data, your eyes are drawn to some suspicious-looking network traffic. It was passing through a **firewall** that had been knocked offline and restarted by Golden Slug's initial DDoS. Closer inspection reveals that it's just traffic for an online game of chess that someone is playing rather than doing any work.

The smell of taurine and cheap deodorant announces the nearby presence of Niko, the reformed hacker, now working as an apprentice in the company, likely on his way to restock his mini-fridge with energy drinks. You can't help but frown; your own request for a mini-fridge was rejected.

As he passes by, Niko points at some nondescript logs and asks, "What is going on here? It looks pretty messed up."

Explore what he is talking about in **Section 330.**

---

338 Phase Three—Attack

As you sit thinking, hands massaging your temples, you are brought back to the real world by your colleague Guillaume tapping you on the shoulder.

"You look like you've got a puzzle on your mind, you know I like puzzles." Guillaume does like puzzles, though you've never actually seen him solve one.

You outline the situation to Guillaume—two brains are better than one, as they say.

"So they made you think that they'd hacked you when they hadn't?"

You nod.

"Well, I have no idea. I'd put more time into this, but I have some networks to bring online or people will start crying."

You glare at the back of Guillaume's head as payback for his half-hearted efforts at assisting you. Behind the glare, your mind continues to attempt to piece together recent events into some kind of jigsaw, but fails.

Vijaya wanders over, notices your expression and immediately looks anywhere but at you to avoid inciting your wrath. She tells Guillaume she has been commanded to get the networks online in 20 minutes.

"No problem. I didn't let myself get distracted, so that will be fine."

You put your headphones on to drone out background noise and decide to move on from the Golden Slug email, instead having a look around the network to make sure everything is running smoothly.

Continue in **Section 130.**

---

339 Phase Three—Attack

Why bring in professionals and then make them sit on the sidelines?

Cecilia is chairing the PR response meeting. All eyes are on you, though, since nobody has dealt with something like this before.

After the normal mundane pleasantries, Cecilia proposes that the company disclose they have experienced a DDoS attack from a cyberadversary, without revealing who is doing it or why. "If we tell people who is responsible they may research Golden Slug and start asking questions."

Cecilia pauses and everyone seems to be in agreement, so she continues. "Should we mention we've appointed an... expert consultancy to aid us?"

You confirm that Generico McCompany can indeed announce they are working with an accredited cyberincident response company. Susan looks at you; reading her mind, you assure the room that the Cyber Pirates were on every government-issued recommended list that you could find.

"Well, that's reassuring," Susan says without meaning it, bringing the meeting to a close.

Check on the Cyber Pirates in **Section 355.**

340 Phase Three—Attack

That's kind of deep.

You agonise over the spelling of "Telephone" for longer than you'd have liked, but manage to submit your answer with time to spare. The onscreen text disappears, before being replaced:

"Thanks for taking part, I will now process your answers and either disarm the logic bomb or unleash hell, depending on your performance. Please do not close the application."

If you want to close the application, go to **Section 345**, otherwise keep reading.

You take your stress ball from your desk drawer and give it a few squeezes, working out the tension of that high-octane situation. Looking around you, you realise that you just underwent an epic, high-stakes ordeal, but life just continued around you. Maybe you should have been more dramatic.

Throw some confetti around in **Section 167.**

---

341 Phase Three—Attack

A message from Susan lets you know that she has had approval to pay the ransom, but adds that if there is further collateral damage, the consequences for everyone will be grim.

You and Ruby carefully craft a reply to Golden Slug's ransom email, confirming you will pay in full and asking for assurances that Golden Slug will not share the contents of the SCAPI database with anyone. You forward it on to Petra and she CCs you in her reply.

Golden Slug's response to the email is actually much more positive and less mocking than expected:

> In response to your fear we will release the data regardless.
>
> We are almost insulted that you would think we are so heartless.
>
> Never fear, we would not commit such a crime.
>
> Besides, when have you ever been lied to by someone who talks in rhyme?

Together, you and Ruby convert Generico McCompany's funds into bitcoin and make the transaction. Golden Slug reply to your email.

> Thank you so much for your custom. As promised, we will never disclose what we found in your data.

Which is great. Except Golden Slug have CCd the well-known cybersecurity journalist Brian Krebs. Smart; they technically haven't broken their promise, but have still managed to throw you under the bus.

Within minutes your phone is ringing and the journalist is on the line, trying to get a comment for the story they are putting together. Before you can even write a message to Cecilia in PR, she has messaged you.

See how things play out in **Section 361.**

---

342 Phase Four—Aftermath

It soon becomes very obvious why Golden Slug have taken such a liking to firewall C-137; the firewall resembles the love child of a colander and Swiss cheese. Based on the ports left open and forwarding rules in place, Golden Slug have likely been using this firewall as their access point into Generico McCompany's network from day one of their intrusion.

You apply updates to the firewall to plug the gaping holes and just like that, Golden Slug are booted off the network. You half expect a rainbow to shoot out of your laptop to celebrate the achievement, but instead you get an impatient messenger chat from Susan.

"Are they taken care of?"

You announce that you found out how Golden Slug were getting into the network and shut the door on them.

"Out of curiosity, how were they getting in?"

You inform her it was a misconfigured firewall—a seriously misconfigured firewall.

"OK, ping me the details and I'll have whoever configured it sent on a training course. One of those that don't provide free lunch."

You do as Susan asks and recline in your chair, suddenly exhausted. The rest of the day passes in a blur. During the afternoon, you overhear a colleague moaning about having to go on a mandatory training course; Susan acts quickly.

Head home, rest up and return to work in **Section 14.**

343 Phase Three—Attack

At some point in the last two months, Golden Slug appear to have compromised a senior recruiter's login credentials and have been using their access to siphon out various files, including employee salaries, interview feedback and annual leave requests. Why Golden Slug would be interested in who takes holiday and when is surprising. On top of that, why would Golden Slug decide to start their payment card data heist when they would have known you as CISO weren't on holiday? Maybe they knew and didn't think you'd be able to stop them? This idea makes you feel a little nervous.

You finally break the silence and ask Charlotte how she is so sure the IP addresses belong to Golden Slug.

"Oh, I am sure, it's them alright."

In response, you point out that aside from the payment card data, none of this activity fits their profile at all.

"Based on what you read in the news?" Charlotte scoffs. "Golden Slug are a lot more nuanced and intelligent than the media gave them credit for. They'll have a plan, I'm certain of it."

Regardless of who did it, you reset the compromised recruiter's password.

Move on to **Section 209.**

344 Phase Two—Preparation

Come on now, did you really think that was going to be considered the "right" choice in a book like this? Say no to crime. But hey, you know you can get paid to do hacking legally, right? Or even if you aren't particularly technically minded, you could get paid to break into buildings? I know, cool. **Penetration testing** *and* **social engineering** *skills are valuable. Get in touch with companies and government agencies in your country for more information on how to enter the industry.*

Anyway, let's pretend you never made this mistake and continue the story.

Shuffle back to **Section 243.**

---

345 Phase Four—Aftermath

You close the tab, and as promised the Golden Slug logic bomb detonates. The Generico McCompany servers resemble sandcastles being ripped apart by a tsunami as a devastating wave of ransomware spreads across the company. Soon, employees are completely incapable of accessing either their email or their work applications, and the entire company has ground to a halt.

Eventually, Generico McCompany recovers from the logic bomb, but with no help from you. Susan promptly fires you in a move that gets officially sanctioned as "damage limitation".

After many days eating breakfast in a robe and dropping your salary expectations lower and lower, you are finally able to find employment again. By the time your first day at your new job comes around, you almost leave the door with no trousers on. Clearly you are out of touch with the norms of the workplace. Things eventually get back on track, but the Golden Slug incident weighs on your mind for many years to come.

The End.

> *They did warn you not to close the tab. You were doing pretty well to begin with, phase two had you well on top of Golden Slug, but things really started to slip away after that. Why not clear your mind by playing again, but picking coffee instead of tea at the beginning? It'll lead you down a completely different path.*

346 Phase Two—Preparation

Things were getting pretty heated; I don't blame you for ending it there.

Using the classic excuse of having to head off for a meeting, you push your chair back and stand up. You look at your watch to reinforce the point, hoping that nobody notices it is now 15:03; as if anyone would have a meeting starting at 15:03. You notice a smirk spread like wildfire across Michael's face and figure that he's sussed you. Regardless, you escape the room and scuttle back to safety.

After putting at least 200 steps between you and Michael's office and sitting with your back against a wall, you wait for your heart rate to return to normal. It takes a long time; you should work out more. As you wait, you reflect on how your investigation is going so far.

Based on what Michael was saying, Project Degrada never happened. You will need to put some time into researching Project Luminec tomorrow to tie off that loose end. You would look into Project Luminec today, except you know that back at your desk a deluge of dull but necessary tasks is going to take up the rest of the day.

You write up a piece for the company newsletter, warning staff about being approached for job roles that sound too good to be true that have hidden agendas. In particular, your piece tells staff to run for the hills if the recruiter asks them to download and install a file with the extension .exe, no matter how much the recruiter says it's necessary. The .exe file will compromise their computer and give hackers access.

This has been done in the past: Google "ATM network hack interview" and read the full story.

The hours tick by slowly until it's time to go home. The evening becomes a blend of reading, growing bored of the book you are reading and browsing the internet, feeling guilty about not reading and then repeating the cycle until it's time for bed.

Brush your teeth and go to work in **Section 323.**

---

347 Phase Two—Preparation

Without knowing whether Golden Slug have any reason to be annoyed with Generico McCompany, looking at the external perimeter for evidence of DDoS attacks serves little purpose. Even if you opened things up and saw that a DDoS attack was taking place, you have no reason to attribute it to Golden Slug as opposed to any other threat actor.

Every time you open up your perimeter protection software program, you get a little thrill and for a minute, you feel like a commander on a space shuttle. The vendor has done an effective job of making the display extremely visual and satisfying to watch. After running a benchmarking exercise in your first week, the program now displays network traffic both internally and externally for Generico McCompany, compared to what a normal day looks like.

This is what is known as a "pew pew map".

The screen shows a spinning globe, and small white dots fly around to symbolise data moving within the company. Red dots are the traffic hitting your external perimeter. This is typically either clients browsing your websites or customers interacting with the company's products.

At first glance, nothing stands out. If a DDoS was taking place, you'd expect to see a massive surge in traffic coming from outside the network. For the moment at least, it seems that Golden Slug aren't interested in Generico McCompany.

Passing co-workers stop to comment on how cool the display on your screen looks. With every co-worker you have to spend at least two minutes explaining what they are seeing, and then telling them that no, you cannot pinpoint their individual laptop on the map. You finally minimise the tab and consider your next steps.

You could switch focus to look at environmentally questionable projects that have been approved, or you could continue down the technical route and review the most recent external perimeter **penetration test** report.

Look into the projects angle in **Section 246.** Peruse the penetration test report in **Section 43.**

348 Phase Three—Attack

Susan messages you on internal chat, confirming the board have accepted the decision to not pay the ransom and are priming the business for dealing with the inevitable public relations fallout.

Ruby points out that Golden Slug are more renowned for their payment card data monetisation and may not have the stomach for actually releasing your documents. You decide to clutch at that straw with all you've got.

Speaking of straws, you could do with getting a soft drink as an energy boost. You venture into the kitchen and witness someone who appears to be trying to shatter the record for the number of sugars in their coffee. You stop counting once it hits double digits.

Fuelled by the oddly addictive fizzy drink, you return to your desk and brace yourself for the surreal task of telling Golden Slug that in fact you will not pay their ransom, a situation you've never received training for. Luckily, Ruby has dealt with similar cases and helps you draft a reply email stating you are not going to pay the ransom and are not afraid of the implications if the document gets released. The second part of that is a blatant lie, but it depends how good Golden Slug are at calling your bluff.

You hit send. You expect fireworks or something to happen, but nothing comes. The hours trickle by until it's time to go home. Ruby lets you know she won't come in tomorrow as there's not much she can input now.

See how things play out in **Section 268.**

349 Phase Two—Preparation

After a commuter coughs directly in your face during your journey into work, you spend the rest of the journey wondering what kind of tropical **virus**es you've been infected with. You selflessly opt to keep your distance from Susan and spare her health during your morning meeting, and sit on the miniature sofa in her office rather than on the chair next to her desk. After outlining the risk that the une**ncrypted** call recordings pose, you detail some potential options for fixing the problem. In the short term you can manually encrypt the recordings that are sitting in the folder, but in the long term you will need to get the call recording software fixed so that it doesn't capture the card details to begin with.

"I will look up the engineer who installed that call recording software. They are going to come back and correct their mistake off their own back. I won't lose money over their failing."

You nod and leave to start encrypting the call recordings immediately. In the interests of your end-of-year performance review, you'd rather Susan didn't lose money over your failings. As you make your way over to your desk, you exchange silent head nods with a few colleagues, the optimum morning greeting for a busy workplace.

Making a start on encrypting the call recordings is delayed, as you are forced to change your password. Naturally, you come up with a completely new password, resisting the urge just to change the number at the end from a 2 to a 3.

If hackers gain access to a password you've used before, this gives them a chance to guess your current password by increasing the number sequentially until it works. This is the same reason reusing a password across multiple websites could eventually come back to bite you.

Get cracking on encrypting those call recordings in **Section 251.**

---

350 Phase Four—Aftermath

*You might want to improve your teaching skills. A CISO needs to be willing and able to take their employer on an educational journey on a regular basis, upskilling end users to avoid traps like **phishing**, but also ensuring the board are educated on relevant information security directives. Like in any role, part of the job is convincing people that problems are big enough to merit investment.*

"Right this way," he says, with all the enthusiasm of a flat tyre. He leads you both through to the checkout section and shows you the store's three PIN entry devices. Two are currently being used by staff on the till, but one is in its charging dock, refuelling before it is sent back to the frontline. The young employee goes back to his greeting post, eager to return to what he was born to do, enticing suckers through the door and bringing them one step closer to emptying the contents of their wallets.

Picking up the charging PIN entry device and wielding it as if it were a television remote, Gesa asks, "What exactly are we looking for?"

You give her the brief: you are both looking for signs of tampering, maybe a loose screw, a piece of plastic casing that hasn't been aligned properly, or perhaps some loose cables. Your reply is more confident than it should be, as you don't actually know.

Gesa hands you the PIN entry device and you begin to inspect it. Although the panelling and screws look fine and there appears to be no sign of any loose cabling, you can hear something inside the device when you rotate it. You wait a few minutes for the store to be less busy, pick up one of the PIN entry devices on active duty and perform the same rotational movement, but hear no sound from within.

After you've carried out your inspections, you remark that you can't be sure of the condition of the devices that are currently serving customers, but you do know that the one in your hand has either been tampered with or just assembled badly. You take the device back to the office so you can get the manufacturer to dismantle and inspect it.

See who the manufacturer sends in **Section 99.**

---

351 Phase Two—Preparation

Good call. Gesa has already proven a dead end, and sometimes talking to your line manager is the best option.

As you sit in the chair outside Susan's office, you can't help but feel like a naughty school child waiting to be told off by the headmaster. A niggle of doubt plays at the back of your mind. Did the folder exist at all? Will Susan even believe you? Someone walks out of Susan's office and you stand up to hover just by her door. Peering inside and seeing her shell-shocked face, you decide to give her a moment. Finally, she shakes her head, resets herself and calls you in.

"Hello again, I didn't expect to see you so soon. Have you learned anything interesting about Golden Slug?"

You let her know you sort of have. Susan looks less than impressed. You describe how you did find a promising lead, but the folder containing all the project details has just vanished.

"Oh dear." She pauses in thought. "What was the project name?"

As soon as you mention the word Luminec, you see Susan's face revert to the shell-shocked expression you saw earlier. As you sit waiting for her to speak, you become very conscious of your arms. You fidget, unsure of whether to fold them or put your hands in your pockets.

Susan doesn't seem to notice your internal struggle. "I'm inviting you to a meeting first thing tomorrow. Nothing to worry about now, it will all be explained then. For the minute, just continue as per normal. It's home time soon anyway."

She smiles at you, but you can see that it's a very forced effort.

You return her smile in an attempt to reassure her. You take her advice to carry on as normal and the afternoon and evening pass in a blur. Before you know it, it's the next morning and you are buried in a stranger's armpit again, hurtling towards the office. Something tells you it is going to be an eventful day.

See just how eventful in **Section 81.**

352 Phase Two—Preparation

"We were asked to hire a ton of scientists with all these weird qualifications and experience. There were so many acronyms I spent half my time on Google."

You ask what the scientists were meant to be doing at the site.

"Beats me, I was just told to hire them, so I did."

Your conversation is interrupted by one of Vlad's colleagues letting out an exclamation. "How could they have been offered more money? We are meant to be at the top of the pay grading scale!"

Vlad's other colleagues gather around the poor fellow to remind him gently that Generico's pay plan is competitive and the world moves on. Besides, the candidate was probably lying.

You decide it's time for you to scarper, and thank Vlad before you head out.

"Any time. Don't be a stranger!" he says, as he walks over to offer his own condolences to his heartbroken colleague.

Your investigation into Project Degrada doesn't seem to be bearing much fruit. Before you get a chance to choose a new avenue of research to pursue, you are called into a meeting to validate the security of a new product being procured. The meeting organiser ignores your protests that without background or context your input is not going to be worth much. A waste of a meeting followed by a waste of a debrief meeting leaves you mentally scarred.

> In companies where information security is seen as a "hurdle" rather than a valued part of the team, this kind of situation can arise. Thankfully, culture shifts are making people aware that this practice is detrimental to a business's long-term cyberhygiene.

It seems wise to go home, recharge your batteries and continue the investigation tomorrow.

Find out if your sleuthing skills will unearth any clues in **Section 100.**

353 Phase Two—Preparation

You look into the finding of the administrative console being exposed and discover it's a bit of a red herring. Whilst the administrator login section shouldn't really be accessible to everyone, the fact it's protected by **multi-factor authentication** and is restricted to login attempts made by Generico McCompany **IP** addresses means that in fact it's not a huge deal.

> *Unlucky, it can be hard to tell exactly what is going on without all the facts. This is probably why the answer to so many questions in information security is "it depends".*

Now a quarter of an hour has passed, you turn a one-minute walk to the meeting room into a five-minute walk, as the company does keep telling you that walking more enhances productivity.

The new starter cybersecurity training session goes as smoothly as ever. A room full of people promise to do a list of things and then you spend the next few months catching them breaking these promises. Upon returning to your desk, you are ambushed by Gesa from the project management team, who has a project she needs to sanity check with you. As baffling as the concept of "virtual water" is, you can't really see any reasons to be concerned from an information security perspective, so you happily sign off on the project for Gesa.

You gossip for a while, dipping back into the virtual water discussion whenever someone senior passes nearby. Before long the clock strikes five and it seems the best course of action will be to pick up the Golden Slug investigation tomorrow.

At home, you eat a microwave meal and watch mindless TV. You go to sleep, thinking that hopefully tomorrow's investigation will bear more fruit than today's. The next morning, your phone rings soon after you set yourself up at your desk.

Pick up the phone and see if this is the fruit you were waiting for in **Section 139**.

---

354 Phase Two—Preparation

> *Wait, didn't I already tell you the vulnerability was a trick?*

You put a call into your account manager. At this point you don't even know what company they work for, they all blur together. Their logo fits the standard "information security" stereotype of being composed mostly of black, white, grey and red. Although they claim to be innovative and different, you're pretty sure that you could peel off their logo and replace it with that of their competitor and you wouldn't even notice the difference.

Francine doesn't pick up, but texts you to let you know she'll call you in 10. Naturally you take this 10 minutes of downtime as the perfect opportunity to go stroke one of the office dogs. Francine calls back 20 minutes into your cuddle session with Max, the lovable golden retriever. Max licks his lips as you pull out your mobile, so it seems wise to take the call elsewhere and you sleuth into an empty meeting room.

"Sorry about that. I was in an internal meeting that overran."

The background noise on Francine's end suggests that she is at a bar, so you suspect that the holdup is actually due to a game of pool or darts that overran. You decide not to bother calling her out. When you let her know you are doing some research into Golden Slug, Francine jumps in before you can finish your sentence.

"Oh yes, we've been doing a lot of incident response work relating to that threat actor lately."

You stay silent, waiting for her to finish the sentence with something useful, but it seems to not be forthcoming. Pressing on, you outline your trail so far leading to the vulnerability on the web app and ask if Francine can press her testing team for some insight.

Find out what insight Francine has in **Section 302**.

---

355 Phase Three—Attack

Captain Dave tips his hat to you as you approach. Pedro the Parrot also seems to nod his head towards you from Captain Dave's shoulder, but that could just be your imagination. As you resume work, the press release goes out and all hell breaks loose.

Cecilia messages you on internal chat. "The press knew about Golden Slug and managed to tie the nuclear fiasco together with this. Our stocks and reputation have taken a small hit. Apparently Petra has received another email from Golden Slug. She is forwarding it to you now."

You feel your phone vibrate in your pocket, before the email popup appears on your screen. For some reason your phone is always those few seconds ahead of the game. You leave Cecilia to worry, as you can't help her now, and focus on the email Petra has been sent.

Dear Petra,

Bad move. Trying to hide a nuclear secret now forces us to activate our next chess piece. The ransom option is now closed.

Golden Slug

As you begin to wonder what Golden Slug's next chess move might be, Ship Cat Tobias wanders over, looking nervous.

See what he has to say in **Section 280**.

356 Phase Two—Preparation

Like a wolf in sheep's clothing, you have the developers smiling and laughing. You gently try to steer the conversation towards the e-commerce websites, and ask the developers if there have been any significant changes to the code.

Suddenly, the developers discern your true intentions and initiate a fight-or-flight response. Seeing as fighting in a professional environment is frowned upon, flight wins out. Four of the five developers you were talking to move away, leaving one who evidently picked "freeze" instead of fight or flight. The cornered developer is Jack, who previously was your karaoke partner on one of the office nights out.

You reassure Jack that you aren't looking to lay blame on anyone and that you are doing reconnaissance because the company is being targeted by a **sophisticated actor**.

"What, like Hugh Jackman?"

Sometimes you want to bang your head against a brick wall. You let him know it's not that kind of actor, and give him some background on the situation.

He seems interested and runs you through the recent changes on the websites, but it's all trivial: moving hyperlinks, changing font sizes and increasing the creepy tracking being performed on customers.

You ask him to quickly show you how new requests come in and he outlines the process. People who want small changes to the sites submit an email to developers@genericomccompany.com, which he then distributes for someone to action. You see that a request has just come in.

Read the request in **Section 76**.

357 Phase Three—Attack

Marshal Marshal provides a briefing to you on what they have been able to attribute to Golden Slug so far, whilst Commander Sasha and Cyberspace Cadet Morgan continue surveillance.

"In summary, they got into your network via a compromised user email and seem to be acting sufficiently noisily to imply they have other ways in if we close off their current route, or perhaps they have already taken all that they need. Aside from stealing payment card data, they have been spending a lot of time reading as many emails as they can that originate from Generico McCompany senior staff, with seemingly no bias regarding the email chain's importance or nature."

You ask him what he means by the last bit.

"Well, they spent a long time reading an email that your CEO sent out to the company, even though it was just an informal update and had nothing sensitive in it at all."

You scratch your chin, wondering why Golden Slug would care about this.

Sasha emerges from nowhere, an impressive feat for a man in a full-body space suit.

"I think we've observed for as long as is prudent. With your permission I would suggest we begin to purge Golden Slug from the network, starting by performing password resets on all the email addresses we know are compromised."

You give Sasha a nod of approval, but notice you are in his blind spot, so voice your agreement instead.

See if he heard in **Section 109**.

358 Phase Four—Aftermath

Personally, I would have gone to check out the procurement tool, since that seems a more likely target for Golden Slug as they are financially motivated. But that's just, like, my opinion, man.

Emails are the lifeblood of most companies and Generico McCompany are no different. Whether it's an email giving the thumbs-up on starting a new marketing campaign or an email with the minutes from a board meeting, inboxes hold a lot of promise for an attacker with the patience to sift through the memes and cat pictures to find what they are looking for.

Generico McCompany's email application works well enough, though it does have a nasty habit of crashing just as you are getting to the end of writing a long message. Maybe that's intentional, though, a hidden defence against people sending long emails.

Golden Slug have been busy. They've made offline copies of three separate mailboxes, allowing them to search through the inbox, sent items, deleted items and junk mail without risking being spotted by the email's true owner. It looks like they'll have access to the last year's worth of mail, given that items older than that are sent to the archive. The three mailboxes Golden Slug have decided to copy belong to you, Susan and Vlad, the head of recruitment. A pretty strange mix.

You cast your mind back over the contents of your own emails, wondering how damaging it would be for Golden Slug to read through them, and come to the conclusion that they'd most likely feel sympathetic towards you. That leaves Vlad in recruitment and Susan. Who do you want to talk to first?

Talk to Susan in **Section 68**. Talk to Vlad in **Section 154**.

---

359 Phase Three—Attack

Ignoring Charlotte's incredulity, you ask Niko if there is any way of checking for devices that steal two-factor authentication codes.

He gives you an enormous smile and dashes off.

"You are wasting your time. We should be looking at what else Golden Slug have been up to," Charlotte lets you know. Whilst that comment makes you more determined to continue your current line of investigation, she may have a point.

Niko returns, holding a black ball with a pulsing red light at the top.

You ask him what it is.

"This little babe is a beacon detector."

Your eyes glaze over, which Niko correctly interprets as an invitation to provide further context.

"It's simple: it blinks red when it detects nothing, but will change to a blue light if it detects a device trying to intercept the signal it emits. It works to a radius of five metres."

This is probably halfway between sci-fi and reality.

You ask Niko why he even has that, and he shakes the question off, asking where you want to hunt. Charlotte looks either disinterested or nervous about the beacon hunt. Either way, this means it would be an opportunity to escape her snide remarks; alternatively, it could be a huge waste of time when you could be looking more closely at Golden Slug's activity on Susan's emails.

Do you want to go and look for a beacon in Susan's office, or move to the less glamorous but potentially more practical line of enquiry investigating her emails?

Keep on beacon hunting in **Section 18.** Look into Susan's emails in **Section 365.**

360 Phase Two—Preparation

I'm not sure congratulations are in order: that was pretty clearly the better choice.

You offer Sonal a sympathetic ear. She tells you how the DDoS itself was manageable, but the knock-on effects were what killed her in the end. You ask her to elaborate, but she tells you she has to go, claiming to have a convenient excuse. You thank Sonal for her time and she hangs up.

You fire up a Google search and try to figure out what she means by knock-on effects from a DDoS attack. In the corner of your eye, you can see a sad-looking colleague approach the IT helpdesk, cradling a mobile phone as if it were a newly born duckling.

"It's broken," they tell a member of the helpdesk.

"Have you put a **ticket** in?" the helpdesk member replies.

You laugh to yourself; nobody submits tickets.

"Well, it's my personal phone, so..."

You continue listening to their conversation, learning that the only option for the personal phone is a factory reset, sending it back to how it was on the day it was first shipped.

"But I'll lose all my pictures of cats dressed as bees."

"Should have thought about that before trying to dry your phone in a microwave."

No joke: don't do this.

The phone conversation, other than being comic relief, gives you an idea as you look at how some of your own devices would cope if forced to restart. Your analysis shows that a large portion of the Generico McCompany **firewall** estate is comprised of Burpafence Model 10s, which have shockingly weak factory settings. If something were to force these firewalls to crash, like a DDoS attack for example, they would restart with very insecure settings, leaving Generico McCompany exposed.

Something you may forgive in a consumer product, but not an enterprise solution.

Glancing at your watch, you see that there is no time to fix this today. Instead, you email Susan and head home for some well-deserved rest.

Head into work for day two in **Section 278.**

361 Phase Four—Aftermath

Things do not play out well, not at all. The cybersecurity journalist has a lead and is not going to let it go. A preliminary breaking news story about Generico McCompany hits and the avalanche begins. Emails, texts, phone calls and even physical mail begin to get directed to the Generico McCompany office from all angles. The regulators want to know what would cause Generico McCompany to pay such a ransom; the public wants to know if their data is safe; and everyone wants to know who is to blame.

The board decide unanimously that you are the ideal person to blame. The company are forced to issue a statement bemoaning your inability to get the Golden Slug incident under control and announce that you are being removed from your position.

As you search for a job, you begin to receive postcards in the mail. First a group of men and women with their faces blurred out, posing on a beach. Next a picture of a garage full of sports cars. Eventually the postcard pictures are giant wads of money. Each time the only message on there is: "Golden Slug give you their thanks."

The End.

Sadly, even paying the ransom is no guarantee of anything. Technically Golden Slug stayed true to their word. The journalist I mentioned writes some excellent articles on hacking activity and hacking groups; if you are interested the website is www.krebsonsecurity.com.

Back to the story. I'll be honest, things went pretty badly for you in phase two, with no clear leads, which made the next portion not exactly work in your favour. Why not start again, but swap some early choices to see how the story changes?

362 Phase Three—Attack

Galactic Cyber by name and by nature, it would seem. Three people dressed in full space suits, including visors, stand in formation at reception.

Incident response staff dress like normal people, sadly. It would be much better if they were themed.

Passers-by can't help but stare at the unusual sight. You'll have to check what made Susan pick Galactic Cyber as the incident response retainer of choice. Regardless, you'll have to work with them.

As you approach, announcing yourself, the middle figure steps forward and offers a gloved hand. "Commander Sasha reporting for duty." His voice is being captured by a microphone inside his visor and then played out through a speaker, making the conversation surreal.

"Introducing Marshal Marshal and Cyberspace Cadet Morgan," he continues, addressing the two other suited figures.

You take a moment to notice that each Galactic Cyber employee has their name stitched onto their space suit, allowing at least some form of identification. You hand each of them a red Generico McCompany lanyard, which they struggle to fit over their comically large helmets, but get there eventually. After convincing reception that you were indeed expecting this group, you take them through the barrier and somehow cram the four of you into a lift.

The walk from the lift to your desk takes longer than usual, as Galactic Cyber walk as if they were on the moon, taking exaggerated and slow, bouncy steps. You would ask them to stop, but is that culturally insensitive to astronauts?

Moonwalk over to **Section 160.**

---

363 Phase Four—Aftermath

It's from hello@goldenslug.com:

> Greetings,
>
> Well done on your efforts so far. We underestimated your intellect and talent. Consider this our surrender. In fact, we have an offer for you: join our fight against those who would happily gorge themselves on our planet's dwindling resources and forsake generations to come.
>
> If you accept, you will not need to do anything, we will transfer funds. Think of them as a prize for proving yourself capable to us. To accept our offer, stay silent for now and we will be in touch in the future with further instructions and our members' contact details.
>
> Yours sincerely,
>
> Golden Slug

This is unexpected, to say the least. You lock your computer and take a walk outside to clear your head. Do you want to side with Golden Slug?

Take the money in **Section 368,** or keep reading.

Alternatively, you could double-cross Golden Slug by taking the money, pretending to be on their side and exposing them further down the line. You could always be a goody two shoes.

Double-cross in **Section 91.** Reject the money in **Section 216.**

---

364 Phase Four—Aftermath

Charlotte's summary of the situation is grim. She lists a number of ways she'd have prevented the initial Golden Slug payment card data attack as well as this business email compromise case. "But don't worry about writing this all down, it'll all be in my final report."

True to her word, Charlotte spares no detail in the final report, which manages to describe you as numerous creative synonyms for incompetent, as well as four counts of the word "incompetent" itself and two cases where Charlotte has tried to call you "trash", but due to spelling mistakes it's morphed to "brash".

The Generico McCompany board, still reeling from losing $20 million to the business email compromise attack, decide to have you removed from your position, which is a polite way of saying you get fired. Many of the Generico McCompany board members were eager to have you literally fired out of the front door using a cannon, but they worried about damaging the sliding doors.

A month after getting fired, you notice that Generico McCompany appoint your replacement. It's Charlotte.

The End

> As resourceful as Charlotte is, she has never seemed to be particularly interested in your short-, medium- or long-term future, so taking her advice always ran the risk of working out poorly for you. In truth, the choices you made in phase two made it unlikely things were going to turn out well, as your initial investigation didn't throw up any solid leads to work on, allowing Golden Slug to steal a march on you. I'd recommend you start again and mix up some of your early choices to see how differently things can play out. Or you could just drink coffee rather than tea—that'll set you on an entirely different path.

365 Phase Three—Attack

> Charlotte does seem to be competent, and she didn't think that was a good idea, so maybe this is a wise decision. She ultimately does have your best interests at heart, right? Right?

You sigh loudly and instruct Niko to put the ball away. If you could somehow harness the look of pure disappointment on his face, you could likely power a small village for years. He trudges off and you realise that you may have just added months to his rehabilitation at Generico McCompany.

"That might be the first sensible thing I've heard you say. I might even give you a gold star on my report for that," Charlotte lets you know.

Not that you care about gold stars, but how many gold stars is everyone else getting? Pushing Charlotte out of your mind, you inspect Golden Slug's activity on Susan's email at a deeper level. You don't find anything of particular interest.

Charlotte seems flush out of ideas, as she's on her phone again. She puts it down and nods to herself, before surprising you. "We may have got off on the wrong foot. How about I buy us lunch somewhere nice as an apology?"

Checkmate. You can hardly say no to what seems to be a genuine attempt at redemption, so you accept. You actually enjoy a pleasant meal with Charlotte, where she divulges that she often finds work very stressful and accidently takes it out on other people. Clearly, displaying weakness isn't something that Charlotte is fond of, so you appreciate the gesture and let her know you felt hopelessly out of your depth when you first joined Generico McCompany.

When the bill arrives, you expect Charlotte to pull the old "left my purse in the office" trick and show she is a monster after all, but no, she takes out her payment card and settles the bill. You joke with her on the walk back to the office that she may need to replace the card if she's bought from Generico McCompany lately, and she actually laughs!

Cement your newfound friendship in **Section 313.**

366 Phase Three—Attack

I suppose that'll work, for now at least.

You instruct the Cyber Pirates to modify port 13337 so that it drops and ignores messages from Golden Slug IPs, and then to reboot the infected servers.

"You are the boss," Captain Dave replies and his team get to work. They write a script to automate this process across the entire business, letting Pedro the Parrot perform the mouse click that starts it. Within half an hour the script has run and there is no sign of Golden Slug. You ask the Cyber Pirates what their view of the situation is.

"Dead men tell no tales," First Mate Gloria informs you. Whilst you are processing whether that is a threat or not, she clarifies. "Annual bonus, remember? It means Golden Slug seem to have walked the plank. The script kind of forced them to, if you like."

You confirm that you do indeed like that. Captain Dave orders the Cyber Pirates to weigh anchor. Whilst you aren't sure what that means, considering they are all packing their bags you assume they are leaving. You escort the Cyber Pirates out to reception and reclaim their lanyards before bidding them farewell.

Captain Dave extends a hooked hand towards you; was that always there? You shake the hook and the Cyber Pirates say their goodbyes. Captain Dave promises an invoice will be arriving as fast as the seas can bring it to you.

"It'll be via email, along with two surveys, one rating our performance and one rating our outfits."

Great, surveys. You return to your desk and work on an internal report on the Golden Slug attack.

Write it up in **Section 89.**

367　Phase Two—Preparation

*Six of one and half of a dozen of the other; both options were valid. A penetration test report is when you pay a company to hack your infrastructure, applications or code, identifying areas of weakness or **vulnerabilities** that an attacker could exploit. With this report, you can then go about assessing which of the vulnerabilities pose a significant enough business risk to justify fixing, as well as timeframes for when the fixes will be implemented.*

You remember the day you picked a company to be the sole supplier of these kinds of services for Generico McCompany; it was a truly significant occasion. Not because of the testing, but because on that day there had been an error in the kitchen supply run and staff were encouraged to take milk, fruit and bread home for free.

When assessing which penetration testing company to use, there are a variety of options available. You could run a selection event where multiple vendors are given access to identical targets over identical timeframes and see who can find the most or most impressive findings. In some countries (but not all), there are accrediting bodies to demonstrate a company is reputable and abides by certain quality metrics. You could make everyone bid their lowest price possible and pick the cheapest. But as they say, pay peanuts, get monkeys. Like with any vendor, a poor decision doesn't only waste money, it creates problems.

Anyway, how much attention to detail would you say you put into your selection of the penetration testing vendor? Give it a score out of 10.

If between 0 and 5, go to **Section 84**; if between 6 and 10, go to **Section 308.**

368　Phase Four—Aftermath

This is going to end well.

Looking around the room, you realise Golden Slug have a point: you work for a company that just leaked radioactive waste into drinking water. You like turtles; maybe if the world continues as it is, there won't be any more turtles.

Golden Slug send a significant sum into your bank account the next day. You spend some on energy-efficient light bulbs to showcase your allegiance.

Work continues to serve up tedium and monotony in equal measures, and you start to appreciate how sparse the vegetarian food options in the office canteen are.

Many months later, the police knock on your door and place you under arrest. Apparently Golden Slug themselves got hacked and the names of all of their agents and accomplices were leaked. As innocent as you would have been, the large transfer Golden Slug made into your account acts as damning proof of your involvement.

You are tried, found guilty and serve two years in prison for being an accomplice to a cyberhacktivist group. Even so, you feel OK about things, knowing you fought for a righteous course. Those days in prison would have been much more infuriating if you'd known that Golden Slug never got hacked at all: leaking your name and removing you from the picture was their plan from the moment they offered you the money. Choose your friends more wisely.

The End.

> *There was no way that was going to end well. You'd done a fine job (up to that last decision), believing in the incident response plan and standing up for yourself under pressure from Petra. If you genuinely thought this was the correct decision, maybe you have that little spark of rebellion in you that would make you suitable for an offensive security career (**penetration tester** or the like). Why don't you consider looking into it?*

Glossary

The items in this glossary are a mix of pure cybersecurity terms and general IT terms. Without the foundation provided by these general IT terms, some of the more niche cyber terms wouldn't tell the full picture.

This glossary first answers the question "What is this?" followed by "Why should you care?" As ever, the internet is there to give you an endless torrent of information on any topic you'd like to explore further. Please note these are not definitive descriptions; I've kept them short and snappy intentionally.

Active Directory

What is this?

First released as part of Windows 2000 and now almost universally adopted, an active directory is a central point where all the user accounts that can access resources on the network are stored. The active directory tells programs and servers whether the user attempting to log in to a system or access data has the required authority to do so.

Why should you care?

Because an active directory holds the keys to the kingdom, all those username and password combinations, and knowledge of which users have authority for doing large-scale changes to an IT network.

© Alexander J. Roxon 2021
A. J. Roxon, *Choose Your InfoSec Path*, https://doi.org/10.1007/978-1-4842-7036-3

Air Gap

What is this?

When two computer networks are completely separated from each other. Even if a virus had infected the entirety of one network, an air-gapped network should be safe, as the virus has no method of crossing this air gap. Air gaps are common in nuclear power plant IT systems or missile launch controls, as needless to say the impact of a successful cyberattack would be enormous.

In practice, malware has been built to cross air gaps by infecting USB devices and waiting for these USB devices to be plugged into the target network. For more information, read about Stuxnet.

Why should you care?

Forget nuclear power plants, if you work somewhere like that you likely aren't learning about the concept of air gaps from this book. Let's talk about data backups. Without an air gap between the normal network and the backup, what would stop a virus from infecting both at the same time, making the backups worthless? This is part of the reason why companies often like to have offline backups as well as online backups.

Allow list

What is this?

IP addresses that have been classed as "safe" to a firewall, allowing the IP's traffic to interact directly with the systems normally protected by the firewall. Often a trusted third party will have their IPs whitelisted so that they can interact with a company's servers directly. If the third party gets hacked, though, they may just serve as a fast track into your company's network. The term "allow list" was previously referred to as a "white list".

Why should you care?

IP addresses in a firewall's allow list are given a lot of access to the network, so make sure you trust each of these IP addresses extremely well.

Authentication/Authenticate

What is this?

The process of proving to a computer system that someone is who they claim to be, typically with a username and password combination.

Why should you care?

Because a huge part of a cybersecurity attack boils down to attackers tricking authentication processes (or people) into believing they are someone else.

Backdoor

What is this?

Getting into a target's network can take a lot of time and effort for a hacker. The last thing the hacker then wants is for their way into a company's network to be closed off, leaving them needing to start from square one all over again. Once a hacker has got their roots firmly planted, they will often look to install backdoors that allow them safe passage back into their target's network, even if the method they were using for access gets closed down, either by an information security team or due to chance.

Why should you care?

If an attacker has installed a backdoor, then there is almost no point in countering the attacker's actions, as they could simply access the system again via the backdoor and perform their actions once more. The backdoor will need to be removed first.

Block list

What is this?

IP addresses that have been deemed "not safe" to a firewall, forbidding data and messages originating from the IP to interact directly with the systems protected by the firewall. This was previously referred to as a "blacklist" (or "deny list").

Why should you care?

Blocking known maliciously owned IP addresses is an easy win for an information security professional.

Brute Forcing/Brute Force Attack

See credential stuffing, except the hackers are working off all words available rather than a previously used password.

Botnet

What is this?

A collection of devices that have been hacked through malware, known vulnerabilities or exploitation of default credentials. Like when you get a new Wi-Fi router and the administrator area can be accessed with username: admin and password: admin. Once infected, these devices can be commanded remotely and are used for things like launching massive distributed denial of service (DDoS) attacks. The extra bandwidth required by an infected device is unlikely to break the bank financially.

Why should you care?

As an industry, we are encouraged to reduce the number of easily infected devices through activities such as **patching** and changing default credentials. Also, vulnerabilities that allow a device to be recruited onto a botnet could be used for other agendas.

Bug Bounty

What is this?

When a company pays information security professionals to report bugs (or vulnerabilities) in its software, hardware or code. This is different to a penetration test, as multiple professionals work on the same project simultaneously, with the bounties being paid to the first person to report an issue.

Why should you care?

For those dipping their toe into offensive information security domains like penetration testing, bug bounties provide a legitimate platform for testing your skill and even offer the potential for earning money.

Business Email Compromise

What is this?

Business email compromise (BEC) is when an attacker has gained access to a corporate email address.

Why should you care?

A significant amount of business communication is done by email, so having access to a senior executive's email may allow an attacker to learn of confidential plans. The attacker can also send emails from the email address, potentially intercepting communications between procurement departments and new vendors to alter payment details to their own bank account. Crucially, this can happen in your personal life. When paying out large sums of money, ideally check the bank details of the intended recipient via a trusted phone number.

Chief Information Security Officer (CISO)

What is this?

The CISO position is often (but not always) the most senior person in an information security chain of command. They handle the strategy for everything security, from coordinating technical assessments of systems to assessing the security risks of potential new suppliers/software, and act as the spokesperson for information security at a senior level. In some businesses information security reports into IT, in others operations, and sometimes the CISO gets a seat of their own at the top table. This person lives and breathes information security.

Why should you care?

Because this is you in the story!

CIA Triad

What is this?

Confidentiality, integrity and availability: the three key objectives when securing data and systems.

Confidentiality is ensuring data is only seen and accessed by those who are meant to do so. Integrity is ensuring data is only changed when it's supposed to be, with a clear audit trail. Availability is ensuring data is accessible when it needs to be.

Why should you care?

Depending on the system and landscape, the importance of the three elements of the CIA triad will vary. For example, the availability of an e-commerce website over the Christmas period is almost as high in importance as it can get. In contrast, if some data is intended to be publicly accessible, then its confidentiality is as low as it can get. Information security programs ideally have the flexibility to treat data and systems with the relevant priority depending on the CIA triad.

Code

What is this?

The language that computer programs are written in that allows computers to do their thing. As with spoken communication, there are a variety of languages that can be used, such as Python, C++ or Go. First a human writes code in their language of choice, then it is compiled into a format a computer can understand.

Why should you care?

Unless you occupy the extremely small crossover of people who both (a) find cybersecurity interesting and (b) never interact with any computer system ever, you will likely be using computers and technology on a daily basis. Knowing exactly how everything works may not be necessary, but having the basics down serves as a strong foundation in a technology focused career path.

Controls

What is this?

The people, processes and products put in place to reduce the likelihood of bad things happening. Compare these to a lock, which is a control to protect a house from being broken into.

Why should you care?

Controls need to strike the balance between protecting the asset in a way that is proportionately related to its value, but also without restricting business operations too much. As an example, a fantastic way to prevent an online bank from being hacked is to disconnect it from the internet completely. Not exactly a suitable control.

Credential Stuffing

What is this?

Credential stuffing is when hackers reuse username and password combinations from previous breaches in new attacks against login pages.

Why should you care?

Imagine hackers steal a database of usernames and passwords from a company you've used in the past, maybe an e-commerce platform; this shouldn't be hard to imagine, as it's a regularly occurring event. Within the records they find your email address, email@hotmail.com, and the password you used for that website, "password2". Hackers can then automatically enter that combination into a selection of commonly used login pages on the internet. So, if this is the same as your actual Hotmail password, the hacker will potentially have access to your email.

Crime as a Service

What is this?

Crime as a service is when complicated technical exploits are sold as an online product to anyone who is willing to pay. This lowers the skill level needed to perform hacking activities.

Why should you care?

As the technical skill required to perform hacking activities is lowered, more people will opportunistically give it a go. This means more phishing emails in our inboxes, more SMS messages loaded with malware and more fraud attempts against us all.

Cryptomining

What is this?

Using computer processing power to mine for cryptocurrency, a very low value for money return on the processing power and electricity involved. Hackers can infect large numbers of machines for this purpose, offsetting the costs because they're increasing someone else's energy bill.

Why should you care?

For your computer to be contributing to a hacker's cryptomining activity implies the hacker has some form of access to the device itself, or you are browsing on a website that the attacker has installed their code on. Whilst the cryptomining may seem harmless, eventually the hacker may grow bored and sell access to your device to someone with more dangerous motives.

Cyberinsurance

What is this?

It does what it says on the tin, really: insurance for a range of cybersecurity scenarios.

Why should you care?

Information security risk, like almost any form of risk, can in some part be transferred to insurance. It's a potential part of the CISO's strategy, but don't get me started on the detail—it's a very, very, very complicated subject.

Dark Web

What is this?

A hidden side of the internet, accessible only with a special browser. All kinds of illegal activities are confined to the dark web, such as selling stolen goods or even drugs. There are perceptions that browsing the dark web happens with complete anonymity, but remember that law enforcement is only ever a trail of breadcrumbs away.

Why should you care?

From a personal perspective, curiosity. From a professional perspective, be aware that there are numerous forums where criminals sell direct access into companies for money, exploiting a technical exploit or making use of a malicious insider.

Data Breach

What is it?

A data breach is when controlled information ends up where it shouldn't be. Breaches are not always caused by hackers; sometimes they are internal accidents. There are reputational, operational and financial impacts at scales dependent on the circumstances of the breach.

Why should you care?

Chances are a company you have dealt with in your personal life has been breached in the past 10 years. That isn't a slight on your personal choices, but instead a reflection on the regularity of high-profile breaches. As a consumer, it is good to be aware of where companies that get breached place their customers' interests when they respond to such a breach.

Data Loss Prevention

What is it?

The practice where software and individuals work together to keep a company's data from being leaked to the outside world either accidently or intentionally.

Why should you care?

Data loss prevention is the reason why sharing files outside of your company isn't always easy to do, even when you feel it should be.

Data Packet

What is it?

When systems communicate, they share data, not as a continuous stream but broken up into packets. Similar to how when humans talk, they break the letters up into words.

Why should you care?

You don't have to, really, but I use the word in the book, so it needed to be in the glossary.

DDoS

What is it?

A distributed denial of service (DDoS) attack is when hackers direct enormous levels of network traffic at a company or individual. This strain puts pressure on applications, which in turn run more slowly and in some cases just crash. This is particularly damaging if you run an e-commerce site, or if the servers in question are used to power services that customers pay for, as you will potentially have to refund them money for not maintaining the server's uptime.

Some hacking groups like to target companies with DDoS attacks and then email senior executives in the business, demanding a ransom payment in exchange for them calling off their attack.

Why should you care?

If you don't care, you probably haven't picked coffee in this story.

Drive-By Compromise

What is it?

A drive-by compromise is when a hacker gains access to a system by exploiting a user's internet browser when they visit a compromised website. Sometimes the website itself doesn't even need to be compromised: hackers can place adverts that contain malicious code on legitimate websites. When a user first browses to the affected website, a scan of the browser is performed, looking for vulnerable versions of software. When the user next visits the website, the right exploit is prepared and deployed. Phishing and social engineering strategies are used to coerce people into visiting the infected websites.

Why should you care?

Because sometimes people are curious when they identify a phishing email and decide to visit the links, thinking they'll be safe if they block any downloads.

e-Commerce

What is it?

Online shops like Amazon or the like. You pay for goods and services using credit or debit cards in an online checkout process.

Why should you care?

e-Commerce websites are a key target for hackers, as the payment cards used on them are valuable. Stolen payment card details are sold to fraudsters, who use them to buy items online, which they can then sell for profit.

Encryption

What is it?

Encryption is a reversible process that makes data useless to any person or computer system that does not have the corresponding key to decrypt it. Encryption can also be used to prove identity in a communication process, like how a website proves its identity using a digital certificate. There are two main types of encryption:

Symmetric – each party involved has one key that encrypts the data and also decrypts the data.

Asymmetric – each party has two keys, one that they share openly (public key) and one they keep secret (private key). If user A encrypts a document with their private key, then the document can only be decrypted using user A's public key. Equally, if user A encrypts a document with their public key, then the document can only be decrypted using user A's private key.

Encryption should not be confused with hashing, which is a one-way process.

Why should you care?

Encrypting data means that an attacker needs to gain access to the associated encryption key(s) before they can plunder the data itself. This is assuming the encryption mechanism is proportionally strong relative to the importance of the data it is encrypting. Weak encryption algorithms can be cracked by even low-skill/resource adversaries.

As computing resource gets cheaper, the strength of encryption standards needs to constantly maintain a high computational cost to stay ahead as older encryption algorithms get made redundant.

Event

What is it?

Put simply, something that happens in the world of IT.

Why should you care?

Events and logs are your audit trail to be able to look into the past and understand exactly how things played out. Incident response crews will almost always want access to this data to help them build a picture of what occurred.

Firewall

What is it?

A piece of software or hardware designed to allow through only certain data traffic. Firewalls use rules to determine what they should do with an incoming piece of data. As an example, if an application is only meant to be accessed from particular countries, then the firewall can be configured to block all traffic originating from outside these countries.

Why should you care?

Firewalls keep the general public away from company-critical systems. You can get a personal firewall for your home network, too.

GDPR

What is it?

The General Data Protection Regulation (GDPR) is a regulation in European Union (EU) law that was implemented in May 2018. it is designed to protect the rights of EU citizens when it comes to how their personal data is collected and used.

Why should you care?

If you are someone who is protected by this legislation, you have the added bonus of having this shield your data when it is being used. For a company, GDPR is another piece of legislation you may need to ensure you are adhering to.

Hacktivist

What is it?

A combination of the word hacker and activist: someone who hacks with an activist agenda. Common parlance, not something I made up.

Why should you care?

Depending on your company's practices, hacktivists may or may not be interested in targeting you.

Honeypot

What is it?

A honeypot is a tantalising trap that is left for hackers to stumble across and exploit. Perhaps it's a seemingly vulnerable server or a router, or even a set of credentials that you've planted that to an attacker look like a worthy prize. The idea is that once the hacker takes the bait, the honeypot can send out an alert to say it's been tampered with and a response can be initiated.

Why should you care?

Many controls focus on keeping attackers out, but once these have been circumvented, they become almost useless. Honeypots are part of the next phase of defence: detection. Ask yourself: If an attacker was on your network, would you have any way of knowing?

Incident Response Plan

What is it?

An incident response plan (IRP) is a guidance document that helps a company's incident response team understand how to act in the event of an information security event. The IRP lays out guidance on topics such as:

- Who the incident response team is
- How to classify an incident and escalate accordingly
- Who the business should notify externally following an incident
- When/how the business should prepare itself for post-notification fallout, i.e. increased email/call centre traffic volumes

In some cases, an IRP will include playbooks that outline granular actions that should be taken when responding to a particular incident. For example, if the incident involves a compromised user account, it will detail the steps that should be taken to contain the user account to prevent further harm.

Why should you care?

If you don't have an incident response plan, go ahead and get one written. If you have one, run regular incident response tabletop exercises to identify playbooks that need to be authored or altered or staff training that may be useful. Try running incident response tabletop exercises where one or multiple key personnel are not present, as this may end up being more representative of a real-world event.

Incident Response Retainer

What is it?

A company that is employed to provide support if your customers get hacked. Particularly relevant for companies large enough to have an interest in information security, but not a large enough team to employ dedicated technical incident response staff.

Why should you care?

A good incident response retainer is a very valuable resource, capable of bringing calm, experience and proven tactics for reducing the impact of a breach and evicting the hackers.

Information Security Policy

What is it?

An information security policy defines how your business views information security and sets the tone for what is and isn't acceptable.

Why should you care?

Aside from being a requirement for most information security compliance/accreditation standards, an information security policy is the foundation upon which all information security decisions are made.

Internal Audit

What is it?

An audit is when you check that the things that should happen do indeed happen; an internal audit is when a company does the audit on itself.

Why should you care?

Companies make a variety of decisions based on assumptions; audits are there to make sure these assumptions are true. Audits are also there to make sure standards don't drop, because you never know when an audit could come around and highlight areas of non-compliance.

Internet Protocol (IP) Address

What is it?

A number labelling system for computer devices. It acts like a postcode to help data know where to go.

Why should you care?

When defending your company, you need to know what IP addresses your servers have so you can make sure they are being scanned, penetration tested and protected by devices such as firewalls.

Intruder Detection System

What is it?

It does what it says, really: software designed to look for intruders, alert the information security team, but take no active action. There is also such a thing as an intruder prevention system, which detects but also puts a stop to such activity.

Why should you care?

Like with any software, an intruder detection system can only be as good as its calibration allows. Uncalibrated, it will alert for every single event happening in the network; too tightly calibrated, and it may overlook genuinely suspicious activity.

Keylogger

What is it?

Malware that sits on your computer and records every keyboard entry you make.

Why should you care?

Username and password combinations for your email, internet banking credentials, the ability to log in to any of your accounts and impersonate/steal from you—all these could be in the hands of whoever plants the keylogger.

Kill Switch

What is it?

A mechanism through which a malicious piece of code can be shut down in the event of the code getting out of control.

Why should you care?

You might read this and think "Yeah, as if that would happen." But it does. In fact, if you remember the WannaCry ransomware attacks that infected hundreds of thousands of devices around the world and crippled countless companies, that malware had a kill switch programmed in.

In essence, once the malware infected a server or computer, it tried to navigate to a really obscure website. If that website didn't exist, the malware would infect the computer and continue to spread. But if the website did exist, then the malware would stop. Thankfully for the world, the people who made WannaCry didn't register the kill switch domain, allowing a security researcher to register the domain and "turn off" WannaCry.

Lanyard

What is it?

That thing you wear around your neck that has your name badge on it; some companies have these worn at the hip. They are used as a quick and easy way to identify who does and doesn't belong in a physical area. Sometimes the cards themselves are used to open doors.

Why should you care?

Obviously not all companies use them, but Generico McCompany do, and knowing which colours are acceptable and which aren't may influence your journey.

Logic Bomb

What is it?

Malicious code that is designed to execute when specific criteria have been met. You could have a logic bomb that is primed to go off when a member of staff is fired, or on a date that is significant to the individual planting the bomb.

Why should you care?

The logic bomb may have a refined, planned outcome, or it might just initiate a ransomware-style mass encryption of files. It can be almost anything, really.

Log

What is it?

A history of all the interactions computer systems have between themselves. An individual interaction can be known as an "event".

Why should you care?

Looking back through logs is what helps an incident response team understand the timeline of activities and identify which events were normal, and which were caused by the hacker.

Macro

What is it?

A snippet of code that performs a singular function, and can be used as an attack vector. For example, Microsoft Office products can be modified to include macros. Hackers can utilise this functionality to create highly sophisticated macros that serve malicious purposes. Macros can allow an Excel or Word file suddenly to turn into a virus. It should be noted that not all macros are viruses.

Why should you care?

Suspicious file types like .exe are more obvious, but what happens when you can't trust file types you've been using for years? As ever, user awareness training is key, not only preventing for this being an issue, but also for creating a culture where an employee will raise the alarm if they suspect they've fallen victim to a macro.

Mail Order Telephone Order

What is it?

A payment card channel where the orders are placed over the phone or mail.

Why should you care?

Anywhere payment card data lives or touches is a target for hackers.

Malicious Insider

What is it?

A person who is looking to launch or enable hacking attempts against a company they work for, from within. These people are often incentivised by money, revenge or shared ideals. A common example of malicious insiders is when staff are made redundant or fired and decide to enact revenge on their employers by leaking data or sometimes planting malicious code designed to activate after they've left.

Why should you care?

Because these people have genuine, legitimate access to applications and data, identifying when an employee has been flipped to the dark side is almost impossible. To defend yourself, screen employees thoroughly before hiring and rotate responsibilities amongst teams. That way, if someone is up to no good on a particular area of the network, there is a possibility that someone may identify this when they rotate roles.

Malware

What is it?

Malicious software. There are all kinds of subclassifications like ransomware, spyware, adware, trojans, worms, wipers etc. To cover all types of malware would need its own book.

Why should you care?

Malware often isn't picky: any computer or smartphone will do, and there are thousands if not millions of strains circulating around the internet.

Mitigation

What is it?

Something that is done to reduce or remove the impact of something else.

Why should you care?

This is common terminology within information security, as there are many vulnerabilities and scenarios that need to be mitigated against.

Multi-factor Authentication

What is this?

Authentication is the process of proving that someone is who they say they are, like a username and password. Multi-factor authentication is when more than one type of authentication is used, for example a username and password combination, as well as a code sent to a phone that is linked to the account.

Some examples include:

- Something you know (username and password)
- Something you are (retina scan, fingerprint)
- Something you have (mobile phone number or a one-time password-generating token)

Remember, having two authentication steps from the same category does not count as multi-factor authentication. For example, asking someone for their username and password and then their mother's maiden name is single-factor authentication; it's only multi-factor if the process is making use of a combination of two authentication methods.

Why should you care?

Hackers have limited time in their day, just like anyone else, and will work through the path of least resistance. If your personal email has two-factor authentication enabled, a hacker becomes much more likely to leave you alone and instead try to break into somewhere less secure.

OSINT

What is it?

Open Source Intelligence Gathering (OSINT) is when hackers or red team crews perform reconnaissance against a company or its employees, allowing more tailored phishing attacks and targeted technical exploits.

Why should you care?

I don't know if you've ever looked at exactly how much data is available about you online, but it can be scary. Whether you care about a hacker being able to impersonate you from a cybersecurity perspective is one thing, but the implications from a fraud angle should be obvious to us all. The more data you put out about yourself, the more ammunition hackers have. People's first school or pet is a common security question, which you can typically easily find from a quick Facebook search.

Packet

See data packet.

Packet Filtering

What is it?

Software that attempts to remove malicious packets before they can be received by the intended recipient.

Why should you care?

Just another potential tool in the CISO arsenal.

Patching

What is it?

Updating software to a more recent version.

Why should you care?

Vulnerabilities and bugs get discovered all the time. Software vendors react to these bugs by updating their software so that the vulnerabilities no longer exist in their software. The problem is, until you apply the patch you will continue to be vulnerable. Patching at an enterprise level can be challenging due to the number of places the patch needs to be applied, but also because patching always runs the risk of causing some other, seemingly unrelated software process to be impacted.

Payload

What is it?

The part of malware that is delivering the intended outcome. There could be many lines of code telling the malware how to behave, how to infect computers and how to spread, but the payload is what the malware executes as its end goal.

Why should you care?

If you're lucky, you'll get infected by a virus where the payload is misconfigured, but don't count on it. Companies can look at what payloads new viruses have and try to come up with counter measures if the virus were ever to infect their system.

PCI DSS

What is it?

The Payment Card Industry Data Security Standard (PCI DSS) is an information security standard that is designed to help merchants and service providers protect debit and card data. PCI DSS is overseen by the Payment Card Industry Security Standards Council (PCI SSC).

Why should you care?

Protecting card data is important, because it's a particularly attractive target for cybercriminals due to its high value. Stolen card details are used to commit fraud, by using them to purchase products from retailers, which the criminals then sell for cash.

Penetration Testing

What is it?

Penetration testing (also known as pen testing) is an assurance activity where technical consultants attempt to discover and exploit vulnerabilities in the functionality, configuration and coding of software or hardware.

Why should you care?

A well-run penetration test helps the business gain visibility about what could potentially go wrong with the in-scope infrastructure and applications. If certain features need to remain for business reasons, then mitigating controls can be put in place to reduce the likelihood of an attacker being able to exploit the associated vulnerability. If a technical exploit leads to compromised data or fraud, the first question asked by an insurance or criminal investigation team will be: When was this last penetration tested? "Never" is not the answer they are expecting.

Phishing

What is it?

Phishing is the practice of sending emails to people to encourage them either to download a malicious attachment, or to enter their login credentials on a fake website, or another nefarious goal.

When it's extremely targeted, it's sometimes referred to us as "spear phishing", and when phishing is targeted to senior members of staff it can be referred to as "whaling". Bad guys will typically attempt to play on emotions with their phishing emails, trying to arouse feelings of panic or guilt by injecting urgency into things.

Why should you care?

Phishing continues to be one of the most powerful and commonly utilised methods for gaining initial access to company networks. Aside from that, phishing poses a huge risk for personal devices, since we receive a deluge of phishing emails and SMS messages.

Plain Text

What is it?

Data that is not encrypted, so is understandable to the human eye.

Why should you care?

If it's readable to your eye, it's readable to a hacker's eye.

Port

What is it?

Think of a port as a pipe that data flows through. Ports are numbered. If you think of IP addresses as a way of identifying a building on a street, a port number would be a specific door or window on that building. You can pass anything you want through that door or window, but convention says you walk through a door and leave apple pies to cool by windows. As an example, port 443 is for HTTPS, which is often how a computer browser will access data about a website before displaying it for you.

Why should you care?

Devices that have unnecessary ports open are at increased risk of being hacked. For example, if a computer is never going to be accessed remotely, it should have all ports that are used for remote access closed.

Privilege Escalation

What is it?

Privilege escalation is when hackers take over increasingly powerful user accounts with the goal of reaching administrator status. As an administrator, an attacker often has full control of the computer.

Why should you care?

That depends, really. Ask yourself: If a basic user can escalate themselves up to administrator, or perform functions normally reserved for administrators, what kind of damage could they do? In some isolated cases you might find that the answer is in fact nothing. But often this kind of scenario opens up all kinds of data loss, operational impact and even direct financial impact scenarios.

Ransomware

What is it?

A strain of malware that encrypts files within a company network or personal computer and demands a ransom payment to unlock the files.

Why should you care?

It's hard to get work done when you can't access any files at all. All work performed between the last successful backup and the ransomware attack will be lost when you restore files from a backup. And if you don't have a backup to restore from, you will have to start from zero.

Risk

What is it?

A term that is used in quite a few ways. In general, a risk is something that could plausibly happen and have a negative impact. Something that could never happen is not a risk, and something that could happen but would have a positive outcome is also not a risk.

Why should you care?

Companies often think about problems in terms of risk, as much of business is weighing up risk and reward. As an example, you could remove the lock from your front door. The reward is that it's now much quicker to enter your home, but the risk is that it's now much easier for a burglar to enter too. Businesses try to boil down many of their decisions into risk-based calculations, balancing costs and benefits.

Risk Register

What is it?

A location where risks are recorded, including when a potential problem was identified and what risk treatment was applied.

Why should you care?

As an information security professional, you will have to accept that you can't fix every problem. Some problems cost too much money to fix relative to their size. The risk register is the source of truth, so if something were to go wrong, the information security professional can show that the issue was raised, but the business decided not to act on it.

Root Kit

What is it?

Software a hacker will look to install on target computers, hiding itself to be used at a later point.

Why should you care?

Denying hackers access to their tools is a smart move.

Script Kiddie

What is it?

A hacker with low levels of sophistication, often used as an insult. The idea is that the hacker can only perform hacking activity through the use of prewritten scripts, as opposed to performing technical exploits themselves.

Why should you care?

The prevalence of such scripts means the amount of technical knowledge a hacker needs to perform a sophisticated attack is lowered, particularly for commonly attacked hardware/software.

Security Operations Centre (SOC)

What is it?

The place from which a company's information security defence is coordinated. This is the place to which alerts are sent. The SOC has a global view of all alerts and incidents and is best placed to recognise when a problem is local, or when a full-blown incident response crisis process is required.

Why should you care?

An SOC is a living and breathing business unit, capable of being run well or badly. SOCs generally are quite expensive to maintain, so you want to avoid having one that isn't fit for purpose.

Server

What is it?

A piece of computer hardware or software that provides a variety of services that enable computers to do their job. One server can provide the resources for multiple people at once.

Why should you care?

Enterprise computer networks, the internet and basically most online things are built using servers.

Shoulder Surfing

What is it?

Shoulder surfing is when someone physically watches your computer activity from behind you, potentially seeing sensitive data or password details.

Why should you care?

Wouldn't you care if your financial or medical records were being paraded publicly?

Social Engineering

What is it?

Tricking someone into doing something they shouldn't.

Why should you care?

Because humans are (often) good at heart, and when someone comes to us with a problem often our first instinct is to help. Hackers take advantage of this to gather intelligence or look to trick people into giving up account passwords or other sensitive data.

Sophisticated Actor

What is it?

A hacking group who have significant capability, generally access to high-quality vulnerabilities, infrastructure and staff.

Why should you care?

A sophisticated actor is significantly harder to keep out of your network compared to a script kiddie.

Stresser

What is it?

The name for online services that send DDoS attacks towards IP addresses in exchange for money.

Why should you care?

Hackers can plug the IP addresses or hostnames for your company into a Stresser to launch a DDoS attack against you. But that's illegal, you say. Yes, and so is much of hacking—that doesn't stop it from happening.

Supply Chain Attack

What is it?

When attackers compromise a company, with a view to using them as a stepping stone to a company it is connected to, or supplies services to. In this situation, if the supplier is less cyberresilient than the overall target, it represents the path of least resistance.

Why should you care?

If you are the supplier being attacked, that isn't ideal. If you are the bigger fish the attackers are really after, this isn't ideal either! The frequency of supply chain attacks has made third-party management an audit point on a number of audit and compliance standards.

Third Party

What is it?

A company other than your own.

Why should you care?

Third-party companies can be seen as an extension of your company, and therefore a potential way in for hackers. Even if there is no direct network connection, a third party is a company that employees within your business expect to receive emails from and therefore are less vigilant towards.

Threat Actor

What is it?

The term used to describe a group that are involved in coordinated hacking activities, as opposed to individuals. Sometimes these threat actors even have backing from a country's government or military.

Why should you care?

Knowing who is targeting you and why is useful when identifying what counter measures to deploy.

Ticket

What is it?

A common term during a support process, when a user calls/emails in with a problem and is assigned a ticket. This ticket is assigned to a member of support staff, providing an audit trail of when the ticket was assigned, what it was for and how it was resolved.

Why should you care?

I mention tickets a few times in the book and didn't want to leave you hanging.

Trojan

What is it?

Software pretending to be something innocent when it's got something hidden inside, like the horse of Troy.

Why should you care?

It's just another way hackers are trying to trick you that it's useful to be aware of.

Virus

What is it?

Malware that is specifically known to self-replicate. So all viruses are malware, but not all malware is a virus.

Why should you care?

Curiosity, really: it's a term that gets used a lot.

Vulnerability

What is it?

A situation that if exploited by a malicious party could lead to some kind of adverse outcome. A vulnerability needs to be exploited in order for there to be an adverse effect; it generally won't self-activate.

Why should you care?

Hackers are looking for vulnerabilities all the time. It's often a race over whether a company can fix them first before a hacker can exploit them.

Vulnerability Scan

What is it?

A scan that looks for vulnerabilities across the target range, things like ports being open or outdated software in use.

Why should you care?

A useful tool for a CISO or their supporting team, but remember that there is actually nothing stopping a hacker from scanning your internet-facing devices using the exact same software (apart from morals).

Zero Day

What is it?

A zero-day exploit is when a previously unknown vulnerability is discovered and weaponised. Until vendors produce a new patch, all systems using the impacted software will potentially be vulnerable.

Why should you care?

A zero-day exploit can potentially allow a hacker to completely bypass a security control within your network. As these vulnerabilities are unknown to the industry, even if your software is up to date it will remain vulnerable until a new patch is produced to counter the zero-day vulnerability.

I

Index

© Alexander J. Roxon 2021
A. J. Roxon, *Choose Your InfoSec Path*, https://doi.org/10.1007/978-1-4842-7036-3

S

SCAPI database, 43, 198, 215, 231, 253

Server ports, 92

Shoulder surfing, 211, 241

Snow globe paperweight, 14

Social engineering, 155, 256

Software services, 86

Sophisticated Actor, 265

Stock exchange, 242

Stresser activity, 87, 172

Stresser campaign, 28

Stresser services, 211

Stress testing, 238

Stringent controls, 103

Stupid Pointless Annoying Message
(SPAM), 87

T

Technical skills, 89

Telephone payment system, 23

Threat actor, 32, 56, 148, 161, 177, 183, 189,
211, 258, 264

TLK2ME, 146, 230

TrainingWheel, 140

Trojan, 72

U

Unemployment, 107

Unencrypted payment card, 128

User account, 51

User awareness training
programme, 4

V

Verbal approval, 80

Vulnerabilities, 96, 225, 274

W, X, Y

Web app, 264

Whiteboards, drawing on, 4

Work meetings, 152

Z

Zero-day vulnerability, 43

Printed in the United States
by Baker & Taylor Publisher Services